Madame Elizabeth

France 1764-1794

Mrs. Maxwell-Scott

Alpha Editions

This edition published in 2019

ISBN : 9789353706135

Design and Setting By
Alpha Editions
email - alphaedis@gmail.com

MADAME ELIZABETH
DE FRANCE

1764-1794

BY

The Hon. Mrs. MAXWELL-SCOTT
OF ABBOTSFORD

WITH ILLUSTRATIONS

LONDON
EDWARD ARNOLD
41 & 43 MADDOX STREET, BOND STREET, W.
1908

PREFACE

———

IN his introductory letter to M. de Beauchesne's *Vie de Madame Elizabeth*, Monseigneur Dupanloup tells us, in his beautiful language, that the Princess's life had not hitherto been really "studied or known; her secondary *rôle*, the modest reserve in which she enveloped herself, the devotedness which characterised her life, had been left too much in the shade. This nature, this heart, this soul, this life had not been observed closely, nor seen in detail." And if this was true of her own country some years back, it is perhaps true in a degree of ours even yet. It is therefore in the hope of more fully revealing the character of this admirable and charming Princess that this book has been written, and the author can only hope that its readers will share with her the interest and admiration she has felt in the study of Mme Elizabeth's character, and the influence it exerted upon those around her— an influence which found its deepest significance, and also its chief reward, in prison and at the foot of the scaffold.

As one reads of the cruel sufferings and in-

dignities undergone by the Royal Family of France
in the closing years of the eighteenth century, trials
sent to the innocent, apparently that they might
expiate the guilt of their predecessors on the
Throne of France, other Royal victims come before
our minds, and we are tempted to compare the
trials or *procès* endured by them which on several
occasions so closely resemble each other.

We see Mary Stuart glancing round the hall at
Fotheringay, and saying sadly to Melville, "Here
are many Counsellors but not one for me," and we
hear M. de Malesherbes in his impassioned appeal
for the life of Louis xvi. utter, the famous words :
" I search among you for Judges and I only find
Accusers."   Louis had indeed been given an official
defender, powerless though he was ; but Queen
Mary and that other royal soul, Joan of Arc, were
left to defend themselves, and when the judges of
the latter, like those of Fotheringay,[1] attacked the
Maid by questions all together, she would say
calmly, "Gentle Seigneurs, speak one after the
other."

As regards our Princess, although a loyal
defender of her cause found himself present almost
accidentally at her trial, she herself was not aware of
the fact till she heard his hopeless appeal to the
judge, and trembled for the danger to which his
words exposed him as she had never trembled for

---

[1] " Like madmen they attacked her sometimes one by one, sometimes all together, declaring her to be guilty."—See " Marie Stuart,"
par Chantelauze, *Journal de Bourgoing*, pp. 522-27.

herself. She too had defended herself with the
gentle dignity which characterised her, and had
acknowledged herself to be "Elizabeth de France
—aunt of your King" with the same calmness as if
she had been at Versailles surrounded by courtiers,
instead of being in prison in the midst of those
who had destroyed "Royalty," as they termed it,
and were, as she well knew, about to send her to
her death.

The chief materials for the Life of Mme
Elizabeth must ever be found in M. de Beauchesne's
fine volumes, but since they were published other
interesting documents have come to light, and the
Memoirs of the Duchesse de Tourzel, that valiant
and loyal *grande dame*, have been published in full.
To these books and to the others mentioned in the
List of Authorities the present writer owes the
material for this little Life of Mme Elizabeth de
France.

M. M. M.-S.

September 1908.

CONTENTS

LIST OF ILLUSTRATIONS

LIST OF AUTHORITIES

———◆———

Vie de Madame Elizabeth sœur de Louis XVI. Par M. A. de Beauchesne. 2 vols., Plon. Paris, 1869.

Louis XVII. De Beauchesne. 2 vols., Plon. Paris, 1879.

Louis XVI., Marie Antoinette, et Madame Elizabeth. Lettres et documents inédits. 6 vols., Feuillet de Conches, Plon. Paris, MDCCLXIV.

Correspondance de Madame Elizabeth de France. Ed. par Feuillet de Conches, Plon. Paris, 1868.

Mémoires de La Duchesse de Tourzel. Ed. par le Duc des Cars. 2 vols., Plon. Paris, 1883.

La Captivité et Mort de Marie Antoinette. Lenotre. 1 vol., Perrier. Paris, 1907.

Le Drame de Varennes. Lenotre. 1 vol., Perrier. Paris, 1905.

La Mère des trois derniers Bourbons (Maria Joséfa de Saxe), Strylenski.

Mémoires de Baron Huë. Ed. par Baron de Maricourt.

The Prisoners of the Temple. O'Connor Morris. Burns & Oates, 1874.

Biographie Universelle. Paris, 1815.

" Tous les coups que reçurent le Roi, la Reine, la Royauté
dans leur puissance, dans leur honneur, dans leur prestige,
Madame Elizabeth les reçut dans son cœur. Quant à elle, elle
a été respectée par la plupart de ceux-là même qui ne respectaient
personne."

DE BEAUCHESNE.

MADAME ELIZABETH
DE FRANCE
1764–1793

———+———

CHAPTER I

CHILDHOOD

THE history of the last days of the French Monarchy in the eighteenth century is inexpressibly mournful, but its sombre pages are illuminated in part by the virtues of a whole group of noble royal women, whose gentle influence was ever exerted for the welfare of their family and their nation. Among these there is perhaps no more admirable or pathetic figure than that of Mme Elizabeth, the sister of Louis XVI., who devoted herself with the most absolute unselfishness to her brother's hopeless cause, and finally gave her life for it.

Born on the eve of the great Revolution, Mme Elizabeth was the daughter of Louis, Dauphin de France, eldest son of Louis XV. and of Maria Joséfa of Saxony. The Dauphin, who

resembled his grandfather, Fénelon's famous pupil,
both in virtue and in his comparatively short life,
died when our Princess was a baby, and was
followed only too soon by his admirable and charming wife. This double loss to the nation and to
the Royal Family vividly recalls the terrible blow
which saddened the declining years of Louis xiv.,
when the sudden deaths of his grandson and
his wife caused consternation throughout France.
Other resemblances may be traced between the
careers of the two Dauphins, both obliged by the
exigencies of the time to live a retired and un-
ambitious life in the very midst of the Court—both
blessed by happy marriages, and both destined to
leave deep and lasting memories in the hearts of
their people.

The Dauphin, who was twice married, lost his
first wife, Marie Thérèse, Infanta of Spain, in 1745,
a short time after their union, and, in spite of
his great grief, was urged by his family to marry
again immediately. The bride now chosen for him
was Maria Joséfa, daughter of the Elector of
Saxony and King of Poland, a young Princess
who, we are told, possessed "piety, knowledge, and
a fine character, and who, from the time of her
arrival at Court, gave proofs of the elevation of her
mind and heart." The poor bride had, indeed, no
easy task. Not only had she to comfort and win
the affection of her husband, still inconsolable for
the death of his first wife, but the circumstances of
her relations with the Queen, her mother-in-law,

were rendered difficult by the fact that Maria Leczinska was the daughter of Stanislaus, the dis-possessed King of Poland. Happily, the thorough goodness and unselfishness of both ladies made their friendship comparatively easy, and the Dauphine, with a charming tact, turned a piece of Court etiquette into an early occasion of offering consolation to the Queen. On the third day after her marriage, custom ruled that the Dauphine should wear a bracelet containing the portrait of the King her father. At first no one had the courage to admire the bracelet or ask to see its contents. The Queen was the first to allude to it, saying, "This, then, is the portrait of your father, my daughter?" "Yes, Mama," returned the Princess; "see how like it is." It was the por-trait of *King Stanislaus.*

The marriage was blessed by eight children,[1] of whom our Princess Elizabeth, the youngest, was born two years after the death of her brother, the charming little Duke of Burgundy, which had cast a mournful shadow on the happy family circle.

Elizabeth Philippine Marie Hélène de France was born at Versailles on Thursday, 3rd May 1764, and was baptized by the Archbishop of Rheims in the Palace Chapel on the same day in presence of the King and the Royal Family, the

[1] Marie Zepherine, b. 1750; Duc de Bourgogne, b. 1751; Duc d'Aquitaine, b. 1753; Duc de Berry, afterwards Louis XVI., b. 1754; the Comte de Provence, afterwards Louis XVIII., b. 1755; the Comte d'Artois, afterwards Charles X., b. 1757; Marie Clotilde, afterwards Queen of Sardinia, b. 1759. The three first all died young.

Duc de Berry representing the godfather, the Infante Don Philippe, and Madame Adelaide the godmother, the Dowager Queen of Spain.

The baby Princess was so delicate that for long her health was the cause of constant alarms. It was supposed that she would be too weakly to live to enjoy "the beautiful destiny that awaited her." "Who could foresee," says her biographer, "that, on the contrary, her fate would be terrible, that she would have the strength to endure it, and that evil days would come when the masters of France would find too long, and would themselves shorten, the life that it was now feared would end too soon?"[1] A short time after the little Elizabeth's birth her parents went in state to return thanks in Notre Dame, and on this occasion the good people of Paris, then still devoted to their Royal Family, saw with grief that the Dauphin, who was usually very stout, had become thin and pale. These symptoms were the forerunners of his fatal illness. Although he insisted in the following summer on joining the camp at Compiègne, and then followed the Court to Fontainebleau, this was his last journey.

Maria Joséfa was the most tender and indefatigable nurse, but both she and the invalid suffered from the terrible etiquette which, as a contemporary author remarks, obliged royal persons "to be ill in public," and, when death drew near, even insisted on the nearest and dearest relations leaving the room. The Dauphin himself was

[1] De Beauchesne, *Vie de Mme Elizabeth de France.*

LE DAUPHIN, PÈRE DE LOUIS XVI.

calm and composed. When his confessor came to him, he said, " Do not be unhappy. Thanks to God's grace, I do not cling to life. I have never been dazzled by the brilliancy of the throne to which I have been called by birth. I have only considered it in the light of the responsible duties that accompany it, and the perils which surround it." After receiving the last Sacraments with great devotion, the Prince had a conversation with the King, in which he begged him to leave the education of his children entirely in their mother's hands. He showed the greatest consideration for all those who attended him, and would express his affection for Maria Joséfa in touching words. " Ah, what a good woman," he exclaimed one day; "after making the happiness of my life, she now helps me to die." And when she feared he was feeling dull and offered to send for someone else to talk to him, " No, my heart," he replied; "can I feel dull when you are there? " When the last moments approached, and his wife had to leave him, he still called for his dear *Pepa*, as he named her,[1] but soon made the sacrifice of not seeing her, and was heard to say, as if speaking to her, " Go, dear Pepa; it would be too hard for you to hear this," in allusion to his terrible cough. The Dauphin expired at Fontainebleau on Friday, 20th November 1765, at the age of thirty-six.

After his death, Maria Joséfa, who was soon to be attacked by the same cruel malady, endeavoured

---

[1] The diminutive for Joséfa in Spanish.

to rouse herself from her grief to devote herself to the education of her children. She sought light and counsel in the papers left by her husband and inscribed by him, "Writings for the education of my son, de Berry." These she looked upon as her "Treasure," and she could never read them without shedding tears. With the help of a few wise friends she made notes, and by degrees evolved a plan of studies for her children, which was submitted for the King's approval. Our Mme Elizabeth was her mother's special care, and the delicate child owed her life in a double sense to her mother's tender watchfulness. Had this wise and loving mother been spared to her family, the future destinies of France might, possibly, have been different; but it was not God's will, and she only survived her husband two years, dying on 13th March 1767.

Mme Elizabeth, who was only three when this sad event occurred, was too young to appreciate her loss or to enter into the family Court life. When the King's death occurred, however, she was ten years old; and on that terrible night of 10th May 1774, when the extinguished light gave notice that Louis, once *le Bien Aimé*, was no more, she, with her elder sister and their governess, accompanied the Court to Choisy. This melancholy journey marked a new stage in the little Princess's life, as in that of Louis xvi. and Marie Antoinette, the youthful royal couple in whom France now beheld its rulers, and whose first impulse, on receiving the news of their dignity, had been to throw themselves on their knees, exclaiming, "My God—guide us—protect us—for we begin too early to reign."

Mme Elizabeth and her sister, Mme Clotilde, who was four years her elder, had been since the death of their mother entirely under the care of the Comtesse de Marsan, "Governess of the Children of France."[1]

The sisters differed much in character. Clotilde was endowed with the most happy disposition, which only needed guiding and developing; while our Princess, on the contrary, was born "proud, inflexible, and passionate;" faults which, however regrettable in an ordinary person, are justly considered intolerable in a royal personage. Such was the nature which Mme Elizabeth had to overcome, and at the beginning Mme de Marsan felt discouraged. Her task as regards Mme Clotilde had been eminently consoling. This little Princess, "who made herself loved by all who approached her," was a most docile pupil in all ways, and had a real taste for study. With Mme Elizabeth things were very different. Endowed with the obstinacy which had characterised her elder brother, the Duke of Burgundy, before he had conquered his faults, she declared, "She had no need to learn or to tire herself, as there were always people at hand whose duty it was to think

[1] Marie de Rohan Soubise, b. 1721, m. in 1736 to Gaston de Lorraine, Comte de Marsan, who died in 1743.

for Princes"; and she would tremble with anger if one of her women did not at once bring her what she wanted. She was jealous of the very natural preference with which Mme de Marsan regarded her sister, and on one occasion, when she had been refused something, remarked coldly, "If my sister Clotilde had asked for it she would have obtained it." This state of matters, however, soon changed for the better. Elizabeth fell ill, and Clotilde pleaded so hard to be allowed to nurse her that their beds were placed side by side for a short time, until Mme de Marsan, for fear of infection, deprived her of this consolation.[1] This illness broke down the little barrier between the sisters, and Clotilde began to teach Elizabeth her alphabet and spelling, and would help her in her struggles with her faults by little counsels which initiated her in the true piety which already influenced her own young life.

Poor Mme de Marsan, who felt herself un-equal to deal with Elizabeth's difficult nature, begged to be allowed to have the assistance of Mme de Mackau, née de Soucy, who had been educated at St. Cyr. The choice of this lady, who possessed "the firmness which bends resistance, and the affectionate kindness which inspires attach-ment," was a most happy one, and she was destined to be the lifelong friend of her royal pupil, whom

---

[1] In Lady Mary Coke's *Journal*, under date 6th June 1772, we find the following allusion to Mme Elizabeth's delicate health : "I forgot to mention the Dauphin's youngest sister, Madame Elizabeth. She is but eight years old, very pretty, but, they say, very unhealthy."

she trained with maternal kindness tempered by firmness. Elizabeth's character gradually softened and developed under her calm rule; her faults became rare, her love for Mme de Mackau aiding her own endeavours for improvement, till little by little her character, once so proud and fiery, became, as we shall see, most steadfast in principle, most noble and energetic in action.

Elizabeth, whose tenderness of heart helped to correct the results of her childish faults, greatly felt the loss of her parents as she grew older. She was devoted to all her brothers, but a special sympathy and affection drew her to the young King, as if she already foresaw his need of her love and support.

Mme de Mackau's daughter, afterwards Mme de Bombelles, was allowed to join the young Princesses, to the great joy of Elizabeth. "When I was presented to Mme Elizabeth," she writes, "I was, in spite of my two years' seniority, as fond of play as she was. Our games were soon settled, and we quickly made friends. Mme Elizabeth was always asking for me, and my presence was the reward of her application or her docility." A few elder ladies were likewise chosen to visit the Princesses at times. These little "Receptions," which they looked upon as great treats, were most useful in initiating them unconsciously in the knowledge of society so necessary in their position, and of giving them the power of discerning the character of those with whom they were to be thrown. This intuitive sagacity became so keen with our Princess, that later on " she rarely made a mistake in the opinion she formed of the character of the persons, or of the wit of the circle in which she found herself."

It was in summer especially, when the Court was at Compiègne or Fontainebleau, that these reunions took place, and they were often enlivened by *Proverbs*, composed by Mme de Marsan, to be acted by her pupils and the other ladies. At this season also the favourite study of the royal children was botany, under the supervision of M. Lemonnier, a celebrated doctor and botanist, who would accompany them and Mme de Marsan in their walks, and tell them the names and qualities of the shrubs and plants and the origin and date of their becoming known in France. These open-air lessons were so delightful to the children that they never forgot them. Their history and geography lessons were given by M. Leblond; while to the Abbé de Montigat, Canon of Chartres and " Tutor to the Children of France," was confided their religious instruction. Mme Elizabeth applied herself with great earnestness to these studies, and owed much of her future piety and fortitude under trial to the admirable training she received.

Mme de Marsan often took her to St. Cyr, where those pupils who deserved it by their good conduct and industry were brought to be introduced to her. She loved this stately school, full of memories of Louis le Grand and Mme de Main-

MARIA JOSEPHA OF SAXONY, SECOND WIFE OF THE DAUPHIN, SON OF LOUIS XV.

tenon. After assisting at Benediction in the Chapel, she would sometimes visit the classrooms and the refectory, when even the menu for the girls' supper interested her.

It would seem as if from the time of her brother's accession Mme Elizabeth began to take her little part in public life, and of this we have pleasant glimpses. On the Whit Sunday and Whit Monday of that year we find that she went with all the Royal Family to Mass and Vespers in the Church of the Minims at Chaillot, and on the following day she accompanied them to St. Denis to visit her Carmelite aunt, Mme Louise, and to assist at Vespers and Benediction, "the populace lining the road in crowds and showing their loyalty by hearty acclamations."

On the Feast of Corpus Christi, the little Princesses joined in the procession in which the Royal Family followed the Blessed Sacrament on foot from the Parish Church of Passy. They and their governesses spent a part of this summer at the Chateau de la Muette, where the King and Queen came to see them from time to time from Marly. On 25th July, for instance, they, Monsieur[1] and Madame, and the Comte[2] and Comtesse d'Artois, spent the evening with the Princesses and supped with them.

On 1st August, the King and Queen took their little sisters to Compiègne, where they made a

---

[1] Comte de Provence, afterwards Louis XVIII.

[2] Charles X.

State Entry, the last of the kind recorded in the French annals of the eighteenth century.

"Their Majesties made their entry towards half past nine in the evening, escorted by their ordinary guard and by four *Red Companies* according to the usage customary on state journeys. The clergy, secular and regular, and all the city magnates met them. The Vicomte de Laval, Governor of the town and castle of Compiègne, received them at the head of the City Guard. The Mayor, M. Decrouy, made them a speech with one knee on the ground. M. de Laval offered the keys of the town to the King, and presented the officers of the Borough to him. The Lieutenant General also made him a speech bending one knee on the ground; but these official testimonies of respect were effaced in the eyes of the Royal Family by the enthusiastic acclamations of the people, who had come in from all parts of the country to salute the youthful Sovereigns."

On 15th August, the Feast of the Assumption, the little girls took part in the procession which was made on that day throughout France, according to the vow of Louis XIII. "The presence of Louis XVI. and of Marie Antoinette lent a special brilliancy to this religious ceremony, in the midst of which the King's two little sisters, walking side by side dressed in white frocks with blue ribbons, brought to mind the figures of the angels who fold their wings in adoration before the Holy of Holies."

The Court remained at Compiègne until 1st September, and the Princesses led their usual regular life of studies, walks in the Park, or drives in the forest. The national atmosphere appeared serene, and all looked bright; yet at this very moment, while the two royal children were "growing up like two white lilies," Mme Roland, still a young girl working in her father's studio, was becoming imbued with revolutionary ideas, and a secret uneasiness—the passion for equality—was beginning to fill men's hearts.

The following year, 1775, brought a sharp trial for Mme Elizabeth in the parting from her sister. Mme Clotilde, who was now fourteen, a marriageable age according to the ideas of her time, became engaged to Prince Charles Emanuel, eldest son of the King of Sardinia, on 12th February, and the event was formally announced at Court on the same day. Mme Clotilde was a general favourite, and to her sister she had become not only her dearest companion, but her counsellor and guide, and the thought of losing her was sad indeed. The sisters became more inseparable than ever during the time that elapsed before the marriage. On 1st May, Mme Clotilde went to St. Cyr to say adieu, accompanied by Mme Elizabeth and Mme de Marsan. They were received by Mme de Mornay at the head of her Community, and Mme Clotilde, wishing to leave a memorial of her affection to the House, presented the Superioress with a portrait of herself; "on her side, Mme de

Mornay offered to her Highness a screen, embroidered by the cleverest fingers in her House,
and which represented the Superioress as presenting
the plan of St. Cyr to the Princess." The hundred
and fifty young lady students then approached, and
one of them, Mlle Dufort de la Roque, read aloud
some verses composed by Ducis, expressing the
regret that the departure of the King's sister would
leave in all hearts.

On 27th May, an unusual function took place
at Court. Sidi Abderrahman Bediri-Aga, the
envoy of the Pacha of Tripoli, was received in
audience by Louis, and pronounced a discourse
"filled with all the flowers of oriental poetry." On
the following day he made his homage to the
Queen in the Gallery of Versailles. The appearance of this stranger, who was not a Christian,
excited the curiosity and pity of the young
Princesses. Seeing that Mme Elizabeth was
looking at him with some emotion, Mme Clotilde
asked her what she was thinking of. "I am
thinking of his soul," she replied. "Ah, my sister,
the mercy of God is infinite, it is not for us to
place limits to it." "You are right, sister," returned Mme Elizabeth. "It is for Christians to
pray for those who are not, as it is for the rich to
give to the poor." On 30th May, the sisters
accompanied the Queen and Madame to the
review on the Plain of Marly. When, after being
inspected by the King and Princes, the troops
passed before the Queen, who sat surrounded by

the Princesses and courtiers, Mme Elizabeth turned to her sister, saying, " Will there be soldiers as beautiful as these in Turin?" " I don't know, sister," replied Mme Clotilde sadly.

The marriage was to take place after the Coronation, which had been fixed for 11th June, and meanwhile the Princesses accompanied the Royal Family to Rheims. According to custom, Marie Antoinette assisted at the ceremony privately.

"The Queen, who had arrived at Rheims accompanied by Madame and whose incognito did not prevent her from receiving the liveliest expressions of affection offered to her by the French nation, was present at all the august ceremonies of this sacred occasion, in a tribune prepared for her and in which were also Mme Clotilde and Mme Elizabeth." [1]

On 19th June, when the Court returned to Versailles, " Mme Clotilde and Mme Elizabeth had already arrived in the morning," and on 29th June they were present at another great review at Marly. But all these festivities did not console our little Princess for her approaching loss. On 14th July, Marie Antoinette writes about her thus to the Empress Maria Theresa, making allusion at the same time to a project of marriage which was never to be realised : " She shows on the occasion of her sister's departure and in several other circumstances a charming good sense and sensibility. When one has such right feeling at eleven years of

[1] *Gazette de France.*

age, it is very delightful. . . . The poor little dear
will leave us perhaps in two years' time. I am
sorry she should go as far as Portugal, but it will
be happier for her to go so young as she will feel
the difference between the two countries less.
May God grant that her sensibility does not
render her unhappy."

The day before this letter was written a
beautiful ceremony took place in the Palace Chapel.
Mme Elizabeth made her first Communion.
"Elizabeth who on the preceding Thursday after
Vespers in the presence of the King and Royal
family had prepared for this solemn action by the
reception of Confirmation, presented herself before
the Altar between Mme de Marsan and Mme de
Guéménée, and offered herself with fervour to God
Who was giving Himself to her."

On 16th August the contract of marriage
between Mme Clotilde and the Prince of Piedmont
was signed, and on the 21st the marriage took place,
Monsieur representing the bridegroom. During the
marriage festivities, which lasted for some days, we
find Mme Elizabeth's name among those of the
rest of the Royal Family, who took part in them
but with no special reference to her feelings until
the day of parting, when she could not tear herself
from her sister's arms.

"My sister Elizabeth," writes the young Queen
to the Empress a few days later, "is a charming
child who has intelligence, character and grace.
She has shown a charming sensibility, much above

her age, on the departure of her sister. The poor little thing was in despair, and being very delicate, she got faint and had a severe nervous attack. I confess to my dear Mama that I am afraid of becoming too much attached to her."

For the next two years there is little of interest to relate about our Princess, except a happy *mot* of hers which has come down to us connected with the Embassy sent by the Emperor of Morocco to France. The Envoy brought rich presents for the King, and the Court was "in ecstasies over them, not knowing how to decide which was the most valuable." "I know which is the most magnificent," said Mme Elizabeth. "I know which it is that the King will most prize; it is the twenty French sailors who were shipwrecked off the coast of Morocco, and whom the King of that country is sending back to my Brother."

CHAPTER II

EARLY YEARS

THE year 1778 was memorable for our Princess, as during it her education came to an end, and she virtually "came out." On 17th May, "Mme Elizabeth accompanied by the Princesse de Guéménée, the under governesses, and the ladies in attendance, went to the King's apartments, and there Mme de Guéménée formally handed over her charge to His Majesty, who sent for Mme la Comtesse Diane de Polignac, maid of honour to the Princess and Mme la Marquise de Sérent, her lady-in-waiting, into whose care he gave Mme Elizabeth."

Mme de Guéménée, the successor of Mme de Mackau, had found her duties pleasant and easy. Instead of having to press the Princess in her studies, she had to moderate her ardour. Mme Elizabeth now hated idleness, and when not occupied by serious studies, she was fond of needle-work, and excelled in this womanly accomplishment.

Some years later, one of her ladies who was admiring her embroidery remarked that it was really a pity that Madame was so clever with her needle. "But why?" asked the Princess. "It would be so useful to many poor girls; such a talent would suffice to gain bread for them and their families." "Perhaps it is for that that God has given it to me," returned Mme Elizabeth, "and who knows? perhaps one day I shall make use of it to support myself and those dear to me." Possibly those words came back to her in the sorrowful days to come, when she devoted her time and ingenuity to mending the clothes of her royal brother and his family in the Temple.

From the moment of her taking her place as a grown-up member of the Royal Family, the question of the Princess's marriage was discussed. As we know, the Infant of Portugal, Prince of Brazil and heir to the throne of Portugal, aspired to her hand. He was about her own age, and the alliance was suitable, but Mme Elizabeth had no desire for it, and although she made no objections, she was relieved to hear that the negotiations were broken off.

Two more *prétendants* soon appeared in the persons of the Duc d'Aosta and the Emperor Joseph II. The latter had remarked the Princess on the occasion of his visit to France in the previous year, and had been attracted by the "vivacity of her intellect and her amiable character." The Duc d'Aosta, the first-named suitor, was not considered of sufficient importance for a Daughter of France; but the offer of the second seems to have caused more serious consideration, and it is said that his interest in Mme Elizabeth was one of the reasons for the Emperor's second visit to France in 1781. Mme Elizabeth's beauty had matured in the intervening years, and "she seemed destined to wear the Imperial diadem," but the anti-Austrian party at Court viewed the proposed alliance with disfavour and managed to prevent the marriage. It has been said, without foundation, that Mme Elizabeth regretted this match. On the contrary, however, she appears to have set no more value on it than on the others which were suggested, but which political reasons caused to be abandoned. She remained heart-whole, and was destined, instead of leaving France for another home and country, to remain as the consolation and support of her family and countrymen.

Among the young girls admitted to Mme Elizabeth's intimacy during her early years we must mention three in particular for whom she had a special affection and from whom she received, to the end, a devoted attachment—Mlle de Mackau, now Mme de Bombelles; Mlle de Causan, who became Mme de Raigecourt; and Mlle de la Riffe, who married the Marquis de Moutiers de Merinville. "Bombelles, Raigecourt, and de Moutiers, beloved names," exclaims M. de Beauchesne, "which were to give so much consolation to Mme Elizabeth, and to reap so much honour from her friendship."

They never lost the memory of the "noble influences which had presided over their youth," and we shall frequently meet with their names in the history of Mme Elizabeth's life and in her correspondence. We have quoted Mme de Bombelles' first impressions of the Princess, and the same memorandum contains further interesting reminiscences from the time that Mme de Marsan obtained the King's leave for her to remain permanently with the Princess. "From that moment," she writes, "I shared all the care given to the education and instruction of Mme Elizabeth. This unfortunate and adorable Princess being able to talk with me about the intimate feelings that filled her heart, found in mine a gratitude and attachment which in her eyes took the place of intellectual gifts and amiability. She showed me an unalterable goodness and tenderness, which then procured me as much happiness, as I now suffer grief and loss. I married M. de Bombelles. The King, at his sister's request, had the goodness to give me a *dot* of a hundred thousand francs, a salary of a thousand *écus* and the appointment of Lady-in-Waiting to Mme Elizabeth. This event caused her sensible pleasure. I shall not forget the tone in which she said to me, 'At last, my wishes are fulfilled, you belong to me. It is sweet to me to think that it is another link between us and to hope that nothing will dissolve it.' "[1]

The picture of the home life of the youthful Sovereigns at this period, which was shared by the

[1] Memorandum given by Mme de Bombelles to M. Ferrand in 1795.

Princess, is graphically drawn for us by Mme
Campan. " The greatest intimacy reigned between
the three *ménages*," she says. "They took their
meals together, and only ate separately on the
days that they dined in public. This manner of
living continued unbroken until the Queen allowed
herself to dine sometimes with the Duchesse de
Polignac when she was Governess, but the evening
reunion for supper was never interrupted, and took
place in the apartment of the Comtesse de Provence.
Mme Elizabeth took part in it when she had
completed her education, and sometimes *Mesdames*,
the King's aunts, were invited. This life of
intimacy, which had no precedent at Court, was
the work of Marie Antoinette, and she kept it
up with the greatest perseverance."

The Princes of the Blood Royal only frequented
the Court when etiquette demanded, with the
exception of the Princesse de Lamballe, whose
position as Head of the Queen's Household, as
well as her affection for her royal mistress, obliged
her to reside there. The old Maréchal de Richelieu
thus pleasantly describes the different tastes of the
three branches of the Bourbons : " The eldest loves
the chase; the Orleans love pictures; the Condés
love war"; and "What does the King Louis XVI.
love?" he was asked. " Ah, that is different : he
loves the People."

Mme Elizabeth early recognised the dangers
and difficulties inseparable from Court life. " The
incessant rivalry, ill nature, envy and untruthful-

ness of the Court atmosphere alarmed the delicacy
of her conscience and her straightforward nature ;
she began to look upon Versailles as an abode to
be dreaded ; and although her charming character
and warm heart endeared her to the family circle,
and especially to her brother the King, the latter,
perceiving that she was wise and prudent beyond
her years, thought he might advance the period
usual for forming the household of a daughter of
France."[1] Another reason assisted this decision.
The Queen was expecting her first child, and it
was arranged that the persons who had educated
our Princess should pass to the household of the
royal infant. Mme Elizabeth therefore became
her own mistress at fifteen, and saw herself surrounded by all the grandeur and pleasures belonging to her state ; but, far from being dazzled by her
liberty, she feared it, and resolved to watch over
herself with the vigilance that her governesses
could no longer exercise. She said to herself,
" My education is not finished. I shall continue it
according to established rules. I will keep all my
masters ; I will listen to their advice more carefully ;
I will follow their example with more docility than
before. I will see only the ladies who have
educated me and who are attached to me. It is
not for myself that I take these precautions, but
against the wickedness of the times, which is so
ingenious in seizing occasions for calumny. As
before, I shall visit my good aunts, the Ladies of

[1] De Beauchesne, *Vie de Mme Elizabeth*, vol. i. pp. 130-31.

St. Cyr, the Carmelites of St. Denis; the same
hours shall be devoted to religion, to the study of
languages and *belles-lettres*, to instructive conversa-
tions, and to my walks and rides."

With rare perseverance she adhered to this rule
of life, and later on, when she occasionally saw her
former governesses, she would say to them, " I want
you always to find me worthy of your smiles and
approbation."

If we would picture Mme Elizabeth to ourselves, we must listen to the description given by
M. de Beauchesne of her appearance, which our
frontispiece confirms.[1]

" She was not tall," he says, " she had not the
majestic carriage of the Queen, and her nose was
of the *Bourbon* type, but her noble forehead, her
soft, penetrating blue eyes, her mouth whose smile
showed teeth of ivory, and the expression of goodness and intellect which shone on her countenance,
made a charming and sympathetic whole." Such
was our Princess at this moment of her life, and
such she remained in essentials to the end, although
her later portraits show the slight difference which
marks the change from girlhood to mature woman-
hood. The apartment at Versailles which was
devoted to her use was situated at the end of the
façade of the south wing, and looked out upon the
Eau des Suisses. The dividing walls have now been
removed and the rooms thrown into one long
gallery. The walls which sheltered the Princess's

[1] De Beauchesne, p. 132.

quiet life are now decorated with a series of battle-pieces.

On 21st December 1778, Marie Antoinette gave birth to a daughter, afterwards the much-tried Duchesse d'Angoulême, but Mme Elizabeth was unable to assist at the rejoicings on this happy event. On the 18th she had been seized with measles, as we learn from a letter of Mme de Bombelles to her husband. M. de Bombelles was the King's Envoy to the German Diet, and we shall often have occasion to refer to the correspondence. The spring of this year saw the beginning of a more intimate companionship between the Queen and her young sister-in-law. "Mme Elizabeth came to see us to-day," writes Mme de Bombelles. "She returned yesterday from Trianon. The Queen is enchanted with her. She tells everyone that there is no one more amiable, that she did not know her well before, but that now she has made her her friend and that it will be for life."

Smallpox seems to have been a veritable scourge in the France of the eighteenth century, and royal persons appear to have suffered from it in a special manner. Mme Elizabeth followed the example of her aunts and brothers and was inoculated this autumn. She begged that twelve poor children might be treated at the same time and receive the same care as herself. M. Goetz, who had attended the rest of the Royal Family, performed the operations, and with all the patients it succeeded perfectly. On 16th November Marie

Antoinette wrote from Versailles to the Empress:
"My sister Elizabeth has been at Choisy for a
month for her inoculation, which has answered
very well. She will return here on the 23rd of this
month." This must have been one of the last
letters addressed by the Queen to her mother, for
the unexpected news of the great Empress's death
reached Versailles on 6th December, causing her
daughter the deepest grief and arousing universal
regret. Even Frederick II. wrote of Maria Theresa
in these terms: "I have wept very sincere tears
for her death. She did honour to her sex and to
the Throne. I made war on her, but I have never
been her enemy."

About this time we find a whole series of
charming letters from Mme de Bombelles to her
husband, which give a pleasant account of the
Court life. On 17th May, after describing all the
doubts and terrors that seized her in leaving her
precious baby, *Bombon*, to accept the Queen's
invitation to Marly, and of the happy return home
to find *Bombon* sleeping happily, she continues, "I
was received most kindly. The Queen paid me
great attention and spoke much of my son, saying
how beautiful she thought him and joking me upon
my alarm at entering the reception room. In short,
she treated me as if she cared for me very much."
"Mme Elizabeth," she goes on, "had the goodness to send a courier just now to ask news of
Bombon. I love her devotedly. If you had seen
how pleased she was with my little success two

days ago! How she gently rearranged my fichu to make it more graceful, and told me in what manner I must thank the Queen for inviting me to the party! I was really touched by her interest in me, and should like to discover a thousand ways in which to show my gratitude." On 23rd June Mme de Bombelles writes : " Mme Elizabeth goes to-morrow to Trianon with the Queen. They will remain there six days. The Queen said to Mme Elizabeth that I must go to see her every morning, that she was *desolée* not to offer me dinner and supper, but that as she had none of her ladies with her, and that only the Duchesse de Polignac would be there, she feared it would excite too much jealousy." On 27th June we find Mme de Bombelles writing again, and much occupied with thoughts of her Princess's possible marriage : " I went to Trianon this morning to see Mme Elizabeth, with some curiosity because all Paris said that the Emperor was there, and that he will marry her. I heard not a word of it, however. He is still at Brussels and it is not even certain if he will come here. So my thoughts have run away with me for nothing. . . . This marriage of Mme Elizabeth has greatly occupied me—for, after all, if she was happy, what a happiness it would be for me to know that, and never to be away from you." By the 4th of August these hopes were all crushed. "I no longer hope that Mme Elizabeth will marry the Emperor. He leaves to-day, and if there had been any idea of it, they would have tried to make them meet and talk together. Instead of that, the Queen did not seem to occupy herself much with Mme Elizabeth during her brother's stay here, and never said anything to her which related at all to the subject. Therefore, it will certainly not take place."

On the 6th this certainty became greater. "We have reasons for knowing absolutely that the Emperor will not marry Mme Elizabeth. I am both very glad and sorry. It is perhaps very happy for her, but not so much so for me, as I could have been always with you if this marriage had come off, but I am so attached to her that it would have been impossible for me to enjoy my liberty, if the marriage had not made her entirely happy." Mme de Bombelles always quitted home and *Bombon* with reluctance, and even a day's amusement at Court could be a trial. On 8th September 1781 she writes from La Muette : " I left my little *Bombon* yesterday at one o'clock ; he was sleeping quietly. I could not help shedding a few tears at the moment of parting. It was foolish, but I can't tell you what I felt. I was depressed, and in spite of all my efforts to be gay I failed. Mme Elizabeth had sent for me to fish with her, so that I had to leave him an hour sooner than I expected. I confess that this upset me greatly. At this melancholy fishing excursion there was a terrible wind and sun ; we stayed there till 2.45. We only left the dinner table at four o'clock. . . . I went back to Mme Elizabeth, and not wishing to appear sulky,

I forced myself to laugh at everything that was said, which must truly have made me seem very *spirituelle*! We left at five o'clock, got here at half past six, and made our *toilettes* to be in the drawing room at half past eight. There I was well received by every one. The King spoke to me. *Monsieur* placed me by him at supper and talked much to me, inquiring about Ratisbonne and you, etc. After supper I played *Truc* with Mme Elizabeth, the Chevalier de Crussol and M. de Chabrillant."

Soon after this all France rejoiced over the birth of an heir to the Throne. The Dauphin was born at Versailles on 22nd October, and on the same day Mme de Bombelles hastened to write to her husband. "I had the happiness of giving this good news to Mme Elizabeth; you may imagine the pleasure it gave her. She could hardly persuade herself that it was really true that she had a nephew; at last so many people assured her of the fact that in the end she gave herself up to her joy. The poor little princess was almost ill; she cried and laughed, and it is impossible to be more interesting than she is. It is she who held the child at its baptism, on behalf of Mme la Princesse de Piedmont, with *Monsieur*; but what touched me to the last degree was the King's happiness during the baptism. He kept looking at his son and smiling to him. The shouts of the people, who were outside the Chapel, at the moment the child was brought in, the joy visible

on all the faces, touched me so much that I could
not help crying."

As this is not a life of Mme de Bombelles, we
must curtail our quotations, and leave out many
allusions to our Princess, but the account of the
great " Secret "—which, like Mme de Maintenon's
famous *peas*, occupies a letter to itself—deserves to
be here given :—

"VERSAILLES, *this* 22 *December* 1781.

" I have had a great pleasure since I wrote to
you," says Mme de Bombelles to her husband,
"caused much less by the thing itself than by the
gracious kindness that accompanied it. Imagine
that Mme Elizabeth has had a superb habit made
for me for the approaching Fêtes. It arrived the
day before yesterday. Some days ago she had
told me that I should soon know a secret which
was much occupying her. In effect, on Thursday
she gave me a large packet which she said came
from Chantilly. I opened it and found envelope
after envelope and no writing, which confirmed me
in the idea that this secret was a joke. At last,
after tearing open many covers, I found a little
letter on which Mme Elizabeth had written, 'To
my tender Friend,' and inside were the words,
'Receive kindly, my dear little Tutelary Angel,
the token of my tender affection.' At the same
instant the great Habit appeared and I remained
confounded, the most lively pleasure succeeded the
first moment of surprise. I began to cry and

threw myself at Mme Elizabeth's feet. She was
enchanted at my joy and happiness. The only
thing which diminished this happiness when I
examined it, was the great beauty of my habit. It
is embroidered in gold and silver and all colours ;
in short it is a habit which must cost nearly five
thousand francs, so you can judge. Although she
told me she could pay for it when she wished, it
will one day hamper her, I fear, and this idea
afflicts me. I would a hundred times rather the
habit was of fifty louis. However, it is done and
I can't help being enchanted. The little letter
charmed me. I find its style full of amiability, but
this is not all. She told me to give her my fur
trimming and that she would undertake to have it
arranged for the Ball which the *Gardes du Corps*
are giving, as one must wear a *dress* for that. I
did all I could to oppose it, but it was no use and
I find myself just now overcome by her benefits.
On one side I enjoy them and on the other I find
them too great, but she puts so much grace and
kindness in conferring them that she almost makes
me believe these gifts do not cost her trouble.
Mme de Causan appeared almost as pleased as I
was at Mme Elizabeth's goodness. She was in
the Secret. . . . Mme Elizabeth is impatient as
well as I, to think that you cannot hear this famous
secret for nine days."

The rejoicing and fêtes in honour of the
Dauphin, interrupted for a time by the dangerous

illness of the Comtesse d'Artois, continued for months, but Mme, de Bombelles, owing to an attack of jaundice, missed some of the gay doings. Her Princess visited her, of course, and was amused by *Bombon*, who on one occasion "began to dance and turn round the room while his mother played on the clavecin." Mme Elizabeth was devoted to the baby Dauphin and to Mme Royale, and the latter especially early became to her aunt an object of tender care and attention, a foreshadowing of the mutual devotion of their prison days. "She became, so to speak, the first instructress of the little Marie Thérèse, inspiring her with ideas of what was good and just, trying to give her a solid judgment, and turning the first movements of her heart to God." Mme Elizabeth was delighted when her friend, Mme d'Aumale, was chosen by the Queen to take charge of Mme Royale, but this appointment caused some jealousy, and was cancelled on the pretext suggested to the Queen, that her daughter was thus under the tutelage of Mme Elizabeth. This incident caused some momentary interruption to the meetings between her and the little Princess, without interfering with their mutual affection.

This "happy year" of 1781, which witnessed the birth of the long-desired Dauphin, was also to give Mme Elizabeth a home of her own. The account of the little conspiracy on the part of the King to give her this pleasure is very charming. Louis had lately become the possessor of the

property of Montreuil, which had formerly belonged
to the Prince de Guéménée, husband to our
Princess's governess. He begged the Queen, who
was aware of his project, to bring Mme Elizabeth
thither during one of their drives. The Queen
was delighted, and on a certain day begged the
Princess to accompany her. "If you like," she
said, "we will stop at Montreuil, where you liked
to go when you were a child." "That will give
me great pleasure," replied Mme Elizabeth, "for
I spent many happy hours there." When the
royal ladies reached Montreuil — which had, of
course, been made ready for them—directly they
were inside the house the Queen said, "My sister,
you are now at home. This place will be your
Trianon. The King, who gives himself the joy of
offering it to you, has left to me that of telling you."

This gift was the cause of immense delight and
profit to Mme Elizabeth, and still more to her
friends and numerous protégés. The park of
Montreuil is situated on the right as one enters
Versailles, and runs along the Avenue de Paris.
Its original entrance still remains, being now No. 2
of the Rue de Bon Conseil. During the Revolution the park was reduced in size, but was restored
in later years, and is still intact. The house, with
its marble peristyle, stood in the midst of a lawn
surrounded by trees and flower beds; the centre
portion of the building still remains as it was, but
the wings were rebuilt after the Revolution. To
the left, Mme Elizabeth's little farm, the source

3

of many of her charities, can still be seen.[1]   One
of her first acts was to detach a small house (in
the Rue Champ la Guide) from her domain and to
give it to Mme de Mackau.   It made her happy
to inaugurate her new life by asking her old governess to share it.   "My mother's little house," says
Mme de Bombelles, "had a door which opened
into Mme Elizabeth's gardens.   M. de Bombelles
had an illness there which caused him terrible
pain.   The Princess, who was extremely kind to
him, visited him daily to encourage and comfort
him, and shared my distress like a most tender
sister."

Montreuil also possessed memories of another
old friend.   Mme de Marsan's pavilion was close
by, and since her death had been inhabited by
Mme Elizabeth's former master, M. Lemonnier.
His pupil was delighted to renew her intimacy with
the venerable Doctor.   "There grew up a constant interchange of interests between them.   The
learned Professor shared his botanical studies in
his garden with the Princess, and even his experi-
ments in his laboratory; and Mme Elizabeth in
return associated her old friend with her in her
charities, and made him her almoner in the
village."

The King had decided that his sister was not
to spend the night at Montreuil until she was
twenty-four, but from the moment she took pos-

---

[1] These details were given by M. de Beauchesne in 1869, and no
doubt there have been many changes since then.

session of the place she spent the whole day there, returning to Versailles in the evening, or, in summer even, only to sleep. After hearing Mass at the Palace, she drove or walked over to Montreuil with some of her ladies, and spent her day as quietly and regularly as if she had been in a country *château* far from Paris. Hours for study and reading, for walks or rides, were settled beforehand, and at dinner-time the Princess and her ladies met at the same table. Before returning to Versailles, prayers were said in common in the drawing-room, and then they went back to the "anxious" Palace, from which they were so near and yet so far in occupation and sympathy.

CHAPTER III

LIFE AT MONTREUIL

As time went on Mme Elizabeth became more and more attached to her home, and the charity she could there quietly practise was one of the special causes of her happiness. She desired to be kept informed of all the cases of poverty and misery in the village and its neighbourhood. If there was illness, a doctor was sent to the sick person and some money to defray the necessary expenses, and her farm gave her milk and eggs for her poor. As the Princess possessed only the allowance due to her as a sister of the King, it is surprising how she managed to support so many good works; but she had already learned to make sacrifices for others and to economise in her dress and other expenses. If at the end of a month her account was overdrawn, she would retrench by cutting off some piece of personal expenditure from the following month's allowance. She considered large sums spent upon things of luxury as mere waste. One day a merchant of bric-à-brac came to offer her a beautifully carved ornament for the chimney-piece of her salon, of which the price

MADAME ELIZABETH SURROUNDED BY THE POOR CHILDREN OF MONTREUIL

was four hundred livres. "It is certainly not dear," she said, "but I can't afford it." "I do not ask for the money down," replied the man, "I will wait as long as Madame wishes." "I thank you, and pray do not be put out with me if I refuse; but, with four hundred livres I can set up two little *ménages*."

Mme Elizabeth was not content to help those belonging to or near her own domain, but asked to be kept informed of any cases of misery which she could assist. Thus we find her begging M. de Calonne to bring before the King the name of a man belonging to Montfleur (Jura) who at the great age of a hundred and sixteen was being supported by the very small earnings of his already aged daughter. He received a gift of money and a pension, and four years later was presented to the King and Royal Family at the General Assembly, being then one hundred and twenty years old.

A young girl of Noyon, who excited deep interest in France by her heroism in rescuing four men who had fallen into a drain and was nearly asphyxiated by the gas, was also helped by our Princess. Having exhausted her own means for the moment, she went to the King and related the incident to him. "I thank you, sister, for having told me of such a fine and touching action," was his reply; "beg Mgr de Grimaldi" (Bishop of Noyon) "to tell Catherine Vassert that I will have 2400 livres sent to her as a marriage portion."

One advantage of her quiet home was that she could see her brothers more frequently. *Monsieur* often came, and made the time pass quickly by the interest of his conversation. "My brother the Comte de Provence," she once said, "is at the same time the best adviser and the most charming *conteur*. He is seldom mistaken in his judgment of men and things, and his prodigious memory furnishes him in all circumstances with a never ending flow of interesting anecdote."

The Comte d'Artois was of a different nature, "*vif*, amiable, enthusiastic, full of grace and chivalry." He was an amusing companion, and there are many stories told of his love of mischief and fun. One day he made a bet with his brothers that he would appear before his grandfather, Louis xv., with his head covered, without causing him displeasure; and accordingly he entered the King's room with his hat on. "Grandpapa," he said, "don't you think that this hat suits me? My brothers pretend it does not and joke me about it. How does your Majesty find it?" "Very nice, my son." "Then, Sire, please tell them so, for they won't believe me."

Mme Elizabeth would sometimes affectionately lecture this brother, and at first he took her words laughingly, but as time went on his love and veneration for her grew. He was proud of being so nearly related to her, and years later, when in exile, he always received her letters with visible emotion.

The royal aunts, too, were ever welcome visitors at Montreuil, especially Mme Adelaide, who had been especially devoted to Louis XVI. in his childhood, and for whom he had felt a grateful affection. *Mesdames*, indeed, were all very pleasant company and "proved that piety is not incompatible with intellectual charm." Mme Elizabeth often visited her Carmelite aunt at St. Denis. She felt thoroughly at home in the convent, where she was welcomed and loved by all the community—so much so, that the King began to fear that she too would be a nun, and said to her, "I ask nothing better than that you should go to see your aunt, on condition that you do not follow her example : Elizabeth, I need you." She had felt this intuitively, and it was the thought of the King which often took her to St. Denis, that she might unite her prayers to those of her holy aunt for this much-loved brother amidst his trials and heavy responsibilities.

The following pleasant little story is recorded of one of these visits to St. Denis, but it probably occurred some years earlier : "Mme Elizabeth arrived at the convent one day quite early, and begged to be allowed to wait on the nuns at their dinner. Leave being granted, she put on an apron and, after kissing the ground, went to the *Tour* to receive the dishes. All went well, till, as she was distributing the portions, the tray slipped and a dish fell." Her embarrassment was extreme. To relieve her, the august Princess said, "My niece,

after such a *gaucherie* the culprit should kiss the
floor." This Mme Elizabeth hastened to do, and
then cheerfully resumed her office of waitress.

Early in 1782 Mme Royale had a sharp illness
which caused alarm. The child soon recovered,
but another and graver anxiety quickly followed.
Mme Sophie, the King's aunt, who had been
ailing for some time, became seriously ill. On
21st February she received the last Sacraments in
presence of the Royal Family, and died on the
3rd of March following. Mme de Bombelles in
a letter to her husband gives us the following
details: "Mme Sophie died this morning. She
got worse on the second. . . . In the morning it
was thought that her sufferings were caused by the
remedies, and everyone was so sure she would not
die yet that there was even a play at the palace
that evening. At its close the King and Queen
were informed that Mme Sophie was very ill; so
they and Monsieur, M. le Comte d'Artois and
Mme Elizabeth went to her and remained till the
end. The poor Princess was perfectly conscious
till the last half hour. It was the dropsy which
moved to her chest and heart that killed her. She
died of suffocation very much like the Empress.
Her body has gone this evening to St. Denis.
. . . Mme Elizabeth is extremely grieved and
impressed by the terrible sight of the death of her
aunt. I have hardly left her since it occurred and
write near her now. She wept much yesterday,
to-day she is quieter. She is in good health, only

very sad. She insists on making her Will and thinks only of death. It is not surprising that with her quick imagination she should feel this so much, but I hope in a few days she will be calmer and will only think of death as much as is necessary in order to live well." The death of the gentle Mme Sophie left many to mourn her memory, and Mesdames her sisters were inconsolable.

Even family losses, however, cannot for long be outwardly mourned at Court, and by the following May the visit of the Grand Duke Paul of Russia and his wife, who travelled under the names of the Comte et Comtesse du Nord, necessitated various gaieties and functions in their honour. At one of these (a supper for three hundred persons) the Baroness d'Oberkirch assisted, and in her Mémoires, published many years later, she thus records her impressions of our Princess: "I had the honour to be placed next Mme Elizabeth, and to watch this holy princess quite at my ease. She was in all the brilliance of her youth and beauty, and had refused all alliances in order to remain with her family. 'I can only marry a King's son,' she said, 'and a King's son must reign over his father's kingdom. I should no longer be a Frenchwoman. I do not wish to cease to be one. It is far better to stay here at the foot of my brother's throne than to ascend another.'"

We have already mentioned Mlle de Causans as one of the three more intimate friends of the

Princess. About this time, this young lady, who was a " Canoness,"[1] was about to quit her for the eight months' residence which her Chapter required by the rule. Mme Elizabeth could not face the thought of such a long separation, and used every endeavour to attach her to her person ; but Mme de Causans could not accept the proposition, declaring it was "a long-established maxim" in her family that none of her daughters should accept a place at Court until they were married.

Nothing daunted, our Princess determined to find a husband for her friend ; and fortunately, M. de Raigecourt, who presented himself with other *partis*, was accepted by the de Causans ladies as a suitable match. Mme Elizabeth now considered how she could help to establish the new *ménage*, and after first thinking of consulting the King, she determined on this occasion to submit her wish to the Queen. One morning, therefore, she visited Marie Antoinette, saying she had come to beg for a favour, and for one that must not be refused.

" Then it is accorded now," was the reply, and after a few more pleasantries the matter was explained and Mme Elizabeth's project revealed. "Causans is going to be married. I want to give her a *dot* of 50,000 *écus*. The King usually gives me 30,000 francs as my New Year's gift. Ask him to advance me this sum for five years."

[1] These ladies are not canonically Religious and are not bound by religious vows. They are therefore at liberty to marry.

The Queen was successful in her embassy, and the King granted the request. For five years our Princess, alone of all the Royal Family, received no present; but, as she cheerfully remarked, "I have no *étrennes* yet, but I have my *Raigecourt*."

In September 1784, Mme Elizabeth met with an accident which might easily have had fatal results. Mme de Bombelles describes it in her usual lucid way. Writing to her husband she says, "Imagine that last Wednesday Mme Elizabeth, when she was out hunting, fell from her horse and rolled under the feet of M. de Menou's, and I saw that the slightest movement of the horse would have broken her head or limbs. Happily, I was alarmed for nothing, and she did not hurt herself in the least. As you may suppose, I jumped off my horse and flew to her rescue. When she saw how pale and frightened I looked, she embraced me, assuring me that she did not feel the least little pain. We placed her again on her horse and I remounted mine, and we followed for the rest of the Hunt as if nothing had happened."

On 1st November, All Saints, when Mme Elizabeth came from Mass in the Palace Chapel, she heard that Mme de Raigecourt was unwell; and from this time her friend and the de Causans family occupied much of her time. Mme de Causans was taken ill in Paris, and our Princess had, with her wonted devotion, to console and encourage the two invalids. On the day that she wrote to inform Mme de Causans that her infant

grandson had died, the Court went into mourning
for the Duc d'Orléans, who died on 18th November,
at the age of sixty.   He was much regretted,
and although, "as Prince, he did not attract much
attention, it may be considered that his loss was a
public misfortune : devoted as he was to the King,
the head of his family, it is possible that later on
he might have controlled his son's leaning to a
Revolution which, in its turn, ruined him."

An anecdote is related of a joke perpetrated
by the Comte de Provence which illustrates the
friendly feeling which then united the two royal
branches.   On 10th August 1785 the Court was
about to leave Saint Cloud to establish itself at
Fontainebleau.   The Queen determined to go by
water, and started from Paris in a beautiful and
costly yacht.   On the same morning the Duke of
Orleans, then at his country place of Sainte Assise,
received a casket addressed to him, but with no
accompanying letter or explanation.   Very curious
to see its contents, the Duke caused the casket to
be opened, and discovered inside a fine net of gold
and silver tissue of great length.   The following
madrigal accompanied the mysterious gift :—

> " A vous savante enchanteresse
> O Montessan l'ancre s'adresse
> Docile à mon avis follet
> Avec confiance osez tendre
> Sur le champ ce galant filet
> Et quelque grace va s'y prendre."

Neither the Duke of Orleans nor his wife,

Mme de Montessan,[1] nor any one of their Court could find the key to this riddle, and the Duke had the net repacked, and gave orders that it should be sent to the Head of the Police with a request that its meaning might be discovered. The explanation was simple. The Duke and Mme de Montessan, hearing of the Queen's voyage, which would bring her under their very windows, had done everything in their power to induce her to stop at Sainte Assise, but in vain; and the Comte de Provence had imagined this ingenious device, which must, he thought, strike her fancy, for arresting his sister-in-law's passage. Unfortunately, as we have seen, no one comprehended the joke. It fell flat, and in his disappointment the Comte exclaimed, "With all their cleverness, how stupid they are at Sainte Assise."

The Duke was a man of large charities, which he carefully concealed, so that they were only discovered at his death. When, according to etiquette, the Duc de Chartres came to announce the sad event to the King, and the latter replied, "Monsieur le Duc d'Orléans, I am very sorry for the death of the Prince your father," he assumed the title, and the Duc de Valois, his eldest son, became Duc de Chartres.

Soon after this, a humbler death-bed made a

[1] After the death of his first wife, Louise de Bourbon Condé, the Duke had secretly married Mme de Montessan, with this very laconic permission of Louis XV.: "Monsieur l'Archevêque, vous croirez ce que vous direz mon cousin le Duc d'Orléans et vous passerez outre."

great impression on our Princess. One day at Montreuil a peasant employed by her was taken suddenly ill in the garden. She had him at once removed to his house, and sent for a priest and a doctor. The illness was fatal and rapid; but the poor man died surrounded by the tenderest care. When all was over and she was leaving the cottage, the curé said to her, "Madame has given a great example here." "Oh, Monsieur," she replied, "I have received a much greater one, which I shall never forget."

The death of Mme de Causans on 4th January 1786 was a sorrow to Mme Elizabeth, and we regret that we are unable to linger over her correspondence with the bereaved daughters. We give two notes, however, to Marie de Causans, who was a special favourite with the Princess :—

"Don't trouble your heart," she writes on 1st March 1786, "by trying to discover what God requires of you. . . . Submit yourself, live *au jour le jour.* Tell yourself in the morning all that you ought to do during the day and why you should do it. Don't anticipate to-morrow, and never change a resolution firmly taken without very strong reasons. Firmness with yourself for a time will bring peace to your heart again, and about everything else drive away scruples, for nothing disquiets or puts one on the wrong road more than scruples."

She writes on 10th April : "I made my Easter Communion to-day. I recalled a certain Holy

Week which I spent with your mother. How happy we were. I never spent one like it. She assured me that I should persevere—she will be the cause: her example, her last words, the letter that she wrote me, all give me confidence. You told her to reckon me among her children. Ah, I am indeed her child in my heart, for I love her very tenderly." Later Mme Elizabeth writes again, urging her friend not to dwell unduly on her grief at the loss of her mother, which she sees is becoming a danger for her. "You dwell too much on just regrets."

Early in January we find Mme Elizabeth, with the rest of the Royal Family, signing the contract of marriage between Mlle Necker and the Baron de Staël. "Although not caring much for M. Necker, Mme Elizabeth could not see without interest this young lady, already known for her wit, and who was to marry the Ambassador of a king devoted to the royal house of France."

Early in the same year we have occasion to admire Mme Elizabeth's very practical good sense. One day the gardeners at Montreuil were alarmed to find an extraordinary number of worms and small cockcroaches in the soil, which threatened the existence of the flowers and vegetables and the beautiful green turf, and went with long faces to their mistress to announce the disaster. "Well," she said, "as you have given us notice of the approach of the enemy, let us be well prepared for him. Warn our neighbours; and tell our magistrate, so that he may send round a proclamation by the drummer to warn the farmers, the officers of justice, and the Curés, to watch and concur in the destruction of the common foe." Thanks to this energy on the part of the Princess, the pest was greatly diminished.

On 9th July the Queen gave birth to another daughter, who was baptized the same evening by the names of Sophie Hélène Béatrice, Mme Elizabeth being her godmother.

On the 1st of August 1786 occurred the centenary of St. Cyr, and it was kept with great rejoicings, the fêtes lasting for a week. As we may imagine, Mme Elizabeth took a special interest in the occasion, and was present on the first day of the rejoicings. She assisted at High Mass in the Chapel, the music for which had been composed by M. Asselin of Versailles and was sung by the pupils of the house. In the evening there were fireworks, which the Princess witnessed from one of the balconies looking into the inner garden. She had a talk that evening with some of the Religious who had been pupils in Mme de Maintenon's time; and as she drove home she conversed with her ladies upon the high qualities of the great King who had taken an equal interest in children who were beginning their lives and old soldiers who were ending theirs, and "who signed with the same pen the foundations of St. Cyr and of the Hotel des Invalides." "It is not without cause," said she, "that Louis XIV. placed this

Institute under the shadow of his palace and under his own patronage. The moral influence of woman is great in France; how important therefore is the education of the young girls who are destined to hold a position in society. What excellent air one breathes at St. Cyr," she continued. "It is there I learnt to love fields and solitude. I always go there with pleasure, because it seems to me that I come back better."

During this conversation Mme de Maintenon's words were also recalled : "Your house will not fail as long as there is a King in France." Mme de Bombelles, to whom we owe these details, adds sadly, "In a few years' time we bade adieu to the glorious past which we were praising that evening." Our Princess could indeed little foresee that shortly the statue of Louis xiv. at St. Cyr would be overthrown, that the prelate who said the Mass would become an exile, that the preacher would be massacred, that the doors of the House would be closed, and least of all, perhaps, that she herself was destined to become a victim to the fury of her own countrymen.

She returned to her quiet life at Montreuil, where her day was spent in study, good works, and correspondence with her chosen friends. It offered a great contrast to the feverish anxiety and publicity of the Court life at Versailles. We do not know whether any voice dared to lift itself to mock at Mme Elizabeth's expense, but in spite of her wish

4

to live unknown, her virtues were known and appreciated throughout France.

On 29th August the Bishop of Alais, at the head
of a deputation from Languedoc, had audience
with the King, and on leaving the royal presence
begged to be allowed to offer his homage to Mme
Elizabeth. He made her, according to the custom
of the times, a complimentary address. Quite con-
fused at his praise, the Princess blushingly replied
that the Bishop judged her too kindly. "Madame,"
he replied, " I am not even at the level of my
subject." "You are right," she returned, "you are
far above it."

The Princess did not care for gaieties, and only
appeared at the Court entertainments when duty
obliged her to do so, or at the personal desire of
the King and Queen. She intuitively realised the
dangers ahead, and regretted the Queen's willing-
ness to show herself in public and the fact that she
drove to Paris without any ceremony. Even the
walks on the Terrace at Versailles in summer, when
Marie Antoinette allowed herself to be surrounded
by the crowd, were subjects of anxiety to her. She
saw that the barrier of regal dignity was a real
and necessary one to preserve the respect of the
populace. She feared that "if sovereigns de-
scended often to the people, the people would
approach near enough to see that the Queen was
only a pretty woman, and that they would soon
conclude that the King was merely the first among
officials." Not daring to impart her sentiments to

CHATEAU DE TRIANON.
Prise dans le Jardin Français.

the Queen herself, Mme Elizabeth confided them
to Mme Adelaide, who tried to impress them on
her niece.

These dangers did not exist at Trianon, and
Mme Elizabeth loved to be there with the Queen.
They then lived alone, as there was no room in the
villa for the Court ladies, and they led the life of
ordinary ladies in a country house : dressed "in
white cotton dresses, straw hats and gauze fichus,"
and delighted in fishing in the lake or seeing the
cows milked. The King and his brothers often
came to supper ; and when the Queen had the
fancy to act comedies, as was done in most
Châteaux of France, our Princess took her share
in the piece : for instance, in *La Gageure Imprévue*
she took the part of the young girl, the Queen that
of de Gotte, and Comtesse Diane de Polignac that
of Mme de Clairville.

But far more serious matters were soon to claim
the attention of the Royal Family. Mme Elizabeth,
as we have seen, was not altogether unprepared
for the sad changes at hand, and she viewed the
political atmosphere with a calm good sense and
wisdom astonishing at her age and in her position.
The financial disorder and the recurring troubles
and discord throughout the kingdom caused the
King to call the National Assembly to meet at
Versailles on 29th January 1787. Owing, however,
to the illness of M. de Verjeunes, it was postponed
to 22nd February. On that day the King opened
the Assembly surrounded by his family. How

Mme Elizabeth looked upon the measure we may learn by a letter of hers dated 15th March: "What will this famous Assembly do for us? Nothing, except to let the people know the critical position in which we are. The King acts in good faith in asking their advice; will they do the same in the counsels they will give him? The Queen is very pensive. Sometimes we spend hours alone without her saying a word. She seems to fear me. And yet who can take a more lively interest than I do in my brother's happiness? Our views differ. She is an Austrian. I am a Bourbon. The Comte d'Artois does not understand the necessity of these great reforms; he thinks that people augment the deficit in order to have the right to complain and to demand the assembly of the States-General. *Monsieur* is much occupied in writing; he is much more serious, and you know he was grave enough already. I have a presentiment that all this will turn out badly. As for me, intrigues tire me. I love peace and rest. But I will never leave the King while he is unhappy."

In the June of this year the little Mme Sophie died, before she was a year old. Mme Elizabeth was with her throughout her short illness, and their mutual anxiety drew the Queen still more to her sister-in-law. A few days later the following note reached our Princess: "Mme de Polignac was very indisposed all yesterday, and this morning, and made me anxious, which is the reason, my dear Heart, that you have not seen my handwriting, as you expected, in your little Trianon. I am anxious to make a visit to mine with you, dear Elizabeth. Let us fix it for the 24th; is that settled? The King promises to come too, and we will weep there over the death of our little Angel. Adieu, my dear Heart, you know how much I love you, and I have need of all your heart to console mine.—MARIE ANTOINETTE, *this 22nd June* 1787."

Mme Elizabeth, of course, accepted the invitation, and from Trianon wrote a long letter to Mme de Bombelles, full of affection for the Queen and her children, especially for the young Marie Thérèse, "who has been charming, she has shown an extraordinary sensibility for her age, and that quite simply." Was it a presentiment of the future which made Mme Elizabeth speak of the little dead niece as "very happy to have escaped all peril: my laziness makes me wish I could have shared her fate," she adds, "when I was younger."

Later in the summer the royal ladies again spent some time at Trianon, where the King and Princes often joined them. "They all seemed to feel the need of seeing each other more and more, as if they felt that separation was at hand."

The need for economy was realised even by the Court and Royal Family, and Mme Elizabeth, who could not reproach herself for undue expenditure in her simple life, still saw a method by which she could save her brother some expense. Sending for the head of the royal stables, she said to him,

"Monsieur, reforms, I know, are indispensable. The King wishes above all to give the example in his own household. I beg that my horses may be the first to be suppressed. I have another service to ask from you. The King is so kind that he might think that my health would suffer from want of my favourite exercise. Promise me that you will keep the secret for me." The secret was kept, but we are glad to know that the sacrifice was not considered necessary; and the Princess, writing to Mme de Bombelles, expresses her naïve joy: "I cannot hide from you that this has given me great pleasure, and I am the more pleased that I am going to-morrow to hunt at Rambouillet with the Duchesse de Duras."

While these necessary reforms in expenditure were occupying her mind, the Princess said one day, "At Versailles they laugh at me sometimes for my modest household expenditure. Well, I am sorry to say it, but the King himself does not possess many servants perhaps who prefer to break their own heads in his service rather than his china. This is, however, what my poor Brisson did. When he was bringing up my dessert, his foot slipped on the stairs and all the china in his *barquette*[1] would infallibly have been broken if this good fellow had not held it up horizontally by pressing his head against the wall. The shock he received was so great that he fainted as soon as his

[1] A sort of stand like a porter's chair, in which the meals of the Royal Family were sent from the kitchen.

barquette was safely placed on the ground." Mme Elizabeth caused this faithful servant to be taken at once to the hospital, but some six weeks later, after he had apparently quite recovered from the accident, Brisson died suddenly, leaving his wife and six children in great poverty. Mme Elizabeth persuaded the Controller of the Royal Household to grant the widow a pension, to which she added a sum from her own allowance.

The winter of 1788–89 was terribly cold, and inaugurated the period of affliction and misery throughout France. Mme Elizabeth joined with the King and Queen, the Archbishop of Paris, and all Christian souls in doing her utmost to cope with the poverty and suffering. She economised in her household in every possible way, so as to give "not of her abundance, but of her necessity," and when other resources failed she sold a watch or bracelet or some other precious object. " It not only brings money," she said, "it is also time gained, for such-and-such poor people will not have so long to suffer."

Parliament had refused to confirm an Edict relating to import duties, and had been banished. In exiling Parliament, Louis was using the monarchical right, but Mme Elizabeth perceived that her brother, who, though " he could heroically resist force, could never use it with discernment or perseverance,"[1] would have done better to have brought Parliament gently to his views than to

[1] *Vie de Mme Elizabeth*, vol. i. p. 272.

have used this extreme measure, and predicted that it would be recalled in six months.

"It seems to me," she wrote, "that it is with Government as with education, one must only say *I wish this* when one is sure one is right—but once it is said one must never change what has been prescribed."

The dark days were at hand, but Court life still continued its course, and one special ceremony demands our attention, as being one of the last joyful occasions on which our Princess appeared in public at Versailles. We feel, as her biographer says, the wish to linger over the details of a period which saw the last gleams of her prosperity, "as if we hesitated to enter the phase of her life in which she becomes greater, but at the price of what trials and what sorrows."

CHAPTER IV

BEGINNING OF TROUBLES

THE ceremony to which we have alluded was the audience granted by the King to the Envoys of Tippoo Sahib, Sultan of Mysore, who sent them to beg his assistance in expelling the English from his domains. On 10th August, after spending the night at the Grand Trianon, they were escorted to Versailles and received with great pomp.

According to the *Gazette de France*, His Majesty, accompanied by Monsieur the Comte d'Artois, His Royal Highness the Duc d'Angoulême, and other princes, went to the Hall of Hercules, which had been decorated and arranged on purpose for the occasion. "The throne was placed on a platform close to the chimney-piece. Two tribunes were arranged in the doorways. The rest of the room was filled by benches for the lords and ladies of the Court. The Queen had preceded the King, and had placed herself in the tribune on the left with Mgr le Duc de Normandie and Madame her daughter beside her. The one on the right was occupied by Madame, Mme la Comtesse d'Artois and Madame Elizabeth de France." The Royal

Princes were near the throne. The King, having seated himself, gave orders to the officers of State to go and fetch the Indian Ambassadors. They were brought through the Hall of the King's Bodyguards, who lined the room under arms, the Queen's Apartments, the Gallery, and the "Grand Apartments." The Envoys apparently were not embarrassed by all this state, and offered the letter they had brought to the King, together with gold coins, after many low bows. As they retired after the King's speech, they begged permission to remain in the doorway for a moment to watch the "brilliant and majestic" aspect offered by the Hall of Hercules. On their return to Paris they were entertained by many festivities, and had the honour of assisting at a meeting of the French Academy, "but had not the patience to remain to the end." On leaving this séance, the Envoys heard of the downfall of Loménie de Brienne, who was replaced by M. Necker, and they very characteristically begged to be allowed "to see the head" of the unfortunate Minister.

These chiefs, dazzled by the magnificence of Versailles, can little have realised that the French Monarchy was on the brink of an abyss, and that their audience was one of the last occasions on which Louis would be able freely to receive a message from another Power.

The tragic events which were to change the face of France were close at hand. On 27th December, the King in Council decided that the number

KING LOUIS XVI
From the original in the Louvre

of the Deputies to the States-General should be twelve hundred—six hundred to represent the nobles and the clergy, six hundred for the "Third Estate." It is related that when he returned to his apartments after this decision, which is attributed partly to Necker's influence, Louis found in his study a picture of Charles I. of England in the place of one of Louis XV., and that he was somewhat moved by the incident, but recovering himself in a moment, he said in a resolute tone, "They may do what they like—the Third Estate will be doubly represented, it is irrevocably settled."

Mme Elizabeth took her part in the ceremonies of the General Assembly at Versailles and at the great Procession of the Blessed Sacrament on Corpus Christi, 11th June 1789, which was the last at which the Royal Family ever assisted there.

By the 23rd of the month the "principles of the Revolution were declared. The Noblesse gave way to the States, certain members of the clergy did likewise, and the three orders found themselves united and confounded in the same Hall where a few days earlier they had been directed to separate. . . . The Third Estate was everything. The Noblesse and Clergy were nothing and Royalty very little. The Assembly had entered into a career of audacity, the Monarchy on one of concessions."

While these gloomy prognostications, of which the echo reached Montreuil, occupied men's thoughts, Mme Elizabeth continued her sheltered life. "After

turning Bourgeoise, she now became a dairy woman"
for the sake of her charities.   She sent to Switzerland for some cows and for a Swiss to look after
them.   Jacques Bosson, from Basle, near Fribourg,
was selected for the honour ; and as he had parents
who were devoted to him, they too were invited by
the Princess to make their home at Montreuil.
" Remember," she said to her cowman when he
arrived, "the milk belongs to my poor children ;
even I will not taste it until the distribution has
been made."   Jacques proved worthy of his
position, and he and his family became devoted to
their mistress.   "What a good Princess," Jacques
said often to Mme de Bombelles.   "All Switzerland cannot produce anyone so perfect."

In spite of his happiness, however, poor Jacques'
heart was in his own country with his cousin Marie,
to whom he was betrothed ; and she, on her part,
was sad and feared he would forget her.   Mme
Elizabeth discovered that something was amiss,
and when she knew the reason of Jacques' distress,
she said, "Without knowing it, I have made two
people unhappy then ; I will repair my fault.
Marie must come here.   She shall marry Jacques,
and be the milkmaid of Montreuil."   On 26th May,
accordingly, just after the opening of the Assembly,
the faithful couple were united in the Church of
Montreuil, and took possession of the home prepared
for them.   This little idyll, which was quite in
character with the period, delighted the Court, and
Bosson's name was rendered historic by some verses

written by Mme de Travannes, sister of Mme de
Bombelles, entitled " Pauvre Jacques," which were
set to music, and became very popular.

Meanwhile, a great sorrow was hanging over
the Royal Family. The Dauphin, who had been
in bad health for some time, became dangerously
ill at the Château of Meudon, where he had gone
for his health, and died on 5th June 1789. Louis
XVI., although prepared for the blow, was inconsolable. Could he have seen what his child was
thus spared, and the fate that awaited his second
son, he would have thought this sorrow a blessing
indeed.

The storm which had been so long gathering
broke over France a month later, on 12th July,
the day of the taking of the Bastille and the
murder of Foulon and Berthier.

Mme Elizabeth, who did not yet know of all
these horrors, wrote on the same day to Mme de
Bombelles.

This letter shows the uncertainty that reigned
at Versailles as to whether the King would leave
the place, and she unselfishly urges her friend not
to come there. Soon the Princess was to say
adieu to her for ever. M. de Bombelles was still
at Ratisbon, where his wife was to join him. Mme
Elizabeth interested herself in every detail of the
journey, etc. ; and the last day they spent together
their talk continued till night : " We are separating for a time," said the Princess, " it is necessary ;
but we shall remain always united by a community

of interests, thoughts, and prayers." They parted in tears, but mercifully without knowledge of the terrible future. "This farewell," said Mme de Bombelles, years later, "was to be eternal. If I could have foreseen it, that moment would have been my last. I should have died at her feet."

A letter to Mme de Bombelles, dated Versailles, 5th August, must be one of the first addressed to her after this parting. It makes one sad to see the illusions still indulged in by the Court.

"The joy of knowing you are in good health," writes the Princess, "is very great in this weary world. The first letters we get will be still better received, and above all the fourth. . . . I have kept my word, my child, I did not regret saying good-bye to you, but—I do not know whether it is from that—I am in a very bad humour. Do not be conceited, however. I am delighted that you have gone to nurse 'Henry IV.' where the climate is warmer, and more suitable for the education you wish to give him. . . . Rejoice at the news I am going to tell you, if you do not know it already. First, the Ministers are chosen, and seem to be approved by the public. The Archbishop of Bordeaux has the Seal ;[1] the Archbishop of Vienne the gift of Benefices ; M. de la Tour du Pin-Paulin the War Office, and the Maréchal de Beauvau is of the Council. Secondly, on the night between Tuesday and Wednesday, the Assembly sat till

[1] Mgr Champion de Cicé.

CHATEAU DE VERSAILLES DU COTÉ DES JARDINS.

two o'clock. The nobles, with an enthusiasm worthy of French hearts, have renounced all their feudal rights, their game rights, and fishing, I think, will also be included. The clergy also have renounced the *dîmes*, the *casuels*, and the possibility of holding two Benefices. News of this Act has been sent to all the Provinces. I trust that this will bring an end to the burning of Châteaux. They number seventy. It was the case of who would sacrifice most, everyone was magnetized. Never was there such joy and shouts. The *Te Deum* is to be sung in the Chapel, and the King is to be given the title of 'Restorer of French Liberty.' . . . I think, my Heart, you will be happy at the good news that I give you."

About this time Mme Elizabeth had to say good-bye also and for ever to Mme de Raigecourt. In her last interview with this dear friend the Princess gave her a beautiful manuscript prayer composed by herself.[1]

The horrors of the 12th July had been a revelation for our Princess, although, as we have seen, she still hoped for good from the new measures proposed in the Assembly. The events of 1st October, in spite of the loyal reception given to the Royal Family at the banquet of the King's Body-guards, left her anxious. When someone spoke of the loud acclamations which had greeted Louis on this occasion, and said that they must

[1] "Prière au Sacré Cœur de Jésus," still preserved in the Bibliothèque Nationale in Paris.

have been heard in Paris: "If only," remarked Mme Elizabeth, "the populace does not reply by insults"; a prophecy which was to be quickly verified.

On the fatal day, 5th October, when the people attacked Versailles, she was on her terrace at Montreuil when she saw the crowd advancing on the Palace, and flew at once to join the Royal Family there. Gifted as she was with an excellent judgment, Mme Elizabeth possessed also an energy of character which one must regret was not shared by the King.

She felt convinced on this occasion that "a vigorous and speedy repression of the riot would save many misfortunes. It seemed to her evident that a few cannon-balls would arrest the advance-guard of anarchy; would cause confusion among the troops which were behind; and — while arousing useful reflections on the part of the hostile portion of the Assembly—would stimulate the courage of the friends of order, who were alarmed at the cowardice of the Government."[1]

Our Princess "developed her views with that firmness of judgment and heartfelt eloquence which characterised her," and likewise urged that the Royal Family should move to some town farther from Paris, where their deliberations would be free from the influence of factions. For a moment these wise counsels, which were echoed by those of M. de la Priest, seemed about to be followed, but M. Necker's observation that " to draw the sword against

[1] *Vie de Mme Elizabeth*, vol. i. p. 308.

rebellion was to give the signal for civil war," caused the King to change, and it was determined to treat the rioters on equal terms.

Mme Elizabeth, unable to do more, retired to the Queen's apartments, and remained with her till two in the morning, when M. de Lafayette affirmed that he could answer for the safety of the Palace.

Early in the morning, the King, anxious for her welfare, sent to look for his sister, and she went to his rooms only to hear how useless had been the assurances given by the General. She remained at Versailles throughout that terrible day, encouraging the Royal Bodyguard by her calmness, and even saving some of their lives by her presence of mind. When the chiefs of the mob demanded "with loud cries" that the King should go to Paris to reside, and Lafayette sent message after message to urge him to assent, Mme Elizabeth took quite another view of the matter. "Sire, it is not to Paris you should go," she said. "You still have devoted battalions, faithful guards, who will protect your retreat, but I implore you, my brother, do not go to Paris."

Had Louis listened to her, the whole future might have been different; but while hesitating between the two opinions, the precious moment was lost — it was too late — and he gave the desired promise.

When the melancholy procession set out for the capital, Mme Elizabeth was in the King's carriage, "in one of the doorways," says the Duchesse de

5

Tourzel, who herself sat opposite the King and Queen, holding the Dauphin on her knee.

As they approached the Avenue de Paris, the Princess, who had a presentiment that she was leaving Versailles for ever, leant out of the window to look at her own little Park.

"My sister, you are saluting Montreuil," said Louis.

"Sire," she replied gently, "I am bidding it adieu."

At this point in the history of Mme Elizabeth the Duchesse de Tourzel's Memoirs become of extreme interest to us, and give many details regarding her till the moment when this devoted lady was forcibly removed from the Royal Family, during their imprisonment in the Temple.[1]

After describing the arrival of the unhappy King and his family in Paris, and the first wretched night in the Palace of the Tuileries, which was utterly unprepared for their reception, she says, "The awakening of the royal family was terrible. The courtyards and the terraces of the Tuileries were filled by an immense crowd of people, who demanded with loud cries to see the King and the royal family, some for the pleasure of realising their victory, the greater number from curiosity, and some from a feeling of interest and

[1] *Mémoires de Madame la Duchesse de Tourzel, Gouvernante des Enfants de France*, 1789-1795. Ed. by the Duc des Cars, Paris, 1883.

attachment. The royal family, even the Princesses, were obliged to wear the national cockade and to show themselves several times to the people from an apartment on the ground floor, which looked on to the courtyard and which was occupied by Mme Elizabeth. Each time she appeared there were cries of 'Long live the King and the royal family.'"

A few days later, several *poissardes* actually jumped through the window into Mme Elizabeth's rooms, and she was obliged to ask the King to give her others, and "ever afterwards had an extreme repugnance for this apartment," adds Mme de Tourzel.[1] The rooms now assigned to our Princess were in the Pavillon de Flore.[2] In this apartment, where "new locks had been made for the doors," she felt secure, although the rooms were neither "elegant nor convenient," we are told. It must be added that, in spite of their rudeness, the *Dames de la Halle* preserved a feeling of special affection for Mme Elizabeth, which survived their former loyalty to the throne, and they called her the Sainte Géneviève of the Tuileries.

The life of the royal family under its changed circumstances was very dull as well as most sad and anxious. "The Queen breakfasted alone, and then saw her children. At this hour the King

---

[1] Mme de Tourzel, vol. i. p. 38.

[2] When Pius VI. was in Paris in 1804 for the Coronation of Napoleon, he occupied the Pavillon de Flore, and, alluding to Mme Elizabeth, remarked that he was occupying the rooms of a saint.

joined her. After Mass she retired to her own rooms. She dined at one o'clock with the King, Madame her daughter, and Mme Elizabeth. After dinner she played at billiards with the King in order that he might have some exercise, worked at her tapestry with Mme Elizabeth and then went back to her rooms till half-past eight, at which hour Monsieur and Madame arrived for supper, and at eleven everyone retired."[1]

During the next two years Mme Elizabeth's correspondence gives us many details of interest, and for long it is evident that she hoped against hope, as we may say, for better times. Her interest in her friends remained as keen as ever, and she often tries to write cheerfully in order to encourage them. Nor was Montreuil forgotten: in a letter to Mme de Bombelles of 8th December 1789 she says, "I don't show any courage in not speaking of Montreuil. You judge me too favourably, my Heart. Apparently I was not thinking of it, when I wrote to you. I often have news from there. Jacques comes every day to bring me my cream;[2] Flury, Coupry, Marie, and Mme du

[1] Mme Dubuquois, who had a needlework shop in Paris, long possessed a small carpet worked by the royal ladies, and which, it is said, the Empress Josephine purchased in the hope of offering it to the Duchesse d'Angoulême in memory of her mother and aunt.

[2] After the 10th August 1792 the Revolutionary Government took possession of Montreuil, and poor Jacques and Marie were imprisoned for a time. They afterwards managed to return with their child to Switzerland, where the honour of having been the servants of Mme Elizabeth brought them the esteem and interest of their countrymen.

Coudray come to see me occasionally. They all seem to love me, and M. Huret, whom I was forgetting, is not very ill. Now for the house. The Salon was being furnished when I left, and promised to be very nice. . . . I don't know if you saw my little study furnished, it is very pretty. My library is nearly ready. As to the chapel, Corille is working at it alone, so you can imagine it does not get on quick ; it is really out of charity to him that I agreed to let him continue to plaster it. As he is all alone, it cannot be considered an expense. I am sorry not to go there, you will easily believe it, but the horses are a still greater privation for me. However, as I cannot make use of them I think of them as little as possible. . . . And poor St. Cyr! ah, it is very sad. . . . Do you remember Croisard, the son of my sister's wardrobe woman? Well! now he is attached to me in the position of Captain. I say *attached*, because he does not leave us any more than a shadow does the body. Do not think that this worries me. As my walks are not varied, it is all the same to me. Still, I take as much exercise as I can, so be happy. This morning again I walked for a good hour."

In February 1790 the judicial murder of M. de Favras, who perished simply for his loyalty, filled the Royal Family with sorrow. Mme Elizabeth especially felt it acutely. Writing to Mme de Bombelles on 20th February, she says, " You will only have one word from me, my poor Bombe.

I heard too late that there was an opportunity for writing, and then my head and heart are so full of yesterday's doings that I feel it hardly possible to think of other things. Poor M. de Favras, of whose case you may have heard by the newspapers, was hanged yesterday. I trust his blood will not be on the heads of his judges, but no one (save the populace, and that class of person to whom one cannot give the name of man without degrading humanity) understands why he was condemned. He had the imprudence to wish to serve his King. That was his crime. I hope that this unjust execution will have the same result as persecution, and that from its embers will arise men who will still love their country and deliver it from the traitors who deceive it. I hope also that Heaven will have forgiven his sins on account of the courage he evinced during the four hours he passed at the Hôtel de Ville before his execution. Pray God for him, my Heart, you cannot do a more blessed work."

The month of March brought the beginning of the active legislation against the Church. Although at first the Assembly, which still called itself Catholic, affirmed its wish to remain in union with the Holy See, it soon passed laws incompatible with this profession, and the strife between principle and scepticism commenced. On the 17th, a decree declared that "the property of the clergy should be sold for the profit of the nation, who would charge itself with their maintenance."

During the discussion regarding the constitution and the clergy, Montlosier, who was defending
the cause of the bishops, said words which find an
echo in our times. "You chase them from their
Palaces," he cried, "they will retire under the
thatched roofs of the poor, whom they have fed.
You take away their gold crosses, they will wear
wooden ones—and it was a cross of wood which
saved the world."

After the clergy it was the turn of the nuns.
"The *philosophes* opened the doors of the convents,
and the nuns were authorised to go out into the
world. All, with a few rare exceptions, declared
that they wished to remain in their cloisters, but
they were turned out in the name of liberty."

Mme Elizabeth was in consternation at these
attacks upon religion. She saw that the Revolution
found its interest in attacking Catholicism, and
"deplored the mad actions of those who opposed
their individual views to the Christian religion, and
who in liberty of thought pretended to find liberty
also to do anything they chose."

On the 1st of May she wrote a letter to Mme
de Bombelles which represents so fully her political
views that we must give it in its entirety :—

"You are much more perfect than I. You
dread *civil war*. I confess that I look upon it as
necessary; first, I think it exists now, because
whenever a Kingdom is divided into two parties,
and the weakest side can only exist by allowing itself to be despoiled, I cannot but call that

civil war ; and further, Anarchy can never finish without that, and I think the longer it delays the more blood will be shed. That is my principle. It may be false ; however, if I was King, it would be my guide, and would, perhaps, prevent great misfortunes. But, as, thank God, it is not I who rules, I content myself, while I approve my brother's plans, with telling him constantly that he cannot be too prudent, and that he must not risk anything. I am not astonished that the step the King took on 4th February has done him harm in the opinion of strangers. I hope, however, that it has not discouraged our Allies, and that they will, at last, have pity on us. Our residence here interferes with our interests greatly,—I would give anything to be out of this, but it is very difficult. However, I hope it may come. If for a moment I thought we did right to come to Paris, I have long changed my mind ; but, my Heart, if we had known how to profit of that moment, believe me that we should have done much good. But it required firmness—it required that we should not fear that the provinces would be angered with the capital—it required that we should resolutely meet dangers. We should have come out victorious."

The quasi-imprisonment of the Royal Family was lightened this summer by a sojourn at St. Cloud. "M. de Lafayette and even the Assembly was very glad to see the King leave Paris," says Mme de Tourzel, "in order that the

MARIE ANTOINETTE
From the painting by Mme. Vigée Le Brun.

provinces might lose any idea of his captivity at the time of the Federation. They felt the necessity of this so strongly that it was they who persuaded the populace of the desirability of the arrangement so that the journey passed off very quietly."

During their residence at St. Cloud, the King and Queen went to Paris twice a week, sometimes oftener. Our Princess was perhaps allowed to remain at home in peace and enjoy the fresh air and flowers, for she writes to Mme de Bombelles on 27th June: " I finish my letter at St. Cloud. Here I am re-established in the garden, my writing desk and book in my hand, and here I take patience and strength for what lies before me." And again on 16th August: "We are still at St. Cloud, just in the same position, waiting with resignation for what Heaven reserves for us."

St. Cloud brought back many memories to the unfortunate Queen. "It was impossible," says Mme de Tourzel, "for this Princess not to compare the happy days she had spent at St. Cloud with those of her present visit. She often thought of this, and one day, when we were together at the end of the gallery from whence Paris is one of the chief points of view, she sighed and said: ' Life in Paris used to be my delight, I longed to live there often. Who could have told me then that my wish would be realised only to be accompanied by bitterness, and that I should see the King and his family the prisoners of a rebel nation?'"

CHAPTER V

FLIGHT TO VARENNES

ABOUT the middle of October Mme Elizabeth commenced a correspondence with Mme de Raigecourt. This faithful friend was in despair to think of the dangers by which her Princess was surrounded, and implored leave to return to her post; but Mme Elizabeth would not hear of her running this risk. In these letters, in which she is obliged to write with great caution, she hints at the state of things in such sentences as "*Everything is in a despairing state*," or alludes to her desire for the King to leave Paris, and his unwillingness to move. She remarks that nothing can persuade the King, though his enemies persecute him in every way, and plans are proposed to him which he rejects. She also speaks of her Will, which she had entrusted to Mme de Raigecourt. Evidently she had no illusions now as to her position and that of the rest of the Royal Family.

On 27th November the Assembly made a decree forcing the clergy to take an oath for the maintenance of the civil constitution of the clergy.

This oath, which violated the consciences of all good Catholics and was formally condemned by the Holy See, met with loyal opposition from the greater part of the French Bishops and clergy, who preferred the risk of death or banishment to compliance with an iniquitous law. The position of the King, whom his enemies pressed to sanction this decree, was terrible; to use Mme de Tourzel's words: "Placed between his own conscience and the misfortunes which he was assured would follow if he refused, he asked to be given time to consult with the Pope, as to what means of conciliation could be employed to meet the wishes of the Assembly without wounding the consciences of the Bishops and priests; he had written to the Pope and wished to await his reply."[1] All who were attached to religion were in consternation.

As the Princess wrote on the 28th November to Mme de Raigecourt:—

"You cannot imagine the consternation depicted on every countenance. Everyone has *la mort dans l'âme* at seeing the fate prepared for the clergy. They wish the Bishops, curés, priests who have any charge, to swear absolute fealty to the Constitution under pain of being made destitute; and if they desire to continue their functions they declare them guilty of lèse-nation. Therefore,

[1] Mme de Tourzel adds the following note: "I have been assured, without, however, being able to affirm it, that the Ministers had intercepted the Pope's reply, and had not wished to give it to the King, in order to obtain, more easily, the sanction of a Decree to which they attached so great a price."

those who sit in the Assembly must decide within eight days between their conscience or martyrdom. Others have a month or two longer to decide, according to distance. You cannot form an idea of the atrocity of those who have spoken in favour of this decree. Even the least religious are indignant. And how can one hope that the anger of Heaven should slacken, when pleasure is taken in incurring it?

"Let us at least endeavour, my Heart, by our fidelity in serving Him, to efface some of the offences which are daily committed against Him. It depends on us to console Him. Ah, how this thought should animate the fervour of those souls who are happy enough to have the faith. Make your little children pray. God tells us that their prayers are pleasing to Him."

A few days later she wrote to Mme de Bombelles as follows :—

" This 6th December 1790.

"Give this letter to your *Honneur*.[1] I have only time to embrace you. We are all well. I am going to gallop this morning. I will tell you in confidence that the other day I went near Versailles, and I felt a great distress at not being able to go in. How stupid they are not to have kept us prisoners there. Gaoler for gaoler, at least the prison would have been pleasanter. But adieu, I embrace you with all my heart."

[1] Cte. Diane de Polignac. The name of *Honour* had come into use for persons attached to the service of the Royal Family.

" This 10th December.

" You are, I guess, very angry with me. Well! and you are quite in the wrong. Your Princess wanted to write all these days, but the post left when she did not expect it, and so she has been obliged to wait till to-day. . . . I went to Saint Cyr this morning. They are all well, and I saw Delpérouse, who spoke of you. I only returned at half-past four. I came by the top of the Park at Versailles. One must allow that it is a very beautiful spot, and that in spite of the unworthy creatures who are there it would be very nice to be back again. But truce to reflections."

Mme Elizabeth urged the King not to allow himself to be intimidated by the fears with which a minister inspired him who was incapable of valuing the true interests of the Monarchy or of religion, its firmest support. After a long resistance, Louis, vanquished by the fear of causing bloodshed, gave this miserable sanction on 26th December 1790.

Mme Elizabeth could not conceal her grief at this weakness in her brother. Writing to Mme de Raigecourt three days later, she says, " I am in mortal sorrow at the assent which the King has just given." Early in January she wrote with greater hope, after the courage shown by the Bishops and priests in the Assembly. " Religion has shown itself mistress of fear," she says. " God

has spoken to the hearts of the Bishops and
Clergy. They felt all the responsibility that
their sacred office confers, and they declared that
they would not take the oath. On the Left at
least twenty retracted. They were not listened
to, but God saw them and will have forgiven them
their error caused by every form of seduction
which could be used. One Curé on the Left
refused with much firmness. . . . I have no
taste for martyrdom, but I feel that I should be
very happy to have the certainty of suffering it,
rather than give up the smallest article of my
faith. I hope, that if I am destined for it, God
will give me the strength. He is so good—so
good. He is a Father always occupied with the
true happiness of His children. What confidence
we should have in Him."

On 12th February Mme Elizabeth announces
to her friend that her aunts are leaving France.
" In spite of all the fuss made at the Jacobin Club,
or at the Palais Royal, they will start in a week."
Mesdames, seeing no prospect of peace or safety
in the future, and perceiving that things would
come to such a pass as to force the King to escape
from his capital, decided to leave the country for a
time and take refuge in Rome. Their departure
was much opposed and they were twice stopped
on the road—at Moret and at Arnay-le-Duc. At
last, after meeting with many insults between
Lyons and the frontier of Savoy, the venerable
ladies—followed by cries and imprecations as

they crossed the Bridge of Beauvoisin—reached the other side, where they were welcomed by salvos of artillery. Escorted by a brilliant guard of soldiers, they set out for Chambéry, where they were greeted as befitted their rank. The contrast between the treatment accorded to them in their own land and in a strange country affected them deeply.

They spent a fortnight at Turin on their way to Rome, " but not even the touching and gracious welcome offered to them by the royal family, the affection shown to them by the Comte d'Artois and the Prince and Princess of Piedmont, their nephew and niece, could make them forget the anguish and perils they had left behind them, and which encircled their family and country with gloom. Mme Victoire wept continuously, Mme Adelaide did not cry, but she had almost lost the use of speech." [1] At this point we wish we could hear some details of the charming Princess of Piedmont, whose early marriage had left Mme Elizabeth so lonely, and it is tantalising to find no trace either of their correspondence during the years that elapsed after their parting.

The departure of her aunts had been the cause of another loss to the Princess, as their chaplain, the Abbé Madier, had been her valued friend and director since her childhood. She now sought for another priest to replace him, and the Abbé Edgworth, who was to be of supreme help

[1] De Beauchesne, vol. i. p. 357.

to the Royal Family later on, was appointed.   She speaks of him in the following letter :—

"My aunts have at last reached T[urin]. After being stopped for ages at Arnay le Duc, they were very well received at Lyons.   But you know all that better than I do.   What perhaps you do not know, is that the municipality at Arnay gave as a reason for their conduct that as the King is no longer free, they required a word in his handwriting to prove to them that he had agreed to my aunts' journey.   Did you ever see such contradictions?   Also, my Heart, I thought I could see in your letters and in others I have received that people are surprised that I have not done as my aunts have done.   I did not think that my duty called me to take this step, and that is what has dictated my decision.   But believe that I shall never be capable of betraying my duty nor my religion, nor my affection for those who alone merit it, and with whom I would give the world to live.   I am miserable at having mentioned you in a letter, especially as I fear that it has weakened your husband's cause with his antagonist,[1] but I did not imagine that the slightest inconvenience could result. . . . In foreign countries people are very severe in our regard and we merit it. . . . What a calumny, my Bombe, your mother did not have the grief of seeing her Confessor take the oath; but she had that of parting with him, for he has gone to Rome with my aunts."

[1] M. de Calonne (note by M. de Bombelles).

A few days later the Princess wrote to Mme de Raigecourt as follows : " I take advantage of M. de Chamisot's departure to tell you a thousand things. I am infinitely anxious as to the attitude my brother is about to take. I think that the wise counsels he has received will not be followed. The little union, agreement, that exists between those persons who should be united by an indissoluble bond—all—makes me tremble. I would wish to see in all this nothing but the Will of God, but I confess to you that I often judge from a personal point of view. I hope M. de Firmont will by his counsels enable me to attain to that point so necessary for salvation. You will judge by this that it is he who has replaced the Abbé Madier in my confidence. . . . I hope to find in him what has long been wanting to me in order to make progress in piety. Thank God for me, my Heart, that by a special mercy of His Providence He has made me know the Abbé, and ask Him that I may be faithful in executing all the orders He shall give me by this means. . . . I have no news to give you from here. Everything is much the same. The bad amuse themselves at our expense. The good are stupid. France is about to perish. God alone can save her : I hope that He will do so. . . .

" Bombe is soon going to Stuttgart. Believe me, little one, that she will be better off there than you think. Her sister-in-law's affection will make her happy, and I can't believe in the

6

sorrow which you say she will feel. Tell little
Chamisot's[1] parents that he has conducted himself perfectly, that his sentiments are excellent,
and that he has shown great prudence. In
short, that shown by the Pages always astounds
me."

In a letter written many years later, the Abbé
thus speaks of Mme Elizabeth : " Although I was
a stranger and very unworthy to approach this
Princess, I soon became her friend and she gave
me her entire confidence, but neither the King nor
the Queen knew me. They had, however, heard
my name, and during the last days of their reign
they several times expressed surprise at the facility
with which I was allowed to come and go in the
Palace, while all round them was nothing but surveillance and terror. . . . Though my presence
excited some murmurs from the guards, I never
received the smallest insult from them. I went
on in this way until the eve of the fatal day on
which the royal family was arrested. It was the
9th August, 1792, I remember it well. Mme
Elizabeth wished to see me, and I spent a great
part of the forenoon in her study, little foreseeing
the horrors which were being prepared for the
next day." On her side, the Princess found in the
Abbé a true friend and guide. " He has intellect,
gentleness without weakness, a great knowledge

---

[1] Adalbert de Chamisot, who had been Page in the King's service.
He emigrated and distinguished himself in Germany as a great
botanist.

of the human heart, and a great love of God," she once wrote.

To return to the spring of 1791. Louis wished to spend Easter at St. Cloud, in order to perform his devotions in peace, but the project evoked a storm of protest. "The King wished to go to St. Cloud," writes Mme Elizabeth, "but the National Guard opposed it, and to such an extent that we could not pass through the gateway of the court-yard. People wish to force the King to send away the Priests of his Chapel, or to make them take the oath and to perform his Easter Duties at the Parish Church. That is the reason of yesterday's riot. The journey to St. Cloud was a sort of pretext for it."

One realises with sadness how much Mme Elizabeth must have suffered from the weakness and indecision of the King in political matters—a weakness with which her loyalty and her deep affection must often have been in conflict. One day she saw one of her ladies looking out of the window and asked her what was attracting her attention. "Madame, I am looking at our good Master, who is taking a walk." "Our Master—ah, for our misfortune, he is no longer that," was her reply. Marie Antoinette, while she shared Mme Elizabeth's anxiety at the King's attitude, kept a hope which her sister could not share. She was per-suaded that the safety of the Royal Family and the Monarchy in France would be assured by Austrian intervention. On her part, Mme Elizabeth had a sorrowful prevision "that the Queen would fall a victim to the Revolution, and this fear inspired her with a feeling of tender commiseration and affectionate devotedness for her."

On Sunday, 29th May, an incident occurred in the Palace Chapel which was much talked about. After Vespers and Benediction, as the ordinary versicle, " Domine, salvum fac regem," was being sung, a loud voice added three times, "*et reginam.*" Every one was struck by the words, and the Queen fainted, thinking that she was menaced by some unknown danger.   It was only the inconsiderate zeal of a loyal grenadier, who, when he was questioned as to why he had made this disturbance, said, pointing to his heart, " It is from there that the exclamation came."

We now approach the moment of the attempted flight from Paris, which is one of the most pathetic incidents in the tragedy. The position of the Royal Family was becoming impossible. After all, Louis had been forced to yield. The Decree of 5th June, which took from him the power of pardoning condemned persons, had profoundly humiliated him. "The King's liberty has long been taken from him," said Mme Elizabeth on this occasion, "and now they forbid him to show mercy."

Louis protested secretly against this and the other decrees he had been forced to sanction ; but would that he had done this publicly, before the face of the world, and forced the Revolutionary party to unmask and show their true colours, which they were still trying to conceal. Absolutely fearless in all that concerned his own safety, the King now determined, for the sake of the Queen and his family, to leave Paris.

Mme de Tourzel, to whom the world is indebted for a most interesting account of the journey to Varennes, in which she took part, stops now and then in her narrative to refresh herself, as it were, with little anecdotes about the Dauphin. At this moment, when the cup of humiliation seemed full, and when the Royal Family was subject to every intrusion, a man called Palloi, "Architect of the City," and who had been at the head of the destroyers of the Bastille, sent word to ask the Queen if he might present the Prince with a game of dominoes made from the stones of the Bastille. *They dared not refuse*, and the Queen replied that if M. Palloi liked to go and find the Dauphin in the garden, he would receive the present. Mme de Tourzel describes the poor child's distaste for such a gift, and how he blushed as he thanked the donor. Directly M. Palloi left he begged to be taken indoors, and sent away the dominoes, asking that they should not be mentioned again.

He loved playing at soldiers or dressing up in the character of some famous French knight, such as Bayard. Even this innocent amusement, however, could only be allowed in private, for fear of exciting comment.

When the preparations for escape were being made, Mme de Tourzel was still weak from a recent illness, and the Queen, with her wonted consideration, thought her unable for the fatigue of accompanying them. Going to see her early one morning, Marie Antoinette said, "It is probable that we shall be obliged to leave Paris and you are still very weak," and counselled her to go to Plombières to take the waters. The Duchess, however, absolutely refused to leave her charges. "If I had been a man, your Majesty," she replied, "you would not have prevented me from storming the trenches. I feel worthy of being the daughter of a father who lost his life for his king and his country. Your Majesty must not worry about me. If I get ill, I will remain at the first inn."

The departure was finally fixed for 20th June, and the Queen, to divert any suspicion, herself took the children to walk in the garden of M. Boutin at Tivoli on the previous evening, and on her return gave orders to the Commandant of Battalion for her walk next day. Mme de Tourzel did the same as regards the Dauphin, and further to prevent any idea of a journey, told her women to prepare her bath at a certain hour next forenoon. She retired to rest about ten o'clock. "A moment later the Queen entered the apartment, and woke the young Prince, who was sound asleep. Hardly had he heard that he was going to a place where he should command his regiment, than he threw himself to the foot of the bed, saying, 'Quick, quick, let us make haste! let them give me my sabre, my big boots, and let us start.' The idea of resembling Henri IV., whom he had taken as his model, excited him so much that he did not close his eyes on the road— it was only after the arrest that Nature resumed her rights, and he fell into the calmest and quietest sleep."

Marie Antoinette and her children, accompanied by Mme de Tourzel, now joined the King in the Queen's rooms. A little girl's cotton dress and cap had been prepared beforehand for the Dauphin, in which he was successfully disguised. The Queen, having gone herself to reconnoitre, and the carriage being ready, she embraced Mme de Tourzel, saying, "The King and I give into your care, Madame, all that is dearest to us in the world with complete confidence. All is ready; go!" The Duchess with the Dauphin and Madame entered an old carriage driven by Count Fersen, and to give the King time to rejoin them, they drove along the quays and returned by the Rue St. Honoré, where they stopped opposite a house there called the Hôtel de Gaillarboise. "I waited there three-quarters of an hour," says Mme de Tourzel, "without seeing any of the royal family arrive. M. de Fersen acted the part of a cabdriver to perfection, whistling, talking to a *soi-disant* companion, and taking snuff from his snuff-box. I was on thorns, although I showed no signs of anxiety, when Madame said to me: 'There is M. de la Fayette.' I concealed Monseigneur the Dauphin under my dress, assuring them both that they need not be uneasy.

I was, however, not happy. M. Bailly followed him at a short distance. They both passed on without any suspicion, and after three-quarters of an hour of anxiety I had the comfort of seeing Mme Elizabeth arrive.[1] The King was the next to join us, and finally the Queen ; directly she got into the carriage the King folded her in his arms and embraced her, repeating, ' How happy I am to see you arrive.' " Every one embraced. They were convinced that the most difficult part of the enterprise had been accomplished, and ventured to hope.

Some interesting details regarding Mme Elizabeth's escape have been preserved. Captain Philippe Dubois, to whom was entrusted the care of the Princess in the Tuileries, made the following deposition regarding this fateful night :—

"On the 20th of June, at half-past ten in the evening, he escorted Mme Elizabeth to her room. . . . One of the pages of the bedchamber

---

[1] " While he [Fersen] was . . . standing at his horses' heads . . . he became aware of a woman sitting on a stone bench at the door of the Hôtel de la Vallière, and thought he recognised Mme Elizabeth. He drew near and found that it was indeed the Princess, who had been brought to the spot by one of her equerries, M. de St. Pardoux. She was dressed in a dark gown, and wore a wide grey hat trimmed with gauze that fell round it like a veil. Fersen went up to her, ' walking as though he were merely sauntering past,' and said in a low voice, ' They are waiting for you.' Either because she did not hear or because she feared to make a mistake, the Princess remained on the bench. Fersen repeated the words as he again passed by, whereupon Madame Elizabeth rose and went to take her place in the carriage."—See *Drame de Varennes*, G. Lenotre, p. 50.

fastened the door on the inside . . . then one of the chasseurs of the guard, having placed a mattress across the door, spent the entire night there. On the 21st, it was only just at eight o'clock that the deponent, going to the window overlooking the Pont Royale, perceived a crowd of people. . . . The deponent, taking his sword in hand, went to find the page and ordered him to take him to Mme Elizabeth's room, where . . . he observed a door or means of exit. . . ." A tapestry curtain had been raised, disclosing a cupboard with a movable back, which opened on the unfinished gallery destined for a museum. The Princess, with the aid of a key which was found on the floor, had opened it and escaped.

It was this door, no doubt, which is alluded to in the following statement of Étienne Trompette, joiner to the King : "About two or three months ago the Sieur Renard, Inspector of Buildings to the King, ordered from him a cupboard, to be made according to the measurements and models furnished by the said Renard. This cupboard, to begin with, is formed of two doors opening in front with one vertical partition in the middle, and a cross partition dividing the cupboard into halves. In this latter partition there is a sliding door running on an iron bar overhead, and hung on wheels to make it move more easily . . . there are several shelves supported on moveable brackets. By removing the shelves it is possible, after having opened one of the two doors in the front of the cupboard and the sliding door in the middle as well as the one at the back, to pass through the cupboard as if it were a door, if the cupboard be placed before a door that opens outwards. The deponent said he had had the said cupboard taken to the vestibule of the old hall of the Comédie Française, Cour des Suisses, in the Palace of the Tuileries, where he left it." [1]

We can picture to ourselves the Princess's feelings as she thus left the home of her forefathers by stealth in the darkness, and with what agitated and rapid movements she must have removed the shelves one by one from this secret egress, which had, no doubt, been carefully prepared for an occasion such as this by the foresight of some of the loyal adherents of the Royal Family, although it is not alluded to by Mme de Tourzel.

We do not propose to enter into a full descrip-tion of the fatal journey to Varennes and the melancholy return of the Royal Family to Paris, of which the history has been often written. The part taken by our Princess, and which perhaps has been somewhat overlooked, is what we wish chiefly to trace ; and here, as usual, Mme de Tourzel is invaluable. Her words regarding the characters adopted by the occupants of the royal carriage are also of interest. After reaching Clichy, where the party changed carriages, she says, " We travelled

---

[1] Documents preserved in the Record Office of the Court of Orleans, Bimbenet, *Pièces Justificatives*, p. 50.   See Lenotre, *Drame de Varennes*, p. 125.

in a large *Berline* which was very commodious but
was nothing out of the common, as people liked
to repeat after the sad ending of this unhappy
journey. I passed as the mistress under the name
of the Baroness de Korff. The King as my valet-
de-chambre, the Queen as my maid, and Mme
Elizabeth as the children's nurse."

During the melancholy journey to Varennes
Mme Elizabeth took no leading part. She suffered
in silence, "agitated hour by hour by the expectation of freedom and the imminence of danger. She
saw disappear hour by hour, minute by minute, the
last gleams of hope." It was only on the return
journey that the Princess appears in the narrative.
At Épernay, where the King stopped to dine at
the Hôtel de Rohan, the crowd was great. M.
Cazotte, a commandant of the National Guard, was
charged with the protection of the King, but his
small troop was unable to disperse the people who
rushed into the courtyard of the inn, carrying the
Royal Family with them. M. Cazotte tried to fight
his way towards them. Mme Elizabeth, who knew
the young officer, was surprised to see him in the
midst of the crush, and exclaimed, "And you too,
Cazotte?" "I am only here to serve you," was
the reply, "and it is essential that you should not
appear to know me." The Princess gave him a
look of intelligence, which she then turned upon
the Queen, as if to make known to their unexpected
protector the person who of all others most required
his help. In fact, the Queen was being pursued by

cries of insult.   "Despise this fury," said Cazotte
in German, looking at Marie Antoinette, "God is
above us all."   "The Queen," he relates, "regarded
me attentively, and began to walk on amidst the
crowd, followed by Mme Royale, Mme Elizabeth,
and Mme de Tourzel."

"The Dauphin, who was being carried by a
garde du corps," says Cazotte, "no longer seeing his
mother, called for her with tears and appealed to
me, throwing his arms round my neck.   My cheeks
were both wet with his tears.   We took him to the
room to which the Queen had been conducted.   She
asked me if I could find a workwoman to mend
her dress, which had been trodden on by the crowd.
In the house itself we found the daughter of the
landlord, a very pretty girl.   I took her to the
Queen, and her respect, her eyes red with tears,
offered to her Majesty a touching contrast with the
scene she had just witnessed."

Soon after leaving Épernay the royal party
were met by three commissaries of the Assembly
—Barnave, Pétion, and Latour-Maubourg.   The two
former entered the royal carriage, and the Queen
and Mme Elizabeth were agreeably impressed by
the moderation and gentleness of Barnave.

The last few days of anguish and the sad reflections she had made upon the position of those
dearest to her now inspired our Princess with a
remarkable speech worthy of a great statesman.

The King's flight was being discussed, and
turning to Barnave she undertook to justify this

measure. "She traced for him with admirable wisdom and courage the King's conduct, which she described in opposition to that of the Assembly in the different periods of the Revolution."

We give a brief *résumé* of this discourse, which, Mme de Tourzel says, lasted an hour and a half:—

" 'I am very glad that you have given me the chance of opening my heart and of speaking to you frankly about the Revolution,' said the Princess. 'You are too clever, M. Barnave, not to have recognised at once the King's love for the French and his desire to make them happy. Misled by an excessive love for liberty, you thought only of its benefits, without considering the disorder which might accompany it. Dazzled by your first success, you went much further than you intended. The resistance you met with strengthened you against difficulties and made you crush without reflection all that was an obstacle to your plans. You forgot that progress must go slowly, and that in striving to arrive quickly, one runs the risk of losing one's way. You persuaded yourself that by destroying everything that already existed, good or bad, you would make a perfect work and that you would then re-establish what it was useful to preserve. Led away by this desire, you have attacked the very foundations of royalty, and covered with bitterness and insult the best of kings. All his efforts and sacrifices to bring you back to wiser ideas have been useless, and you have not ceased to calumniate his intentions and to humiliate him in the eyes of

his people, in taking from royalty all the prerogatives
which inspire love and respect. Torn from his
palace and taken to Paris in the most disgraceful
manner, his goodness never failed. He opened his
arms to his misguided children, and tried to come
to an understanding with them in order to co-
operate with them for the welfare of France, which
he cherished in spite of its errors. You have forced
him to sign a Constitution not yet completed,
although he represented to you that it would be
better not to sanction an unfinished piece of work,
and you have obliged him to present it in this
form to the People before a Federation of which
the object was to attach the Departments to you
in isolating the King from the nation.'

"'Ah, Madame,' interrupted Barnave, 'do not
complain of the Federation. We should have been
lost, had you known how to profit by it.'

"The royal family sighed, and Madame Elizabeth continued, 'The King, in spite of the fresh
insults he has received since then, could not
make up his mind to do what he has now done.
But, attacked in his principles—in his family—in
his person — profoundly afflicted by the crimes
committed throughout France and seeing a general
disorganisation in all departments of Government,
with the evils which result; determined to quit
Paris in order to go to another town in the kingdom,
where, free in his own actions, he could persuade
the Assembly to revise its decrees and where he
could in concert with it make a new Constitution,

in which the different authorities could be classified
and replaced in their proper place and could work
for the happiness of France. I do not speak of
our own sorrows. The King alone, who should
make one with France, occupies us entirely. I will
never leave him unless your decrees, by witholding
all liberty to practise religion, force me to abandon
him to go to a country where liberty of conscience
enables me to practise my religion, to which I hold
more than to my life.'

" 'By no means, Madame,' here exclaimed
Barnave, 'your example and your presence are
too useful to your country.' "

Mme Elizabeth's words, spoken " with a
persuasive eloquence and grief," made an immense
impression on Barnave, and he was changed from
that moment, says Mme de Tourzel.

At Dormans, where the night was spent, an
incident occurred which makes one wonder if even
yet the royal cause could have been saved. After
supper, when the Royal Family were about to
retire for the night, a waiter carrying refresh-
ments managed to enter the room where they were
assembled. He saw " the King seated on a small
straw armchair in the middle of the room ; the
Queen sitting near the bed against which she leant ;
the Dauphin and Madame playing with Mme de
Tourzel."

The man, without saying a word, offered his
tray to Mme Elizabeth, and the latter, raising her
eyes, recognised him as a young officer called Jean

Landrieux. Landrieux explained that he was the son-in-law of the proprietor of the inn, Truet, and together they had planned a method of escape of which he begged the Princess to speak to the King. Sentinels were placed at the door of the apartment, but the windows opened upon the garden at the back of the house, from whence the river was reached by a little staircase. Here a boat could be ready to carry the King and his family to Vincelles, where Truet possessed a vintage. Here a cart, "commodious, filled with mattresses, covered and harnessed to three good horses," would await them, and he would drive them himself as far as Fère en Tardonois, and from there other arrangements were made for the party to reach the frontier. The idea. was hopeful although somewhat hazardous ; but the King absolutely refused, "saying that he relied on the good town of Paris, which he had quitted with regret and upon false information." The Queen, "who was leaning on the bed, rose quickly and told the King angrily" how much it cost her to renounce this chance of safety, but he remained inflexible.[1] The description of the King's words and the Queen's ill-humour are not convincing, and Mme de Tourzel does not allude to this incident. She remarks that this night was terribly noisy. "The King did not undress and only slept for three hours in his chair. The cries of *Vive la*

[1] From the MSS. of Jean Landrieux ; *Le Drame de Varennes*, by Lenotre, pp. 238-40.

Nation—Vive l'Assemblée Nationale, which began with daylight, so impressed the Dauphin in his sleep that he dreamt he was in a wood with wolves, and that his mother was in danger. He awoke sobbing and could only be quieted by being taken to the Queen."

CHAPTER VI

IMPRISONMENT IN THE TUILERIES

THE Royal party reached Meaux the next night, and slept at the Episcopal Palace—Bossuet's home. On the following day they made their mournful entry into Paris. At the Barrier an immense crowd was gathered to see the King pass—all with heads covered.[1] "When we reached the Place Louis xv.," says Mme de Tourzel, "they made us enter the Tuileries by the Suspension Bridge (*Pont tournant*) in order to get out under the Archway where His Majesty's officers awaited him. The National Guards surrounded him on the spot, and one of them took possession of Mgr the Dauphin to carry him to his apartment, but as the child began to cry at finding himself in strange hands, he gave him to M. Hüe who took him to the King's rooms."

[1] Lord Sutherland was Ambassador in Paris at this time, and his eldest daughter, Lady Charlotte Gower, afterwards Duchess of Norfolk, recalled walking with her governess one hot summer day, when they were stopped "by a crowd surging round a large carriage full of people without and within. This was no other than the famous 'Berline' with its royal captives on its way back from that ill-starred flight to Varennes."—*Records and Reminiscences*, Lord Ronald Gower, p. 41.

There was a large crowd outside the Palace, and the moment was critical. Shouts arose for the death of the three faithful *gardes du corps* who were still with the royal carriage, but they were saved and taken to the *Abbaye* for refuge.

All at once there was a great silence, and when the door of the carriage opened and the King walked quietly into the Palace, no one said a word. When the Queen followed murmurs were heard, and M. de Noailles hurried to escort her. The Dauphin and his sister were applauded : " There goes the hope and support of France." Mme Elizabeth and Mme de Tourzel then entered, escorted by Barnave and Latour-Maubourg—and the gates of the Grille were shut. It was seven o'clock in the evening of June 25.

The King and Queen went up the big staircase and retired to their rooms—the King smiling, according to Barnave. The latter adds that, owing to the great heat, Pétion begged Mme Elizabeth for a drink, and that she sent for beer for him.[1]

On the following day the King was visited by three members of the Assembly, who came to receive his explanation of the motives which had led to his leaving the capital. He read a short declaration aloud, in which he again protested that he had not intended to leave the kingdom. They then begged to see the Queen, to receive

---

[1] Pétion has also left a report of the journey from Épernay in which he flatters himself that Mme Elizabeth was impressed by him. See Lenotre, *Drame de Varennes*, etc.

from her a similar declaration. "Elizabeth," said the King, "please go to the Queen and ask her if she can see these gentlemen, and she must not keep them waiting." The Princess obeyed, but returned shortly to say that the Queen had gone to her bath, and it was arranged that the Deputies should return next morning at eleven o'clock. The Queen's short declaration did not give any more satisfaction than the King's, and it was received with murmurs by the Assembly. The King was soon forgiven, but the rancour against *the Austrian* was implacable. This the Queen felt and knew. The next day when she rose, and one of her women remarked that she was looking well, she took off her nightcap, and it was seen that, as a result of the anguish she had undergone during the last few days, her hair had become quite white, "like that of a woman of seventy."[1]

On returning to the Tuileries, the King, the Queen, and the Dauphin were put under surveillance by M. de la Fayette, who selected certain officers to be responsible for them. Mme Elizabeth and Madame were alone excepted, but out of affection and respect for her brother the former refused to make use of her liberty to leave the precincts of the Palace. Poor Mme de Tourzel was closely watched. "I remained for more than a fortnight in the Dauphin's apartments," she says, "and it was only after my interrogation that I was permitted to speak to a few persons. The Queen and

[1] *Mémoires de Mme Campan.*

LE PALAIS DES TUILERIES.

Mme Elizabeth always full of kindness, found a way of saying a word to me now and then, or would pass me little notes when they went through the room to go to Mass. I knew by this means what the King and Queen had said in their declaration, which it was of great importance for me to know. I was also allowed to read the *Moniteur*, which informed me what was going on in the Assembly. My only consolation during this time was that I was permitted to hear the King's Mass, which was said daily in the *Galerie de Diane*, and there I also saw, together with the royal family, my relations and friends, who never failed to assist."

Meanwhile, congratulations reached the royal family, congratulations which must have been heart-breaking for them to receive. The courier who took the news of the King's start for Varennes to Mesdames his aunts in Rome bore also the news of his arrest; but by some extraordinary confusion—caused, it is thought, by Monsieur's successful escape—he was quickly followed by another messenger announcing that Louis had been delivered by M. de Bouillé and escorted by his troops to Luxembourg. At this news "the whole of Rome shouted with joy; the crowd massed itself under the windows of the Princesses crying out: Long live the King."

Pope Pius VI. addressed a letter of heart-felt congratulation to the King, in which the following passages occur: "Words cannot express, very

dear son in Jesus Christ, the lively consolation with
which this happy news has filled my paternal heart,
and this rejoicing is not mine alone. All Rome
shares in it, it is felt by the citizens of all classes.
All, from the highest rank to the lowest, are
enchanted to see that, through the Mercy of God,
you have escaped the greatest dangers. Our
streets, our public squares, re-echo with the shouts
of joy of the Romans, who congratulate themselves
on your escape. Do not think that I exaggerate
these feelings; We have as witnesses of this
universal joy our very dear daughters in God, the
royal Princesses Marie Adelaide and Victoire
Marie, your excellent Aunts, and our venerable
brother, Cardinal de Bernis, who in this universal
and heartfelt rejoicing could not restrain their tears."

Mesdames, wishing to show their gratitude to
the Roman nobility for their sympathy, invited the
most distinguished of them to a great banquet; but
alas! on the very day it was to take place, a third
courier reached them with the news that turned
their rejoicing into mourning.

As we may believe, Mme Elizabeth sent news
to her friends as soon as it was possible. On 29th
June she wrote a few words to reassure Mme de
Raigecourt, promising to write *if she could do so.*
A second laconic note followed this one on 9th
July. On the same day two hundred members of
the clergy and nobility protested in the Assembly
against the Decree relating to the Oath which they
had severally taken a short time previously.

On 10th July the Princess wrote more fully to Mme de Bombelles. In this letter she says, "Paris and the King are in the same position— the firstnamed is quiet and the second is guarded 'at sight,' and so is the Queen." The last part of the letter is written in invisible ink and runs as follows : "No, my heart, I am far from permitting your return. It is not that I should not be charmed to see you, but it is because I am convinced that you would not be safe here. Take care of yourself for happier days when we may perhaps be able to enjoy in peace the friendship that unites us.

"I have been very unhappy ; I am less so now. If I could see an end to all this I could bear things better, but this is the time in which to abandon oneself entirely into the hands of God. . . . Our journey with Barnave and Pétion passed off very ludicrously. You believe no doubt that we were in torments ! Not at all. They behaved very well, especially the former, who is very intelligent, and not fierce as is said. I began by showing them frankly my opinion of their doings, and after that we conversed for the rest of the journey as if we were not concerned in the matter. Barnave saved the *Gardes du Corps* who were with us, and whom the National Guard wished to massacre on our arrival here."

The life of the royal prisoners—for so they now were—was most monotonous. The King and Queen, unwilling to show themselves in this cruel position even to the National Guard, no longer walked in the Dauphin's little garden, but remained shut up in their rooms, where the very hot weather added to their discomfort.[1] Mme Elizabeth, as we have said, would not profit by her greater freedom. "This angelic Princess," says Mme de Tourzel, "was their consolation during their captivity. Her attentions to the King and Queen and their children always redoubled in proportion to their misfortunes."

The only recreation in which the Royal Family indulged was to watch the children playing, and during the first days of their return they could see the Deputies of the Right, who as they passed and repassed the windows of the Palace saluted them with sorrowful respect; but the Assembly took offence at this, and caused the Tuileries to be shut even to the Deputies—so this small alleviation was taken from them.

The preparation of the new Constitution now occupied the Assembly, and every effort was made to persuade the unfortunate King to sanction it. The draft was brought to him, and he was given ten days in which to consider it. As it was necessary for him to appear free on this occasion, the officers who guarded him were withdrawn and the usual honours were rendered to him once more. In consequence, Louis and his family appeared at

---

[1] It was possibly at this time that a picture now in the possession of the Duke of Buccleuch was painted by our Princess. It is a view of a Seaport in oils, rather in Vernet's style, and is inscribed at the back, *Elizabeth, pour mon frère d'Artois*, 1792. The Comte d'Artois was often at Dalkeith, and no doubt presented the picture.

Mass in the chapel of the Tuileries on the Sunday following. The populace went there in crowds, and showed great joy at seeing him again. From all sides was heard " *Vive le Roy*," but one voice added significantly, " Yes, *if he accepts the Constitution.*" The brothers of the King and the Princes of the House of Condé united in imploring Louis not to accept the Constitution, which they foresaw would be fatal to his cause and that of the true interests of France ; but the King, persuaded by the Ministers that he alone was in a position to judge events,—"tired of their insistence, of his present position, afraid of that in which he might find himself, and fearing above all to bring about civil war in France,"—determined to accept it, and another step on the downward path of the Monarchy was accomplished.

Yet the question was so difficult that it is impossible entirely to blame the King for his decision. Had he refused to ratify the Constitution, he would at once have ceased to reign, even in the very limited way in which he still exercised power. As he said in a letter to the Princes, written a few days later, most of the population believed that their misfortunes would end on the day that the Constitution was promulgated ; to delay this promulgation was to declare himself an enemy to his country.

Mme Elizabeth did not blame her brother. She suffered more from a new danger which threatened the family union. When the King's captive condition was understood abroad, the Princes who had emigrated looked upon it as their duty to direct the political future, and the Comte d'Artois seems to have thought that the necessity for a Regency might occur. Under these circumstances, Mme Elizabeth thought it her duty to write to her friend, Mme de Raigecourt, urging her strongly to see that the Comte d'Artois was informed of the fresh change in the position of affairs. In this letter the King is indicated under the name of the *Père de famille*, the Queen as the *Belle Mère*, and the Comte d'Artois as the *Fils*.

The Constitution was received with enthusiasm, and the Royal Family was obliged to take part in the rejoicings ; the King, indeed, seeing the general joy, "kept some of his illusions." He gave a fête to the Parisians, distributed large alms to the poor, and a *Te Deum* was sung at Notre Dame.

He and the Queen, moreover, now free in the eyes of the people, appeared at the theatre once more. Mme Elizabeth, who was little disposed to rejoice over the late events, thought it her duty to accompany them on these occasions. "We have been to the Opera ; to-morrow we go to the *Comédie*. What pleasures ! I am enchanted !" She refers also to an illumination which was to take place with little lamps, "and with those machines of glass that one dares no longer speak of after the horrible use to which they have been put for two years. You recognise lanterns." And in another letter she says again, "Do you know that we were taken to the Opera on Tuesday, and that on Monday we went to the *Français*. We are going through a course of Theatres. When it is over I shall be charmed."

There was for a moment a return of loyal feeling, and on 8th October, wishing to associate their children in their joy, the King and Queen took them to the *Théâtre Italien*. They were applauded several times, but the cheers were mingled with sobs. The crowd was "gentle and compassionate" and full of respect. The royal parents and Mme Elizabeth rejoiced that the children should see the people under this aspect, after all they had witnessed of another nature.

Not long after this the Assembly sent a deputation to ask the King to beg the foreign Powers to disperse the crowd of emigrants on the French frontier, and, in case of refusal, to declare war. An allusion was even made to Louis XIV., which aroused Mme Elizabeth's indignation. "It is pretty, is it not," she writes, "that they should speak of Louis XIV.—that despot—at this time!"

But more serious anxieties occupied her. "The Decree against the priests who refused the Oath has been passed with all possible severity," she writes; and once more the position of the King, face to face with this Decree, "which he could not sanction without disobeying the Church, or refuse without endangering his Crown, and perhaps his life," filled her with the gravest apprehensions. Another incident about this time brought home to

the Royal Family their utter powerlessness. A
rising in the island of San Domingo had brought
destruction on the French inhabitants, and some
of the Colonists then in Paris drew up an address
which they begged to be allowed to present to the
King to beg for his protection. Headed by M.
Comier, they were admitted to the royal presence
on 2nd November. Louis listened to the address
with deep emotion, and promised to do all in his
power to send succour to the unfortunate island.
The Colonists asked to pay their homage to the
Queen and Mme Elizabeth, and were received
with the greatest sympathy. The Queen tried to
speak, but was overcome by emotion, and they
withdrew. It was only on her return from Mass
that Marie Antoinette was able to address them.
"Gentlemen," she said, "it was impossible for me
to answer you, but the cause of my silence has
said enough." When they saw Mme Elizabeth,
M. Comier, after referring to the misfortunes which
brought these "faithful Frenchmen" before her,
and stating that they sought comfort from the
Royal Family, added, "but in appearing before
you, Madame, they can feel no other sentiment
than that of veneration for your high virtues. The
interest which you will deign to feel for their fate
will sweeten its bitterness." Mme Elizabeth was
no less moved than the Queen, but replied gently
and calmly, "Gentlemen, I have keenly felt the
misfortunes which have visited the Colony. I
very sincerely share the interest taken in it by the

King and the Queen, and I beg you to assure all
the Colonists of this." Alas! the unfortunate
Royal Family was in no position to help others.
"These poor Colonists, who are drowning," said
our Princess, "call those who are already drowned
to their aid." In her correspondence at this date
she refers with great sorrow to the hostility which
was manifested against religion and the clergy
who remained faithful in the Assembly, but
remarks with thankfulness on the piety still openly
practised in parts of France. "The Churches are
filled, the Communions innumerable, and all goes
on in perfect peace. May God grant that evil
spirits do not come to upset all this, at which I
should not be surprised, for God has given them
very great power over our unhappy country."

At the close of this sad year a happy and
tender memory was evoked by the anniversary of
Mme Louise, and Mme Elizabeth writes to Mme
de Lastic : "It is four years on the 23rd of this
month that my pious aunt, Madame Louise, died
in peace, tenderly cared for by her dear Carmelites.
How merciful God was to her in calling her to
Him on the eve of the disasters and misfortunes
which were about to fall on her family and her
convent itself. She lived in peace and she died
very happy. It was for that reason, no doubt, that
the Court did not go into mourning for her."

Pétion was now Mayor of Paris. Mme
Elizabeth had not seen him since his elevation,
but she remembered "certain strange remarks of

his during the journey from Varennes." This is an allusion, probably, to Pétion's absurd fancy that he had made a favourable impression on the Princess, simply because she made him talk in order to discover his political opinions.

On 1st January 1792 Pétion refused to offer the usual New Year's wishes to the Queen. He remarked that the town of Paris owed nothing to a woman, and if his colleagues persisted in wishing to present themselves before the wife of Louis XVI., his principles would forbid him to have the honour of being at the head of the deputation.

Early in January the two Decrees concerning the priests and the *émigrés* were, according to the Constitution, presented to the King for his sanction ; but this time Louis was not to be intimidated. He calmly opposed his Veto to both Decrees—one of which wounded his conscience, the other his family affections. Even according to the Constitution he was within his rights, but this refusal "appeared as a blow to the National Sovereignty"; it was bitterly resented, and the revolutionary disorder grew from day to day.

"We are watched like criminals," wrote the Queen to Mme de Polignac on 7th January, "and in truth this restraint is terrible to bear. To be in continual fear for one's belongings—not to approach a window without being insulted—not to be able to take the poor children out of doors, without exposing these dear innocents to the vociferations of the crowd : what a position, my dear Heart! Again, if one had only one's own sorrows to think of—but to tremble for the King, for all one possesses most dear on earth, for the friends who are present, for those who are absent, is a burden too hard to bear ; but, as I have said, you all help me.   Let us hope in God, who sees our consciences and knows we are animated by the truest love for this country."

On 20th February the Queen again took the children to the Italian Theatre, and for the last time received a warm and respectful welcome. Mme Elizabeth alludes to the occasion as follows : "There was tremendous applause.   The Jacobins tried to have their way but were beaten.   The audience insisted on having the Duet between the Valet and his wife (in the *Événements Imprévus*) in which the love which they bear their Master and Mistress is mentioned, repeated four times.   At the moment at which they say '*We must make them happy,*' a large part of the audience cried '*Yes, yes.*' Can you understand our nation? but one must agree that it has charming moments.   Upon this I wish you good-night.   Pray to God for us this Lent that He may have pity on us, but, my Heart, take care to think only of His glory and put aside all that has to do with the world."

Her correspondence was Mme Elizabeth's one pleasure.   As she would not leave the Tuileries or enjoy the freedom she still possessed, her inter-course with chosen friends like Mme de Lastic, who now spent the evenings with her, and her letters to absent ones, were her great resource.

On 6th April she writes to Mme de Raigecourt in delight at the news that the latter was about to return to Paris, but she adds a sombre word referring to the news of the murder of Gustavus III. of Sweden. "Here is the King of Sweden assassinated—each one in his turn."

This tragic event "caused a great sensation in France," says Mme de Tourzel. "The King and Queen were in consternation on hearing the news. I was with Mgr the Dauphin, and M. Ocharitz, Minister for Spain, sent to ask me to go down to my apartment, as he had something to tell me. I found him looking much shocked and he told me of the misfortune of which the news had just come. He said, 'The King's Ministers have perhaps not informed him of this terrible event, and I think it would be well for you to let him hear of it at once.' I went down to the Queen's rooms with Madame, who supped every evening with the King and Queen, and I begged Her Majesty to let me have a word with her in private. I was miserable at having to inform her of such a misfortune. She knew it, however, and said to me : 'I see by your face that you already know the cruel news that we have just heard. It is impossible not to be filled with sorrow, but we must arm ourselves with courage, for no one can feel assured he will not undergo a similar fate.' The Queen told Madame, who threw herself into her arms and those of the King in the most touching way." [1]

[1] Mme de Tourzel, vol. ii. p. 73.

About this time Mme Elizabeth was urged by one of her correspondents, the Abbé de Lubersac, to join her aunts in Rome, but her reply shows her constant resolution never to abandon the King. "There are certain positions in which one cannot dispose of oneself, and such is mine. The line I should follow is traced so clearly by Providence that I must remain faithful to it." She trembled at the fresh dangers which menaced those dear to her, and looked forward with dread to the anniversary of the journey to Varennes (which coincided with that of the Oath taken by the Third Estate at Versailles in 1789), fearing that popular feeling would be aroused afresh and that the people would seek to punish the King for his inflexible *Veto*, which neither pressure nor threats could now make him change.

The thrilling events of 20th June are so graphically described by her in a letter to Mme de Raigecourt that we must give large extracts from it. The Princess, in her humility, however, leaves out one or two incidents of special interest to us, which we must relate. When she joined the King at the moment that the wretches were forcing him to put on the red cap, she was mistaken for the Queen. "You don't understand," was said to her; "they take you for the *Austrian.*" "Ah, would to God it were so," she exclaimed; "do not enlighten them, save them from a greater crime." Later, turning aside a bayonet which almost touched her heart, she said gently, "Take care,

8

monsieur. You might wound some one, and I am sure you would be sorry." Seeing a poor man who was faithful to the King faint in the crowd, she managed to reach him and gave him her smelling-salts, which revived him. The incident struck all present, and even Pétion was touched.

Afterwards a woman of the people, relating in her way the failure of this attempt on the Royal Family, which she attributed to Mme Elizabeth's presence, said naïvely, "There was nothing to be done to-day ; their good Ste. Généviève was there."

The Queen, with her usual heroism, had likewise hastened to the King. "Don't stop me," she said ; "it is my place, I repeat, to be in the same dangers as the King. It is me they are calling for. It is my head they desire."

"For three days," writes Mme Elizabeth, "a great movement was expected in Paris, but it was thought all necessary precautions had been taken. On Wednesday morning (June 20th) the courtyard and the garden were full of troops. At midday it was known that all the Faubourg St. Antoine were on their way to present a petition to the Assembly, but nothing was said of their project of going through the Tuileries. Fifteen hundred men entered the Assembly. . . . Soon after the outer doors of the garden were opened in spite of orders. Soon the garden was filled. At three o'clock the crowd seemed to wish to burst open the gate of the great Courtyard. The National Guard, who had not been able to get orders since the morning, had the

sorrow to see them pass through the Court without
being able to bar their passage. . . . We were now
at the King's window. The few persons who were
with his valet came also to rejoin us. The doors
were closed and a few minutes later we heard
someone calling. It was Aclocque and some
Grenadiers and Volunteers he had brought. He
asked the King to show himself alone. The King
passed into the first ante-room. . . . At the moment
that the King went into his ante-room some of the
Queen's people obliged her to go back to her rooms.
Happier than she, there was no one to force me to
leave the King, and the Queen had hardly been
dragged back when the door was burst open by
the pikemen. At that moment the King got up
on some chests which stood in the window, and the
Maréchal de Mouchy, MM. d'Hervelly, Aclocque,
and a dozen grenadiers surrounded him. I remained near the wall encircled by Ministers, M. de
Marsilly, and a few of the National Guards. The
pikemen entered the room like lightning, they looked
for the King, one in particular who, they say, said
horrid things, but a Grenadier caught his arm,
saying : '*Unhappy one, it is your King.*' They
at the same time cried *Vive le Roy.* The rest of
the pikemen answered the cheer mechanically. The
room was full in quicker time than I can write, all
asking for the Sanction (for the decrees) and that
the Ministers should be sent away. For four hours
the same cry was repeated. Some members of the
Assembly came soon afterwards. MM. Vergniaud

and Isnard spoke very well to the people, telling
them they were wrong to ask the King in this way
for the Sanction, and tried to persuade them to
retire, but their words were useless. . . . At last
Pétion and other members of the municipality
arrived. The first-named harangued the people,
and after having praised the *dignity* and *order* with
which they had come, he begged them to retire
with the *same calm*, so that they might not be
reproached with having given way to any excess
during a *fête Civique*. . . . But to return to the
Queen, whom I left being forced back, against her
will, to my nephew's apartment. . . . She did
everything in the world to return to the King, but
MM. de Choiseul and de Hauteville and our women
who were there prevented her. . . . The Grenadiers
entered the Council Chamber, and put her and the
children behind the Table. The Grenadiers and
others who were much attached to them, surrounded
them, and the crowd passed before them. A woman
put a red cap on the Queen's head and on my
nephew's. The King had one almost from the
first. Santerre, who led the file, harangued her,
and told her people had misled her in saying that
the people did not love her; they did, and he
could assure her she had nothing to fear. 'One
never fears anything when one is with good
people,' she replied, holding out her hand at the
same time to the grenadiers near her, who all
threw themselves upon it to kiss it. It was very
touching. . . . A real deputation arrived to see the

King, and as I heard this and did not wish to remain in the crowd, I left an hour before he did. I rejoined the Queen, and you can guess with what pleasure I embraced her. I had, however, not known what risks she had run. When the King returned to his rooms, nothing could be more affecting than the moment when the Queen and his children threw themselves into his arms. Some deputies who were there burst into tears. Deputations succeeded each other every half hour until calm was restored. They were shown the damage which had been done by the violence of the crowd. They all behaved very well in the King's apartment, and he was perfect to them. At ten o'clock the Palace was empty and everyone retired to their own rooms. . . . These are the details of the day of June 20th. Adieu: I am well; I love you; I embrace you and I am very glad you did not find yourself here for this squabble."[1]

[1] A contemporary—Mme de Lage de Volude—writing of Madame Elizabeth, who with all the world she considered "the perfection of perfections," says, "She spends her days in prayer and in devouring the best books on our situation. She is full of noble and generous sentiments: her timidity changes to firmness when it is a question of speaking to the King and of informing him as to the state of things." Another lady, a friend of Mme de Lage, told her that an eye-witness of the horrors enacted on 20th June, and who found himself close to the King, heard some one say to Madame Elizabeth, "Ah, Madame, Heaven will avenge such crimes." But the Princess, turning round, replied with angelic sweetness and in a tone of voice which deeply touched her hearers, "Do not speak of vengeance. Do not forget that we are Christians. Let us hope that God will change them and forgive them."—*La Marquise de Lage de Volude* [1764–1842], pp. 47–8 and 155–56, par la Comtesse H. de Reinach-Foussemagne, 1908.

CHAPTER VII

FALL OF THE MONARCHY

AFTER the terrible day of 20th June, the King himself felt that the Monarchy was nearing its end. He saw that "the People who had humiliated it at Varennes had now broken its effigy in pieces," and he realised that there was no hope in this world. "Come and see me this evening," he wrote to his Confessor, "I have finished with men, and will now occupy myself only with heaven." To Mme Elizabeth the future appeared "as an abyss from which they could only escape by a miracle of Providence." The Princess's correspondence now brought her chiefly sinister warnings of danger, which she sometimes imparted to her brother. They suffered together, and she tried in vain to encourage him with hopes in which she herself had no faith. Constant in her desire to save her friends pain, Mme Elizabeth continued to write cheerfully to Mme de Bombelles and Mme de Raigecourt as long as she had the power to send letters.

On Saturday, 7th July, Lamourette, Constitutional Bishop of the Rhone, made a speech in the National Assembly calling upon all parties to unite

in defence of the Constitution. The Hall resounded
with the cries of " *Yes, yes, we only want the Constitution.*" He ended his speech with these words :
" Let us swear," he said, " to have only one
sentiment, one mind . . . equally averse to anarchy
and to the feudal system. I beg the Assembly to
put to the vote this proposition, *That those who
abjure equally* the Republic and *the two Chambers
should rise.*" The Assembly rose like one man to
applaud and to embrace each other. This scene
is known as the *Kiss of Lamourette.* On the next
day we find Mme Elizabeth recording her views on
the subject in a letter to Mme de Raigecourt with
all the *verve* of the famous lady whose name she
humorously suggests :—

"It would really require the eloquence of Mme
de Sévigné to describe all that took place yesterday,
for it is certainly the most surprising thing, the
most extraordinary, the greatest, the smallest, etc.
etc. But happily experience helps us a little to
understand it. Here are the Jacobins, the
Feuillants, the Republicans, the Monarchists, who,
abjuring all their discords and reuniting close to the
immovable Tree of the Constitution and Liberty,
promise very sincerely to walk with the law in
hand and not to deviate from it. Happily, August
is approaching, the moment when all the leaves
being well out the Tree of Liberty will offer a better
shade. Our town is quiet and will be for the Federation. I tremble for fear there should be a religious
ceremony ; you know how I feel about this. Beg

of God, my Heart, to give me strength and light. Adieu. I embrace you and love you with all my heart."

After the dreaded day of the Federation was over, she wrote again : " Your prayers, unworthy as you deem them, have brought us happiness. The famous 14th of July has passed off quietly. . . . When we came back all the Guards who escorted the King cried continually ' *Vive le Roy.*' " The intense heat of the weather added to the gloom of the Tuileries, and Mme Elizabeth confesses to her friends that she finds it very trying.

On 22nd July she wrote a letter—which proved to be a farewell one—to the Abbé de Lubersac in Rome, which is a striking testimony to her faith and courage under the pressure of constant anxiety and anguish, although she calls herself weak : "You will soon receive a letter from me which is a veritable jeremiad ; from my style you would suppose that I had foreseen what followed. Now, I do not wish, Monsieur, that you should think that this is my usual state. No, God gives me the grace to be quite different ; but at moments the heart needs to let itself go to speak of what occupies it. . . . Since the frightful day of June 20 we have been quiet, but we have no less need of the prayers of holy Souls. Let those who, sheltered from the storm, only suffer as it were from the after effects hold up their hands to God. Yes, God has only given them the grace of living in peace that they may make this use of their liberty. Those upon whom the storm falls feel at times such concussions that it is difficult to know and to practise this great resource of prayer. Happy is the heart that in the greatest agitations of this world can feel that God is still with it—happy the saints who though pierced by blows do not cease to bless God at each moment of the day. Beg this grace, Monsieur, for those who are weak and unfaithful like me ; it will be a real work of charity."

A short time after this letter was written, the Princess's correspondence with Mme de Bombelles, from which we have learnt so much of interest, was closed for ever by the following letter. The date needs some comment, as it is that of the fatal 10th of August ; but comparison with the facts related and with the original manuscript, where the date has been evidently altered by Mme Elizabeth from the 9th to 10th, shows that the latter date must have been put by mistake. As M. Feuillet de Conche remarks, the fatal tocsin began to ring at midnight of 9th August, and the letter must have been finished before then. It is written in the playful style often used by Mme Elizabeth to comfort her friends :—

"If you do not think I am submissive to your orders, Mademoiselle Bombe, you are wrong, for, look you, I have just received the letter in which you beg me for all the news, and here I am writing at once to tell you that this day of the 10th (9th) which was to be so lively, so terrible, has been the quietest possible, that the Assembly has not decreed the Abdication or Suspension, that it occupied itself with the Federals whom one party wishes to send away and the other to keep, and that they restricted themselves to summoning the President to answer why the Camp at Soissons was not ready to receive them; to-morrow this reply is to be given. The President said that he had given orders to the Municipality to see to the order. The Mayor (Pétion) then appeared to complain that the Dt.[1] had given the order to him only, and not to the Municipality, and to ask that he should be enjoined to give precise orders to the Municipality. There, my Heart, that is all that passed that is interesting. It is very hot, but in spite of that she who writes to you, your Mother, and all you are interested in are well. How happy I am, my Heart, that you find peace and happiness in your Home—enjoy it well. A visitor is arriving, so I conclude, embracing you with all my heart. Tell your sister-in-law I am much touched by her message." This letter is thus endorsed by Mme de Bombelles :—

" Last letter from the Princess. On the following day [the 13th, not the 11th] she was taken prisoner to the Temple with the King, the Queen, and their children, and only left it on May 9, 1794, to be executed on the 10th."

During those last days Mme Elizabeth was cheered by a memory from the past. One morning while she was in her apartment in the Pavillon de

[1] Meaning possibly " Defendant."

Angélique de Mackau
Marquise de Bombelles
1762-1801

Flore, the Princess thought she heard some one outside singing the song of *Pauvre Jacques* : opening her windows, she listened ; but although the air was that of her old favourite, the words were changed. The *Pauvre Peuple*, who had no longer a king, and who were in misery, was substituted for *Pauvre Jacques*. This little incident was the "last reflection from old happy days" for our Princess.

About this time Mme de Tourzel relates this interesting anecdote, which shows the state of terror and alarm in which the constant rumours of danger kept the friends of the Royal Family :—

One day a gentleman, M. de Paroy, brought the Duchess three cuirasses made of several plies of taffetas or silk, which he had caused to be made, and which were impenetrable to bullets or daggers, and begged her to offer them to the Queen, for herself, the King, and the Dauphin ; giving her also a dagger, that she might prove them. " I took them to the Queen," she says, " who at once tried on the one intended for her, and seeing the dagger in my hand, said calmly, ' Hit me to prove it.' I could not hear of such an idea, it made me shudder, and I declared that nothing would induce me to strike. She then took off her cuirass ; I put it on over my dress, and I struck it with the dagger ; as M. de Paroy had said, it remained impenetrable to the blow. The Queen then agreed with the King that they should all three put them on at the first appearance of danger, and this was done."

All was now ready for the triumph of the

revolutionary party. The programme for the assault of the Tuileries was arranged and publicly distributed a week before it took place, and a copy was even given to Mme de Tourzel, so that the Royal Family knew to a certain extent what was coming upon them.

On the evening of 9th August, after supper, they retired to the Council Chamber, where the ministers and some of the persons attached to the Court were to pass the night. The imminent peril in which they were placed broke, for the first time, the usual etiquette, and the *Coucher du Roi* did not take place. "The Queen," relates Mme de Tourzel, "spoke to each one in the most affectionate manner, and encouraged the zeal they testified to her. I spent the night, as did also my daughter Pauline, near Mgr the Dauphin, whose calm and peaceful slumbers formed the most striking contrast with the agitation which filled our minds." At eleven o'clock the Revolutionary Municipality, after turning out the former Municipality, established itself at the Hôtel de Ville, and declared itself in a state of insurrection. When midnight struck, Camille Desmoulins, Chabot, and some others gave the signal, and the tocsin began to ring at the *Cordeliers*. The sound of cannon and beating of drums could also be heard. "Towards three o'clock," writes one who was present in the Tuileries, "we heard the tocsin. The number of persons in the King's room had now increased still more; they had finished by sitting on the arm-

chairs, the floor, the tables, the *consoles* ; in fact,
wherever they could find rest, although at first
some of the Subalterns of the King's Household
held that it was against etiquette to sit down in his
room."[1]

"Yes," remarks M. de Beauchesne, "it was
still a question of etiquette, though the life of the
King and the very existence of the Monarchy was
in peril. From the King down to his son, none
was to be spared. Elizabeth was not the prey
they sought for, but she offered herself. She
wished to brave the death that menaced the King,
the Queen, and their children."

As the day dawned, the Queen, in her terror
that the children should be discovered in bed by
the mob, had them awakened and dressed. Absolutely fearless for herself, she went about from the
King to her children and to the Council Room
accompanied by Mme Elizabeth, encouraging
every one by her calmness and courage. When
the King went round to visit the guards in the
interior of the Palace, Marie Antoinette, Mme
Elizabeth, and the children, attended by Mme de
Lamballe, followed him. In the *Galerie de Diane*
they were received with enthusiasm—here in the
midst of the Revolution was a sight worthy of the
best days of French chivalry. About two hundred
gentlemen, hearing of the King's danger, had
hurried to protect him. They had no uniforms,

[1] *Mémoires inédits du Comte François de la Rochefoucauld.*
See *Mme Elizabeth*, de Beauchesne, vol. i. pp. 456–57.

and carried their arms under their dress, which won for them the name of the "Chevaliers du poignard." Some begged the Queen to touch their weapons to render them victorious, others asked to kiss her hand so that death might be sweeter. "*Vive le Roy de nos Pères*," cried the young men. "*Vive le Roy de nos Enfants*," exclaimed the veterans, lifting the Dauphin in their arms. Outside the Palace, when the King, unaccompanied here by the ladies, made his rounds, he was by no means well received. The National Guard cried "*Vive le Roy*," but the loyal words were soon drowned in shouts of, "*À bas le Veto.*"

At nine o'clock the gates of the Palace were forced, and the mob filled the courtyards. From that moment all was lost, and messengers of woe found their way to the Royal Family. "The People demand abdication or death ; they want abdication," said one. "Madame," cried another to the Queen, "the People are the strongest. What carnage there will be. Your last day has come." At last the Procureur-Générale, Roederer, wearing his scarf of office, rushed into the King's presence. "Sire," he cried in terror, "the danger is beyond all expression. No fighting or defence is possible. The National Guard only possesses a few faithful members. The greater part are intimidated or bought over. They will unite themselves to the mob at the first blow. The Artillerymen, who were simply asked to be on the defensive, have already discharged their guns. Sire, you have not a moment to lose. There is safety for you only in the midst of the Assembly. There is no certain shelter for your family but amid the representatives of the People."

The King was silent, appalled by this suggestion ; but the Queen, lifting her head, proudly exclaimed, "What is this you say, monsieur ? you propose to us to seek refuge with our most cruel persecutors ? Never, never ! Let them nail me to these walls before I consent to leave them ; but tell me, monsieur, tell me, are we then totally abandoned ? "

"Madame," replied Roederer, "I repeat that resistance is impossible ; do you wish the King, your children and attendants to be massacred ?" "May God avert it," replied the Queen, "may I be the only victim."

"Another minute, another second perhaps," said Roederer, "and it will be impossible to be responsible for the King's life, yours, or those of your children." "Of my children," she replied, encircling them in her arms, "no, no, I will never give them up to the knives." Then, turning to the Ministers, the Queen said, "Well—it is the last sacrifice, but you see the object."

Mme Elizabeth now approached. " Monsieur Roederer," she exclaimed, raising her voice so that all might hear, "you will answer for the lives of the King and Queen ?" "Madame," was the reply, "we answer for it that we will die at their side ; that is all we can guarantee."

The fatal resolution taken, the sad procession was formed and the Royal Family left the Palace of their forefathers for ever, escorted by a large number of armed gentlemen and by some members of the Assembly. As they passed through the halls and galleries they were surrounded by loyal sympathisers. " Let there be no excitement," cried Roederer, " it would endanger the life of the King."   " Be tranquil," said Louis ; and Marie Antoinette added, " We will soon return."   Mme de Tourzel gives some further details of interest. She says that the Queen felt much anxiety at abandoning the faithful gentlemen and guards, and the King, who shared the feeling, turned to them and said, " Messieurs, I beg you to retire and to give up a useless defence.   There is nothing more to do here, either for you or for me."

Mme de Tourzel followed the Royal Family, leaving her daughter Pauline "with death in her heart " to the care of the Princess de Tarante, who promised never to separate from her.   " We crossed the Tuileries sadly to reach the Assembly," continues Mme de Tourzel.   MM. de Poise, d'Hervilly, de Fleurien, de Bachmann, Major of the Swiss guard, le Duc de Choiseul, my son, and several others followed His Majesty, but they were not allowed to enter. At the door there was a crush which made one fear for a moment for the lives of the King and Queen.   At last a passage was made for them, and they were received by a deputation sent by the Assembly.   The King walked through, accom-

panied by his Ministers, and placed himself beside
the President ; and the Queen, her children, and
suite stood opposite. 'I come, gentlemen,' said
the King, 'to prevent a great crime, thinking that
I cannot be in greater safety than in your midst.'
Vergniaud, who presided just then, replied : 'You
can count, Sire, on the firmness of the National
Assembly. Its members have sworn to die in
support of the rights of constituted authority.'" M.
de la Rochefoucauld supplements Mme de Tourzel's
narrative with further details. He says that as
they passed out of the Palace, the King looked sad
but calm ; the Queen was weeping, although she
essayed from time to time to show an air of confidence. The Dauphin did not seem much alarmed,
but Mme Elizabeth, who gave her arm to Madame,
"was the calmest. She was resigned to everything,
and it was religion that supported her. When she
saw the fierce crowd, she said : 'All those people
are misled. I desire their conversion, but not their
punishment.' The little Madame Royale cried
quietly, and Mme de Lamballe said to her : 'We
shall never return to the Palace.'"

During the hours of agony that followed, the
sound of cannon and musketry filled the royal party
with terror for the fate of their followers, and the
King sent a pencil message to the faithful Swiss
to cease firing. "The poor little Dauphin," says
Mme de Tourzel, "cried, thinking of the fate of
those who had remained at the Palace, and threw
himself into my arms to embrace me. Several

9

Deputies were struck by this, and the Queen said to them : ' My son is tenderly attached to the daughter of his governess, who has remained at the Tuileries. He shares the anxiety of her Mother and that which we feel for the fate of those we have left behind.' "

Some faithful servants managed to make their way into the Assembly and reassured the King as to the fate of Pauline de Tourzel and the rest of the ladies, and the Dauphin "was charming in his satisfaction at the good news."

In the midst of the horrors of this day it is interesting to come across the name of Mme Elizabeth's old and faithful friend, Dr. Lemonnier. As the King's physician he had rooms in the Tuileries, and had no intention of quitting the Palace. The mob found him sitting quietly in his library. "What are you doing there?" they cried. "I am at my post. I am the King's doctor." "And you are not afraid?" "Of what?" "Where do you wish to go?" asked the men, astonished at his calmness. "To the Luxembourg." And thither he was escorted by them, through a lane of pikemen and the infuriated mob. "Let him pass," said his protectors. "He is the King's physician, but he is not afraid."

Another surgeon, Dessault, the head of the Hôtel Dieu, rescued several wounded soldiers and other victims and hid them in the beds of the sick in the hospital. When the mob came to search for them he evaded their questions, and none of his helpers in the wards or the patients betrayed him.

As the terrible day wore on, signs of the pillage of the Tuileries reached the Assembly. Some of the mob, and the more honest of them, came in, covered with blood, and placed on the President's table the silver plate, diamonds, gold pieces, etc., which they had found, and which were saluted as trophies. Deputations also arrived demanding the Abdication of the King, and uttering threats against him. The Royal Family, worn out by the intense heat, as well as by the agony of their position, had to bear sights such as these. Heart-broken but calm, Mme Elizabeth witnessed these terrible scenes, "and bowed her head as if in submission to God's Will."

Night brought no cessation to the horrors. Great fires were lit to consume the corpses, and by their light the Assembly prolonged its sitting till two in the morning. At that hour the Royal Family were conducted to lodgings which had been hastily prepared in the ancient convent of the Feuillants. "They crossed the garden," says d'Aubier, "in the midst of a crowd of pikemen who were covered with blood; the way was lit up by candles placed on the ends of muskets; ferocious cries for the heads of the King and Queen added to the horror of the scene; one wretch, raising his voice above the others, announced that if the

Assembly delayed to give them up, he would set fire
to the building in which they were to be placed.
As we crossed the garden I carried the Prince
Royal in my arms.   Seeing these murderers
covered with blood coming near us, the Queen
feared, as I did, that the Prince would be struck
at in my arms.   She was too tender a mother
to leave to her servant the honour of shield-
ing her child, and forgetting that she herself
was in the greatest danger of all, she ordered
me to give the Prince—who was trembling with
fear—to her, and whispered a few words in his
ear.   At that happy age, calm is easily restored,
and we had hardly reached the staircase [of the
Feuillants] when he began to jump for joy, saying
to me : ʻMama has promised me I shall sleep in
her room because I was very good before those
bad men.ʼ ” [1]

The rooms assigned to the Royal Family consisted of four of the monks' cells, paved with brick
and opening on to a passage.   The architect of
the Assembly had furnished them in haste with
his own belongings.

In the first room the few faithful attendants
kept watch, in the second the King took some
rest, half dressed.   The Queen and her daughter
occupied the third, with the Dauphin—as promised
—for the first night also ; after that he slept in the

[1] Lettre de M. Aubier de la Montille, gentilhomme ordinaire de
la Chambre de Louis XVI., à M. Mallet Dupan.—See De Beauchesne,
vol. i. p. 467.

fourth cell with Mme Elizabeth, Mme de Lamballe, and Mme de Tourzel.

Supper had been prepared, but no one but the children could touch it. The poor little Dauphin began to think of his dog, and made anxious inquiries for it and was very unhappy. Mme Elizabeth said to him sadly and gently, " Come, dear child, be consoled ; there are more cruel sorrows than that, continue to love God so that He may preserve you from them."

M. d'Aubier shared with M. de Tourzel the honour of passing the night in the King's room, and describes how a band of wretches in the corridor outside cried through the door near the bed, that they would remain there all night ready to murder the King if Paris made any movement in his favour.

Outside, matters were even worse. "Furies under the window screamed to those in the corridor : 'Throw us his head, or we will come up.'" The King's calmness never deserted him except at one moment, when the noise redoubled and he heard them cry for the heads of the Queen and Mme Elizabeth. "What have they done to them ?" he said brusquely.

Presently the Queen came into the King's room. She evinced no anxiety about her own danger but much for her children. "The Queen retired and the King got into bed. Tourzel, overcome by fatigue, went to sleep in an armchair at the foot of the bed, and I remained near the bed."

Louis was saying his prayers, but interrupted them to ask the cause of the increased noise in the passage, fearing that his attendants, some of whom were in the corridor and some in the anteroom, might be attacked. D'Aubier reassured him, and, hoping to persuade him to take some rest, remarked that things might still change for the better ; but to this Louis only replied, " Charles I. had more friends than we have." After this the King slept peacefully till awakened by another burst of shrieks from the garden, when his first words were, " Do you know if the Queen and my children have slept ? " No, Marie Antoinette had not yet slept ; her anguish was too deep : and Mme Elizabeth passed the night in prayer, kneeling on her poor mattress.

About six o'clock the Queen fell into a doze, and Mme Elizabeth, hearing no sound from her room, woke the children very quietly, and helped them to dress to be in readiness to return to the Assembly.

When she took them to the Queen's room, their kisses roused her from her brief slumber, and she embraced them, exclaiming, " Poor children ! How cruel it is to have promised them such a beautiful inheritance, and now to say : This is what we leave to them. Everything ends with us."

At ten o'clock the misery of the day before recommenced for the Royal Family. They were taken back to the hot, close tribune or *loge* they had before occupied, and were forced to remain during the whole day and to witness the new developments in the Revolutionary procedure. The King, when offered his choice of a place of abode, had fixed upon the Luxembourg. This wish was now set aside because *the Luxembourg offered means of escape by its subterranean passages.* Several other places were suggested by the Assembly, but the Commune, by the voice of Manuel, demanded that the Temple should be assigned to the King for his dwelling, declaring that he would be safer there than elsewhere. The wishes of the Commune, now paramount, triumphed ; and by this decision another act in the fatal drama was closed.

We have come to a point in our story when it may be said that the history of Louis XVI. no longer possesses a claim to our attention. His reign was now over; but it is impossible to separate the thread of Mme Elizabeth's life from that of her brother. Dante's words might with too much truth have been inscribed over the portal of the Temple : *Let those who enter here leave hope behind !* But our Princess brought to the prison the sunlight of her presence and her sympathy, and, after devoting herself to the King and Queen, and undergoing the anguish of seeing them taken away to die, she still remained to cherish her little niece until her own turn came in the terrible tragedy—so that we may almost call her the central figure in the history of Royalty in the Temple, and of the transformation effected by suffering in the character of the King.

"The tower of the Temple," says M. de Beauchesne, "not only witnessed the virtues of Mme Elizabeth. It shows us in the place of the weak irresolute Prince, the calm, patient Man, and steadfast Christian. God, who had called him to be the innocent expiator of the crimes of the last two reigns, was about to place an ineffable crown upon his life. The day was coming when in the sombre light of his death all the failures of his life would be effaced."

LA TOUR DU TEMPLE.

CHAPTER VIII

THE TEMPLE

WHEN she heard the Temple proposed as the royal residence, the Queen could not forbear a shudder, and whispered to Mme de Tourzel, "You will see they will put us in the Tower, which they will turn into a real prison for us. I have always had such a horror of that Tower that I begged the Comte d'Artois a thousand times to have it pulled down, and this was surely a presentiment of all that we shall have to suffer there." When Mme de Tourzel tried to reassure her, she repeated, "You will see if I am mistaken."[1] "The event, unfortunately, only too truly justified this extraordinary presentiment," adds the Duchess. The Commune, going further than the Assembly had done, now "degraded Royalty." The few faithful friends who had remained by the King were ordered to leave him. "I am a prisoner then," said Louis,

[1] The Comte d'Artois, in his position as "Grand Prieur du Temple," occupied the Palace attached to the buildings. It was in the great salon of the Palace that the Royal Family supped the evening they reached the Temple, and the "subterranean passages" alluded to by Mme de Tourzel were in reality the rooms and vaulted galleries which connected the Palace with the Tower.

"Charles I. was happier than I am, as they let his friends remain till he ascended the scaffold." Then, turning to these loyal gentlemen, he expressed his grief at losing them, and bade them retire. The Queen, with tears in her eyes, said to them, "It is only at this moment that we feel all the horror of our position. You softened it for us by your presence and your devotion, and they now deprive us of this last consolation." The gentlemen, who knew that the Royal Family had neither money nor linen, offered them all the gold and notes they possessed. "Messieurs," said the Queen, "keep your pocket-books; you need them more than we do; you have, I hope, a longer time to live." On Monday, 13th August, the Royal Family were excused from appearing at the Assembly, and the morning was spent in settling the arrangements for their departure to the Temple.[1]

According to the decision of the Assembly, the King made out a list of the persons he wished should accompany them, who numbered about eleven in all; but he forgot that the Commune was now in the ascendant. In fact, the new Mayor of Paris, together with Manuel and others, came to see him, and declared that none of the persons

[1] Lady Sutherland, wife of the British Ambassador, hearing of the destitution of the Royal Family, sent some linen to the Queen and some of her son's clothes to the Dauphin. Lady Sutherland, it is thought, kept a journal while in Paris which would have been of exceeding value to future generations, but it is supposed that she destroyed it at the time she and Lord Sutherland were forced to fly from the French capital.

mentioned should be allowed to follow the Royal Family. At last, however, the King obtained that M. de Chamilly should be permitted to attend him, and that Mme Thibaud should follow the Queen, Mme de Navarre, Mme Elizabeth, and two other ladies to attend the children. M. Huë, who had been previously named as first *valet de chambre* for the Dauphin, and who had long known Pétion, begged him so earnestly to be allowed to follow the child that he obtained this favour. "The Queen," says Mme de Tourzel, "who was always occupied with the thought of what could soften the sorrows of those around her, wished to procure for me the consolation of taking my daughter Pauline with me, and offered to ask this favour of Pétion. I was petrified with fear at the proposition, fore-seeing only too plainly that we should not be allowed to remain long in the Temple . . . but M. le Dauphin and Madame, who saw I was in doubt, threw themselves on my neck, begging me hard to give them their dear Pauline. 'Do not refuse us,' cried Madame, 'she will be our consolation, and I will treat her as my sister.'" Mme de Tourzel yielded, and the Queen obtained the necessary leave from Pétion, who now seemed much more considerate in his behaviour to the Royal Family, and gave it with "a good grace." At five o'clock in the evening of 13th August, the melancholy procession started for the Temple, through a dense and menacing crowd. There were two large court carriages "with only two horses each." The coachmen and footmen were in grey, and now served their royal master for the last time. The Royal Family occupied the first carriage, accompanied by Mme de Lamballe and Mme and Mlle de Tourzel. They were escorted by a battalion of the National Guard, who bore their arms reversed. In the middle of the Place Vendôme,—where later on the great crime was to be consummated,—the carriage was stopped for a moment in order that the deposed and outraged monarch should see the statue of Louis XIV., which had been thrown from its pedestal and was being broken and kicked by the mob, who shouted, "This is how we treat tyrants." Manuel, turning to Louis, repeated the sentence in this way : "See, Sire, that is how the People treats its kings." "May God grant," replied the King, in a calm and dignified manner, "that its rage be only exercised upon inanimate objects." The drive lasted more than two hours, and there were moments when Pétion and the other officers were terrified for the safety of their prisoners, and harangued the mob, imploring them, "in the name of the law," to let the carriage pass. Much as they dreaded arriving at their destination, the Royal Family was reduced "to desire it, to bring to an end a scene so odious and prolonged," says Mme de Tourzel. "The Temple," she continues, "presented a festive appearance. Everything was illuminated, even to the battlements on the garden wall. The salon was lit by endless candles, and was filled by the members of the infamous

Commune, who, with hat on head and dirty dress, treated the King with a revolting familiarity. . . . This Prince and the royal family always preserved the same noble manners, and replied to their questions with a kindness which ought to have made them ashamed of themselves." The poor little Dauphin was overcome by sleep and fatigue, and begged hard to go to bed; but there was a long delay and a great supper, during which he went to sleep so soundly, while eating his soup, that Mme de Tourzel had to take him on her knee. At last word was brought that the room was ready, and a Municipal Guard hurried off with the Dauphin in his arms, anxiously followed by Mme de Tourzel and Mme de Saint Brice, who were terrified at seeing him borne through gloomy subterranean passages, till they reached a chamber in the small Tower. Here the Duchess put her charge to bed at once, and sat beside him, "full of the saddest reflections." She trembled to think the child might be separated from his parents, and was filled with immense consolation on seeing the Queen enter the room. "She pressed my hand, saying, 'Did I not tell you so?' and approaching the bed looked at the dear child who was sleeping profoundly; the tears came to her eyes as she watched him; but far from letting herself be overcome, she summoned again to her aid the great courage that never abandoned her, and occupied herself with the arrangements of the rooms in this gloomy place."

The Royal Family at first inhabited the smaller Tower, until the large one was ready. It consisted of two rooms on each floor, with a small passage-room between. The Queen and the Dauphin were given the first-floor rooms, with Mme de Lamballe in the little room; the King was lodged above, with a guard stationed next to him. Mme Elizabeth was put in a kitchen, which was very dirty, next to the guard-room. " This Princess, who joined to an angelic virtue an incomparable kindness, said at once to Pauline that she wished to take charge of her, and had a bed for her placed next hers. We shall never forget all the marks of kindness which she received from her, during the time we were permitted to dwell with her in this sad abode."[1]   Mme de Tourzel, whose Reminiscences, unfortunately for us, are nearing their end, tells us some interesting details of the daily life of the royal prisoners. As the Queen's room was the largest, she says it became the general sitting-room, and the King came down to it every morning; but the family were not permitted to be alone. One of the Commissaries of the Commune was always there, changed from hour to hour. To these men " they always spoke so kindly that one or two were softened." The meals were taken in a room below the Queen's apartment, and about five in the evening " their Majesties walked in the garden, for they dared not let Mgr le Dauphin walk alone, for fear of

[1] Mme de Tourzel, vol. ii. p. 243.

giving the Commissaries the notion of carrying
him off. Next to the dining room was a library,
from which the King and Queen chose some
books for themselves and the children." Outside,
the walls of the Temple garden were being
rapidly heightened. The architect, Palloi, who
had so distressed the little Prince by his ominous
gift, was in charge of the work and of preparing
the big Tower, and he brought the plans of the
royal apartments to the King for inspection, an
attention which must have brought back all the
Queen's fears. In writing of these last days passed
with her charge, the Duchess dwells as usual
on the kindness shown to her and her daughter.
"Mgr le Dauphin and Madame were charming to
Pauline—they showed her the most touching friendship, and the King and Queen overwhelmed her
by their kindness. We both endeavoured to give
back to their hearts some ray of hope."

On the 18th the Duchess perceived that dis-
cussions were going on between the Municipal
guards, and one of them, who was friendly, tried to
give her a hint that they were about to be taken
away, but it was so unintelligible that she could
not understand it.

"We went to bed as usual," she says, "and as
I was about to fall asleep, Mme de Saint Brice
woke me, telling me that Mme de Lamballe
was being arrested. The next moment a guard
entered my room and told us to dress quickly, as
he had received an order to take us to the Com-

mune to be questioned, after which we should
return to the Temple. The same command was
intimated to Pauline, who was in Mme Elizabeth's
room. We could only obey. We dressed and
went to the Queen, into whose hands I gave the
dear little Prince ; he was brought in his bed, without his being awakened. I did not even look at
him, in order not to shake the courage of which
we had now such need, so that we might give no
handle against us, and be able to take up again, if
possible, the duties we left with such regret. The
Queen went at once to Mme de Lamballe's room,
and took leave of her with great sorrow. She
showed a most touching sensibility to Pauline and
me, and whispered to me : ' If we are not so happy
as to meet again, take great care of Mme de Lamballe ; on all important occasions speak yourself, and
spare her as much as possible from having to answer
embarrassing or capricious questions.' Madame
was silent with surprise, and very unhappy at seeing us taken away. Mme Elizabeth arrived, and
joined the Queen in encouraging us. We embraced these august princesses for the last time,
and tore ourselves away—with death in our hearts
—from a spot which the thought of being able to
afford some consolation to our unhappy Sovereigns
rendered so dear to us."[1]

---

[1] Of all those who were removed with Mme de Tourzel, M. Huë
was the only one permitted to return to his post, and that not for
long, as he was imprisoned afresh, and only escaped by a miracle
from the September massacres.

This is not the place to follow the Duchess and her daughter in their further trials and dangers, which at first they shared with the unfortunate Princesse de Lamballe, but from which it is a happiness to know they eventually escaped. Mlle de Tourzel, the charming Pauline of the *Mémoires*, in a letter written after her imprisonment was over to her sister, the Comtesse de St. Aldegonde, adds a few interesting particulars to her mother's narrative. She tells us that half an hour before the departure from the Feuillants Mme Elizabeth called her, and, taking her apart, said, "Dear Pauline, we know your discretion and your attachment for us. I have a letter of the greatest importance which I wish to get rid of before leaving here. Help me to make it disappear." They took the letter of eight pages, and tore some pieces which they tried to crush in their fingers and under their feet; but as it took too long, Pauline courageously put one page in her mouth and swallowed it. "Mme Elizabeth wanted to do the same, but the prospect made her feel sick, which I perceived, and, begging for the two last pages of the letter, I swallowed them so that no trace remained of it." As her clothes had been "pillaged" in the sack of the Tuileries, Mlle de Tourzel possessed, in the Temple, only the gown she had on. "Mme Elizabeth, to whom some had been sent, gave me one of hers. As it did not fit me, we employed ourselves in undoing it to remake it. Every day the Queen, Madame, and

10

Mme Elizabeth had the extreme goodness to work at it, but we could not finish it before we left them. The next morning we received a parcel from the Temple; it contained our belongings, which the Queen sent to us. She, with that kindness which never left her, sent us word that she had put them together herself. Among them was Mme Elizabeth's dress. It is for me the token of an eternal remembrance. I keep it with a holy respect, and will preserve it all my life."

On 20th August, two days after his arrest, M. Huë was allowed to return to the Temple. On the same evening Manuel presented himself before the King to announce not only that he had failed in his endeavours to restore the ladies to their service, but that Mme de Lamballe, Mme and Mlle de Tourzel, Chamilly, and the women had been sent to the prison of La Force.

As this sad news took away all hope of the return of the ladies, Mme Elizabeth came down from the third floor and took possession of the Dauphin's empty room, and the bed of the young Princess, which had hitherto been in the Queen's apartment, was removed to her aunt's room.

From this time the Royal Family spent their days with a certain regularity, as follows: At six o'clock Mme Elizabeth rose, and her niece got up soon after. Although they helped each other with their dressing, Mme Elizabeth taught the little Princess how to do without assistance; thus gradually accustoming her to what she no doubt

feared might come to pass later. About eight
o'clock, when M. Huë's steps could be heard
coming down from the King's room to tidy that of
the Queen, the Princesses unlocked their door, the
Queen did the same, and M. Huë and the Commissaries entered. These officials spent the day
in Her Majesty's room itself, and passed the night
in the room which separated it from that of Mme
Elizabeth. At nine o'clock the latter followed the
Queen and her children to the King's room for
breakfast. At ten o'clock the family assembled in
the Queen's room to spend the day. The King
taught the Dauphin, and gave him lessons in Latin,
French, geography, and history. The Queen
taught Madame, and Mme Elizabeth gave her
lessons in drawing and arithmetic. About one
o'clock, if it was fine, the Royal Family, escorted by
four Municipal officers, walked in the garden, and
the children generally played with balls or quoits.
At two o'clock they went back to the King's room
to dine, and then back to the Queen's apartment.
This was the time for recreation, and the children's
games brought a ray of brightness to the whole
party. At this hour Mme Elizabeth often suggested to her brother a game of picquet or back-
gammon, to keep him from his books and work,
from which it was difficult to distract him and to
which he was ever eager to return.

At seven o'clock they established themselves
round the table, and our Princess and the Queen
took turns in reading aloud. It often happened

that something unforeseen in the books they chose brought home to them their sad position and evoked painful memories. Miss Burney's *Cecilia*, it is said, in particular, caused these reflections.

At eight o'clock M. Huë arranged the Dauphin's supper in his aunt's room, and the Queen and all the family assisted. Louis himself, in order to make this time cheerful for the children, would ask riddles or conundrums which he had found in an old copy of the *Mercure de France* in the library. Presently the little Prince said his prayers and was put to bed by M. Huë. The Queen and Mme Elizabeth took turns in watching by him, and supper was brought to the bedroom for whichever lady remained. After his supper the King would return to his son's room, and, after embracing his children and secretly pressing his wife's hand and that of his sister, went up to his own room. After this the Queen and her sister worked at their tapestry or took advantage of this moment to mend their clothes. The King did not go to bed till midnight, when the Commissary whose duty it was to relieve the guard at that hour had come. "Then night enveloped the old Donjon," and all slept, unless it were Mme Elizabeth, who often sat up to sew and mend. "Sometimes for a great part of the night a woman secretly watched, and unknown to any one but Huë, her necessary accomplice, mended by the light of one candle the only garments possessed by the King and the Dauphin, which the faithful servant had brought her at midnight. More than once the Commissaries of the Commune searched some garment which had left Mme Elizabeth's room at six o'clock in the morning."[1] The strict poverty and absence of necessary things entailed by their position was only one of the trials borne by the Royal Family. Mme Elizabeth could not see without indignation that the King and Queen were now insulted during their short walks in the garden. The men at the gateway would watch them pass out " between two puffs of their tobacco," and the men on duty outside affected to cover their heads and sit down as they passed and to rise and uncover after they had gone. Owing to the number of workmen about, the walks were restricted to a portion of the "Chestnut Avenue," where the little Prince indeed could get some exercise, but this advantage was purchased by his parents at a price which "filled Mme Elizabeth with grief."

The King, in spite of repeated demands, could not obtain leave to see the newspapers, so a plan was invented by which the news could be reported to him. Every evening, when the newsmen came to cry their news outside the Temple, M. Huë would ascend the turret and climb up to a window, where he held on until he had heard the chief items of news. He then went down to the Queen's anteroom. At the same time Mme Elizabeth would go to her room; Huë followed her on some pretext, to communicate what he had heard. On

[1] De Beauchesne, vol. ii. p. 25.

returning to the Queen's room, the Princess would go on to the balcony—the only one which had been left more or less in its original state. Here the King joined her by way of taking the air, and learnt what she could tell him. Amongst the noise made by the newsmen or *colporteurs*, other and friendly voices were heard at times. Thus one day the King could distinguish a well-known air : "*Henri, bon Henri, ton fils est prisonnier à Paris*" ; and Mme Elizabeth could only suppose that it was by means of friends that the tune of *Pauvre Jacques*, played more than once by the violin, reached her ears.

The faithful M. Huë was presently joined by Cléry, who had been attached to the Dauphin's service from his childhood, and who now obtained leave from Pétion to follow him to prison. He entered on 26th August, and as long as M. Huë remained, devoted himself chiefly to the young Prince. "You will serve my son," said the Queen, "and you will consult with M. Huë as to what regards us." He obeyed, and for the time did nothing for the King beyond dressing his hair ; but we owe much both to M. Huë and him for their interesting reminiscences of those sad days, and shall often have occasion to quote them. Turgy also, who managed to get leave to enter the prison as cook, was able to render great services to the Royal Family, but he only gained admittance to the Temple in the following year. In the meanwhile, M. Huë bore the whole burden of service, and

devoted himself in the most admirable way to the
care of his Sovereign and his family, in spite of
much abuse and insult from the municipal officers.
As these men often spoke loudly, Mme Elizabeth
overheard them several times, and took occasion
to thank M. Huë for his patience under trial. The
King also comforted him. "You have had much
to suffer to-day," he said one evening as he was
going to bed. "Well, for love of me, continue to
bear everything; do not retort." Mme Elizabeth
herself, under the constant supervision of the
officials, could rarely speak freely to Huë. One
day when he entered her room, he found the Princess at prayer, and made a movement to retire.
"Remain," she said, "do your work; I shall not
be disturbed"; and when she had finished she
remarked, "It is less for the unhappy King than
for his misguided people that I address prayers to
Heaven. May the Lord deign to allow Himself
to be entreated, and send a look of mercy upon
France." Then, seeing the emotion caused by her
words, she added, "Come, courage; God never
sends us more trials than we can bear." The
Princess gave M. Huë a copy of the beautiful
prayer she was saying, and which she recited daily.
It runs as follows :—

Prayer

"I do not know what will happen to me to-
day, O my God. All I know is that nothing will

happen to me but what You have foreseen from all
Eternity.   That is sufficient, O my God, to keep
me in peace.   I adore Your infinite designs.   I
submit to them with all my heart.   I desire them
all : I accept them all.   I make the sacrifice to
You of everything.   I unite this sacrifice to
that of your dear Son my Saviour, begging You
by His Sacred Heart and by His infinite merits for
the patience in my troubles and the perfect submission which is due to You in all that You wish
and permit.   Amen."

It has been long supposed that this prayer,
known as "Mme Elizabeth's prayer," was composed by her, but in a manuscript book which
belonged to the Duchesse de la Rochefoucauld
a copy has been found inscribed as follows :
"Prayer composed by the Bishop of Beauvais,
and which Mme Elizabeth, sister of Louis xvi.,
recited every day."   We may therefore conclude
that it may originally have been given to the
Princess by its author.

Mme Elizabeth herself was the best example
of the courage she spoke of, and her serenity
remained unshaken in the midst of the sorrows
that afflicted her and those so dear to her—so
much so that those who observed the Princess were
misled by her calmness and would say, "Doubtless
she is aware what efforts Europe will make to
deliver her brother.   No doubt letters from the
ci-devant Princes keep alive this hope, and she

believes that the hour of deliverance is approaching." As we know, however, the Princess had no illusions; and those who thought she had, mistook her resignation in suffering for mere earthly hope.

CHAPTER IX

THE PRISONERS' DAILY LIFE

A TERRIBLE crime was now about to add to the sufferings of the Royal Family. On 2nd September there was much noise and tumult round the Temple, but it did not penetrate into the prison; and as it was Sunday and a fine day, the King and his family went down into the garden after dinner. The officials appeared anxious and talked together, and suddenly drums beat the call to arms. The prisoners were hurried indoors, and the faithful M. Huë was arrested and taken off in a cab to the Hôtel de Ville. The King could not account for this fresh loss except by repeating the words, "He is attached to me : that is a great crime." Next morning while dressing he questioned Cléry, now the only person left to attend on the Royal Family. "Do you know anything of what is going on in Paris, and especially, have you any news of M. Huë?" "During the night I heard vague rumours that the people were attacking the prisons, but I know nothing else. I will go and try to find out," replied Cléry. "Take care not to compromise yourself," returned Louis, "for then we should be left alone."

Towards eleven Manuel came to assure the King that M. Huë was in no danger, but that it had been decided that he should not return and that some one else should be sent in his place. "I thank you," replied Louis, "but I will make use of the services of my son's valet ; and if the Council refuses this, I will attend upon myself. That I am resolved." As Cléry conducted Manuel to the door, he asked if the tumult still continued. "You have taken a difficult task upon yourself. I exhort you to have courage" ; was the ominous reply, and Cléry feared the mob were about to attack the Temple. In fact, Manuel was aware that the massacres commenced the day before were still continuing.

The municipal officer, Danjon, who was on service in the Temple, adds some details to this account of Manuel's mission : "Charged with the duty of announcing the commissaries to the prisoners, I invited them to come up. Arrived in their rooms, the declaration of the Council-general was read to them. Capet complained bitterly of this severity, saying that the *Corps Legislatif* would be far from approving it if they were informed of it. The Women were bitter too. Elizabeth especially walked rapidly up and down, showing her anger openly, and occasionally throwing us menacing looks. Marie Antoinette seemed much affected at this separation. 'They wished then,' she said, 'to take away the persons who were most attached to them, and in whom they placed

confidence,'" etc.   Then one of the Commissaries,
who was impatient at the complaints of the Royal
Family, now addressed the King "in a very loud
voice," says Danjon, "and said : 'The alarm gun
has sounded, the tocsin is ringing, and the Drums
are still beating.   The Enemy is at our gates ; he
seeks blood, he seeks heads.   Very well, yours
will be the first he shall have.'   At these words,"
continues Danjon, "all the family uttered a cry.
'Save my Husband,' 'Have pity on my brother,'
said the women, approaching us."[1]

An eye-witness gives the following striking
description of Paris on the day that preceded these
horrors : "Let us imagine to ourselves," he says,
"populous and busy streets suddenly becoming
empty and silent as death on a beautiful summer
evening near the hour of sunset. . . . All the shops
are shut, everyone has taken refuge at home,
trembling for their lives or their property.   All are
waiting in expectation for the events of a night in
which no one seems able to hope for help in their
despair."   In the midst of so much bloodshed
comparatively few women were killed, and it is a
consolation to find that several of those most devoted to the Royal Family escaped.   Mlle Pauline
de Tourzel and Mme de St. Brice were miracu-
lously set at liberty on 2nd September ; Mme de
Tourzel, Mme de Navarre, Mme Thibaud, and
Mme Basire on the 3rd.   Mme de Mackau, the

[1] See Rélation de Danjon, Lenotre's *Captivité et Mort de
Marie Antoinette*, pp. 56-59.

devoted governess of our Princess, was set at
liberty the same day. The unhappy Princesse de
Lamballe's fate is too well known to need description here. The prison register itself contained an
indication that she was not to escape the fate of
the royal persons to whom she was allied by her
relationship and rare devotion. Her name comes at
the end of the list of ladies, and the last words are
ominously underlined—thus : Marie Thérèse Louise
de *Savoi de Bourbon-Lamballe.* Even yet history
cannot tell us exactly why this good and charming
lady was put to death, but in the above words and
in the significant entry below them, written by the
same unknown hand, we may see that her fate was
predetermined : "Conducted on September 3rd to
the Grand Hôtel de la Force." Here she was
asked to "swear hatred to the Queen," and on her
refusal was brutally murdered.

On the same day the Royal Family had just left
the dining-room to return to the Queen's room, and
Cléry was taking his dinner with the attendant
Tison and his wife, when Mme Tison uttered a cry
of horror. The head of Mme de Lamballe, pale
and bleeding, had appeared at the window. The
wretches outside thought they recognised the
Queen's voice, and welcomed the scream with
terrible laughter. Cléry rushed upstairs and
whispered the horrible news to Mme Elizabeth,
but his countenance was so changed that the King
and Queen observed it. "What is the matter,
Cléry?" exclaimed the latter. The two Com-

missaries were at their post, but a third now
entered, crying out to the King, "The enemy are
at Verdun ; we shall all perish, but you will perish
first." Four other officials now appeared, one of
whom urged that the prisoners should show themselves at the window. "Oh, no, no, in mercy,"
cried one of the men on guard ; "do not go there,
do not look—what horror." Seeing this charitable
opposition of the guard, one of the deputation
said, "They want to hide from you the head of
Lamballe, which was being brought to you to show
you how the People revenges itself on tyrants. I
advise you to appear if you do not wish the People
to come up here." The Queen fainted with horror.
Cléry flew to assist her, and with Mme Elizabeth
placed her in an arm-chair. The children burst
into tears and tried to restore their mother by their
caresses. The man who had uttered the fatal
words still remained, and the King, turning to him,
said with energy, "Monsieur, we are prepared
for anything." The guard then left the room,
together with his comrades. When the Queen
recovered consciousness she wept with her children,
and they all went into Mme Elizabeth's room,
where the clamour of the mob was less distinctly
heard. From all sides crowds flocked to the
Temple. The extra troops which were asked for
three times by the warders did not arrive for six
hours, and during all that time it seemed doubtful
whether the Royal Family might not be massacred.
About eight o'clock calm was restored, and the

officer who informed Cléry of the events of the
day demanded from him *forty-five sous* for tricolor
ribbon bought for that day's use.   When the King
retired to rest he questioned Cléry about the events
of the day, and asked the names of those who had
tried to quiet the people and prevent them entering
the Temple.   Cléry named Danjon, whose words
we have already quoted, and who, on his arrival to
take up his duty four months later, received the
King's thanks.   As to the officer who dissuaded
the Royal Family from approaching the window,
Louis had asked him his name at once, and in his
last days he expressed again to M. de Malesherbes
how much he had been touched to find such com-
passion in the midst of the horrors of that day,
adding, " Unable to do more, I asked for his name
and address."   " Did you also ask that of the man
who wished to drag you to the window ? " asked de
Malesherbes.   " Oh, for that one," replied Louis,
" I had no need to know it."

After this cruel scene, the smallest object which
had belonged to Mme de Lamballe became a
sorrowful memento for the royal ladies.   Mme
Elizabeth collected some things which she had left
behind her in the tower and hid them away, and
later she gave these articles to Cléry, begging him
to make them into a parcel and send them with a
letter to Mme de Lamballe's woman-in-waiting ; but
neither letter nor parcel reached its destination.

About this time the name of the shoemaker
Simon—afterwards too well known in connection

with the poor little Dauphin's last days—comes before us. He was one of the Commissaries, and distinguished for his rudeness and vulgarity. One day Mme Elizabeth, who had heard that his wife was ill at the Hôtel Dieu, inquired for her. "She is better," he replied, adding, "It is a pleasure to see the ladies of the Hôtel Dieu now. They take great care of the sick. I wish you could see them; they are dressed to-day like my wife, like you, Mesdames, neither more nor less." [1]

During the first sitting of the Convention on 21st September, on the motion of Collot d'Herbois and almost without discussion, Royalty, already dead in fact, was abolished officially, and the Republic was proclaimed. On the same day this decree was publicly read outside the Temple, so that the Royal Family might hear it. Hébert, well known by his sobriquets of Père Duchesne and Destournel, who was on guard that day, was seated near the door of the King's apartments, and he and the other officers tried to read the expression on the prisoners' faces when the fatal words were heard. The King, who saw by their look what they wished, went on reading his book without the slightest change of countenance; and the Queen remained calm and dignified. In the evening Cléry asked the King for an order for curtains and

[1] The hospital of the Hôtel Dieu had been, for thirteen centuries, under the care of Augustinian nuns, who were allowed to remain, even during the Terror, in lay dress. Our generation, alas! has witnessed their expulsion.

covers for the Dauphin's bed, as the weather was getting cold. Louis told him to write the demand, and signed it. Cléry had used the ordinary formulas : "The King asks for his Son," etc. "You are very bold," said Hébert, "to use a title abolished, as you have heard, by the People ;" adding afterwards, "You may tell *Monsieur*, to cease to use a title which the People no longer recognise."

On the following day Mme Elizabeth advised Cléry in future to ask for things in the following terms : "It is necessary for the service of *Louis XVI.*, of *Marie Antoinette*, of *Louis Charles*, of *Marie Thérèse*, of *Marie Elizabeth*, etc." These requests were necessarily frequent. The Royal Family possessed only the linen which the English Ambassadress, Lady Sutherland, had sent to the Feuillants for their acceptance ; the Dauphin still wore her son's clothes, the boys being of the same age. After much pressing Cléry obtained that some underlinen should be made—but as the workwomen had embroidered crowns on the things, the officials insisted on the royal ladies unpicking these. Some of these men, however, were more sympathetic. One who came on guard for the first time found the King giving the Dauphin his geography lesson. When asked where Lunéville was situated, the child replied, "In Asia." "How in Asia ?" exclaimed the officer, smiling. "Do you not know a place over which your ancestors reigned ?" The way in which this was said pleased the King and Queen, and the latter began a conversation with

11

him in low tones, ending thus: "Our misfortunes would be more easily borne if more of your colleagues were like you." On another occasion, when the Royal Family were in the garden, a guard —a young man of pleasing aspect—showed by his gesture and look that he wished to tell them something. Mme Elizabeth took the opportunity of walking near enough for him to address her. Whether out of respect or fear, he seemed afraid to do so, but with tears in his eyes he indicated that he had hidden a paper among the débris of the building. Cléry, while affecting to look for one of the quoits belonging to the Dauphin, searched for the paper, but being observed by the Commissaries, was warned not to approach the sentinels, and had to retire, and it was never known what the paper contained. Another day Cléry thought he recognised Mme de Tourzel in a lady who seemed to be anxiously watching the little Prince, and informed Mme Elizabeth. The Princess, who had feared that this faithful friend had perished in the September massacres, could not restrain her tears. "What," she exclaimed, " can she still be alive?" Cléry had been mistaken, but he was able to ascertain next day that the Duchess was safe and in one of her country places.

Our Princess did not escape the insults suffered by her family. M. Huë gives us these odious words used by one of the guards later on: " Marie Antoinette showed pride, but I forced her to come down. The daughter and Elizabeth bow to me

against their will. The doorway is so low that in
order to pass through they are obliged to lower
themselves before me. Each time I give that
Elizabeth a mouthful of smoke from my pipe ; did
not she say the other day to the Commissaries :
'Why is Rochu always smoking?'   'Apparently
because it pleases him,' was the reply."

The work in the big tower, although far from
completed, was progressing, and the rooms destined
for the King were now ready. Meanwhile another
indictment was being trumped up against Louis in
the absurd story of the "Cupboard of Iron." The
real facts were these : A short time before the
fatal 10th of August, the King—who, as we know,
was an excellent mechanic—had made a secret
place between the door of his room and that of
the Dauphin, in which he had concealed his most
important papers. At the end he had sent for a
locksmith to complete the work, and this man now
denounced Louis's action to Roland, and it became
a fresh cause of accusation. The poor little "iron
cupboard" became of public importance, and was
supposed to be the link in a great conspiracy. On
29th September, at ten in the morning, six municipal
officers entered the Queen's room, where the Royal
Family were sitting, and one of them, Charbonnier,
read aloud an order of the Council of the Commune
commanding them to "take away paper, ink, pens
and pencils, and even written documents from the
persons of the prisoners and from their rooms, and
also from the valet and other persons in service in

the Tower; to leave them no weapon of any kind, offensive or defensive; in a word, to take all necessary precautions to prevent all communications between Louis *the Last* and anyone but the municipal officer." Then, fixing his eyes on the King, the man added, "When you want anything, Cléry will go downstairs and write your requests on a register which will be kept in the Council Chamber."

Without making any remark, the prisoners searched themselves and gave up their papers, pencils, the contents of their pockets, etc. The Commissaries looked into the boxes and cupboards and took away everything mentioned in the order. One of them said to Cléry, " The *ci-devant* King will be transferred this very night to the Tower." Cléry communicated this painful intelligence to Mme Elizabeth, and she found a way of warning her brother. After supper, as Louis was leaving the Queen's room to go up to his own, the Commissaries told him to wait a moment to listen to a fresh order from the Council. It declared that in view of the increasing difficulty in guarding the prisoners, because of their being together and the plans they might concert, the following had been decreed :—

" 1. That Louis and Antoinette be separated.

" 2. That each prisoner shall have a separate cell.

" 3. That the Valet shall be placed under arrest, etc."

The Commune had not before dared to show
such a bitter tone in its decrees, and although
prepared for this event, Louis was moved by it.
The Queen and Mme Elizabeth sought to read in
the eyes of the officers how far their orders were to
go. In bidding good-bye to his wife and sister,
the King pressed their hands as if to say, " Let
us resign ourselves." The ladies wept bitterly, and
for once Mme Elizabeth found no words of comfort
with which to support her sister. Next morning
she and her niece went to the Queen's room earlier
than usual. As Cléry had followed his master,
Mme Elizabeth wished to dress the little Prince.
All were sad and discouraged, and when at ten
o'clock they were obliged to sit down to breakfast,
they wept at the sight of the King's empty place.
They asked for news of him, but no one could
give any. However, soon after, one of the officials,
having gone to the big tower, told Louis that he
had just assisted at his family's breakfast and that
they were well. " I thank you," he replied, "and
I beg you to give them news of me and to say that
I am well. Could I not have some books I left in
the Queen's room ? " he added, " you would do me
pleasure by sending them." The man agreed, and
as he could not read, bade Cléry accompany him,
thus giving him a welcome opportunity of seeing
the royal ladies. He found them in deep sorrow,
and was plied by questions to which he had to
reply with reserve. Their grief touched the
Commissaries, and when they begged to be

permitted to see the King at least once in the day,
if it were only at meal-time ; one of them said
authoritatively, "Very well, let them dine together
to-day ; but as we are under the orders of the
Commune, to-morrow we will do as it prescribes."
At these words "a feeling almost of joy came to
relieve these sad hearts.   Marie Antoinette pressed
her children to her, and Mme Elizabeth, with eyes
raised to heaven, seemed to thank God for this
unexpected favour.   Some of the officers wept.
Even Simon said; 'I think these women could
make me cry'; but, addressing the Queen, he
added : 'When you had the people massacred on
August 10th you did not cry.'   'The people are
much misled about our sentiments,' she replied
sadly."[1]   Dinner was served in the King's room,
and his family were taken up to join him.   By the
transports they showed, the fears they had undergone could be estimated.   As the officials who had
given them leave to come did not wish to disavow
their concession before those who succeeded them,
the permission continued, and happily there was no
further question of the order of 29th September.

    After dinner the Queen and Mme Elizabeth
expressed a wish to see the rooms which were
being prepared for them above those of the King,
and were conducted thither.   They begged the
workmen to make haste, but it took another three
weeks to complete the work.

    During this period Cléry was able to divide his

----

[1] *Vie de Mme Elizabeth*, de Beauchesne, vol. ii. p. 50-1.

time between the prisoners—he attended to their rooms, made up their accounts, and strove to keep up some communication between them. The position of the prisoners in separate towers rendered the duty of the warders harder, and they were consumed with anxiety lest any efforts to escape should be made. The smallest thing excited suspicion. A poor priest of Fontenay de Vincennes sent some verses to our Princess, addressed to " Madame Elizabeth, at the Temple"; but the paper was seized and sent to the Council of the Commune as a possibly dangerous document. As we have said, no newspapers were permitted to the prisoners, but horrid pamphlets, which vilified the Royal Family, sometimes found access, and were placed designedly on the chimney-piece or elsewhere to attract their attention. One declared that " the two little wolf-whelps," as they called the royal children, must be suffocated, and another heaped insults on Mme Elizabeth, to try and destroy the admiration felt for her by the public generally. About this time a little difference arose between Cléry and Tison as to their mutual duties, and the Council took occasion to arrange how the Royal Family's demands were to be presented in future. One of the officers said to Tison, " Be happy, the Ministry is formed ; you have the Department of the Women." This decree in fact presaged the more complete separation of the Royal Family.

On Friday, 26th October, the Queen, Mme

Elizabeth, and the children were installed in the big tower.

This moment, which had been so ardently desired, was embittered by an act of cruelty towards Marie Antoinette. The Council of the Temple, in a motion suggested by a personal enemy of the Queen's, decided that the Dauphin should be taken from her care except during a short time in the afternoon and given over to that of the King. No notice of this was given to the unfortunate mother, and the boy was taken away on the very evening they entered the Tower. The Queen's grief was intense. Since they had been in the Temple she had devoted herself absolutely to the child, and had found consolation in his great love for her. It was the last joy of her sad life. She still hoped he would be given back to her prayers and tears when they should be settled in their new rooms; but when the next day came, she was presented with the decree of the Council for their separation. The Dauphin was inconsolable, and took an opportunity of showing his feelings while talking to one of the workmen, who thought that the Prince did not treat him with sufficient respect, and said to him, "Don't you know that *Liberty* has made us all free, and that we are all *equal*?" "Equal as much as you like," replied the royal child, with precocious wisdom, "but it is not here," he added, looking towards his father, "that you can persuade us that *Liberty* has made us free."

Cléry at the same time was suddenly carried off

LOUIS CHARLES DE FRANCE, DAUPHIN.

Né le 27 Mars, 1785, mort dans la Tour du Temple le 12 Juin, 1795.

to the Hôtel de Ville, where he spent six hours in a dungeon ; but after a long interrogation he was fortunately sent back to the Temple, and allowed to take up his duties again. Before describing the new and last prison of the Royal Family, we may give a pretty anecdote about the little Dauphin, relating to the legend of the "Cupboard of Iron" which had brought such fatal results to the Royal Family. The story had somehow reached the boy, and one day when a tempting cake was brought in at dinner-time, he said, " Mama, here is a beautiful and excellent *brioche* ; there is a cupboard here in which, if you approve, I will put it, and where it will be safe, for I assure you no one will be able to take it out." Every one looked about, but there was no cupboard in the room. The Commissaries were full of suspicion, and no doubt thought of fresh denunciations ! " My son," said the Queen, "I do not see the cupboard you talk of." "Mama," replied the boy, pointing to his mouth, "here it is."

CHAPTER X

THE GREAT TOWER

THE Great Tower of the Temple, which now formed the prison of the Royal Family, stood one hundred and sixty feet high. Its walls were nine feet in thickness, and it contained four storeys of vaulted rooms, which were supported in the middle by a huge pillar reaching from the bottom to the top of the building; the interior measured about thirty-four to thirty-six square feet. The ground floor remained in its original state of severe yet dignified architecture. It was used in turn by the officials on guard, and it was this apartment which was later on called the Council Chamber. There were turrets at each angle, one containing the staircase, which went up to the roof. The first storey was a repetition of the ground floor, and served as guard room, and here were piled the arms of the Temple. The second storey, devoted to the King's use, originally formed one room like those below, but was now divided into four by wooden partitions with false ceilings of cloth. The first room formed an antechamber, which had three doors. The King's room faced the entrance of this room and contained a second bed for his son. Next to it was the dining-room. The King's room had a fireplace, and each room possessed a window; but the iron bars and the wooden shutters which had been placed outside effectually prevented the air from entering freely. The room was hung with a yellow glacé paper covered with white flowers. On entering, the chimney-piece was in front, the window and turret on the right; at the left was the King's bed, with his son's little bed at its foot. On the mantelpiece stood a clock, which still bore the inscription: *Lepaute, Clockmaker to the King*—but some zealous patriot had covered the word King with a wafer; while the words *Liberté, Égalité, Propriété, Sûreté* were written on the beams of the fireplace. The turret served Louis as a study and an oratory; its walls were grey, and it was warmed by a small stove. Cléry occupied a room to which access was obtained by a door near the Dauphin's bed, and which led into a short passage.

The third storey, occupied by the Queen and the Princesses, was arranged in the same way minus the passage. The Queen's room was just over the King's, and her bed in the same position, with Mme Royale's near it. It was papered with stripes of green and soft blue, and the clock on the mantelpiece represented Fortune and her wheel. Mme Elizabeth's room was hung with the same common yellow paper which adorned Tison's apartment, and was furnished in much the same style as his: an iron bedstead, a walnut table, a common cupboard—such were the chief pieces of furniture. The Queen's bed had pillars of green damask, and both ladies had piqué counterpanes.[1]

The fourth floor, which was uninhabited, was left untouched; and above again was a gallery running between the battlements and the roof, which could be used as a promenade; but as each opening in the wall was carefully closed by planks and wooden shutters, persons walking there could neither see out nor be seen from below.

The changes in their lodgings, and even the absence of the Dauphin from his mother's rooms, made little difference in the even tenor of the life led by the prisoners. Louis, who remained calm and serene in the midst of his trials, sought distraction in his books. The Queen, less calm by nature, occupied herself with the children, and strove to soothe her anguish by manual work. As for Mme Elizabeth, she turned her thoughts more and more from the evils surrounding her. Sometimes during the day, in the midst of the oaths and blasphemies which she could not escape hearing, she would retire to her room to pray and meditate. Often after dinner, while the children played in the anteroom, their aunt would assist at their games, sitting at the table book in hand. Cléry generally remained in this room, and by the Princess's orders

[1] This description of the furniture of the royal apartments is absolutely authentic, and is taken from two contemporary inventories.

would also seat himself and take up a book, so as to appear occupied. This division of the family worried the guards. They had orders never to leave the King and Queen alone, and moreover distrusted each other, and they could not always be present here. Mme Elizabeth would profit by their absence to talk to Cléry, who replied without lifting his eyes from his book; while the children, who understood the manœuvre, would help their aunt by playing noisily or by making signs that the guards were approaching.

In other ways the watch kept was terribly minute. After meals the Princess sometimes handed her knife, which had a gold blade, to Cléry to clean. More than once one of the officials snatched it from him to make sure that no paper was concealed in the handle. On one occasion she gave Cléry a ˙pious book to return to the Marquise de Sérent; the officials seized it and cut off all the margins for fear that something might be written on them in invisible ink. The linen also was minutely examined on its way to the wash, and on its return, and the washing account or any paper, was held before the fire to make sure it contained no writing.

One day when the little Princess Royal was unwell, and the doctor had brought some medicine and a prescription to the Queen, the Council took alarm, sent for the medicine, and summoned Dr. Leclere to answer for his action.

His reply is worth recording, as it shows the

difficulties which the most ordinary attentions met with : "The wife of Louis Capet," said the doctor, "spoke to me of the necessity of finding remedies for her daughter, who has an eruption on her cheek and asked me what they should use for it. One must respect those in sorrow, and the daughter should not be punished for the faults of the father. Besides, she has a pretty face, and it would be a pity for the eruption to remain, as it is a *chef-d'œuvre* of nature." Here he was interrupted by the President, who said, "*The skin of the serpent is also a* chef-d'œuvre *of nature* ; the Council invites you to *continue without digression.*" The result of all this was that the Council decreed that the prisoners were to receive no succour in illness except from physicians approved by itself. Soon after this, however, on the 14th November, the King became unwell with an abscess in the mouth. The Queen begged that his dentist might be sent for, in vain ; but on the 22nd, when he was worse and fever set in, the Commune became alarmed, and allowed our old friend, M. Lemonnier, to come to the Temple, accompanied by M. Robert, a surgeon, and even demanded a daily bulletin of the King's health.

M. Lemonnier was greatly affected at seeing his royal master and Mme Elizabeth, for whom he had a profound affection and respect. He visited the invalid twice a day for a week. At this time, as the Dauphin had whooping-cough and fever, the Queen implored the Council that he might be moved to her room at night, but was refused. Then she and Mme Elizabeth begged at least to nurse him. "You have refused him the favour of coming up to us ; permit us to have that of going down to him." But no—the Revolution wished to persecute the mother as well as the Queen, and her request was refused.

Mme Elizabeth, Mme Royale, and also Marie Antoinette herself, took the whooping-cough ; and presently the faithful Cléry became ill with fever and pain in the side, and was obliged to remain in bed. Meanwhile the King looked after his son ; and as by now the latter was well, he in his turn sat in Cléry's room and brought him his *tisane*. In the evening the King seized a moment, when he was freer than usual from surveillance, to visit Cléry and give him his drink, saying, "I wish I could take care of you myself, but you know how we are watched : to-morrow my doctor shall see you." The royal ladies came to see him at supper-time, and Mme Elizabeth was able, unobserved, to give him a little bottle containing a *leech*. She had a bad cold herself, but insisted on giving him this her own remedy. After supper, the Queen had the happiness of undressing her son and putting him to bed, while Mme Elizabeth arranged the King's hair for the night. For six days Cléry lay ill, and only his extreme desire to be about enabled him then to resume his work. One evening when he was better, and had just put the Dauphin to bed, the Queen and Princesses came to bid the child good-night, and he withdrew. Mme Elizabeth, unable to speak to him herself without attracting the attention of the guards, gave her nephew a little box of ipecacuanha, saying, "This is for Cléry. I beg you to give it to him when he returns." Cléry, however, had gone to his supper, and did not return till eleven o'clock. When he came to prepare the King's bed, he was surprised to hear the Prince call to him in a low voice, and asked why he was awake so late. "It is because my aunt gave me a little box for you," was the reply, "and I did not want to fall asleep without giving it to you, it is time you came, as my eyes have closed several times." "Mine filled with tears," added Cléry, when he told the story. "The Dauphin perceived this and embraced me, and two minutes later he was sound asleep."

In December the guards were doubled; in future two at a time were in attendance on the King and on the Queen, and their vigilance became still more oppressive. Cléry was treated with more rigour, and Turgy was forbidden to speak to him. The only way now in which news from without could reach the prisoners was by Mme Cléry, who was permitted access to the Temple once a week on the pretext of bringing clean linen and other necessaries. She was always accompanied by a woman friend who passed for a relation.

On 6th December Mme Cléry arrived with her faithful accomplice, and while, in order to disarm the suspicions of the new warders, she talked to her husband in a loud voice, her friend whispered these fatal words: "Next Tuesday they will take the King before the Convention; his trial will begin; the King can procure a counsel; all this is certain." That evening, at Louis's bedtime, Cléry managed to tell him what he had heard; he also mentioned that probably he would be separated from his family during the trial, and that only four days remained in which to concert measures for a correspondence between the third and fourth storeys. Next day at breakfast the King informed the Queen, and she in her turn told Mme Elizabeth. Signs which confirmed the bad news soon followed. The King and his son had just returned to his apartment when an officer arrived at the head of a deputation from the Commune, and read aloud in a voice of emotion a decree ordering that all weapons or sharp instruments were to be taken from the prisoners and from all who were about them: "in general, everything of which prisoners presumed to be criminals are deprived." The King took a knife and a pair of scissors and penknife from a case in his pocket, and gave them to the officer. The rooms were then searched, and razors and all the little toilette necessaries were seized. The officials went upstairs on the same errand. "If it is only that," said the Queen disdainfully, "our needles ought also to be taken, for they prick very sharply." She might have said more had not Mme Elizabeth nudged her elbow. The Queen

12

and Princesses then gave up their scissors, and the men took all their little work implements. " Do you know," remarked one of them, "that we have orders also to take Tison and Cléry from you, and to taste all the food that is served to you?" The deprivation of their work things was bitterly felt by the royal ladies, especially as it forced them to give up various pieces of work which had helped them to pass the long days. One day while our Princess was mending the King's coat, having no scissors, she bit off the cotton. "What a contrast," said Louis, who was watching her affectionately. "You wanted for nothing in your pretty home at Montreuil." "Ah, my brother," she replied, "can I have regrets when I share your misfortunes."

On 8th December Cléry was summoned before a Commission that had met to verify the prisoners' expenses, and heard from a well-disposed official that the order for the King's separation from his family had not yet been finally pronounced. Turgy, on his side, managed to get a newspaper which contained the announcement that "Louis Capet would be called to the Bar of the Convention." He gave this paper, and a memorandum published by Necker on the King's trial, to Cléry, who was able to hide them in an old piece of furniture and to warn Mme Elizabeth. On Tuesday, 11th December, the drum beat the call to arms in all quarters of Paris, and cavalry and cannon were massed in the court of the Temple. The Royal Family would have been alarmed at

these preparations had they not known the cause.
They had to feign ignorance, and asked for an
explanation, but in vain.   At nine o'clock, as usual,
the King and the Dauphin went up to the Queen's
room for breakfast, where they all remained
together for an hour; but the presence of the
officials prevented any private conversation, and at
ten o'clock they separated, "their looks expressing
what their lips could not utter." The Dauphin,
according to custom, went down with his father,
but at eleven o'clock two officers came to take him
back to his mother.   Louis embraced his son and
bade Cléry accompany him.   Almost immediately
an official announced to the King that the Mayor
of Paris was below with a large retinue and would
soon come up.   Louis, however, spent two long
and sorrowful hours of waiting.   An important
paper, which had been forgotten and which had to
be sent for, was the cause of the delay.   At one
o'clock, Chambon, the Mayor, accompanied by
Chaumette, Procureur Générale, Coulombeau,
Secretary, and Santerre, Commandant of the
National Guard, appeared.   The Mayor told the
King that he had come to conduct him to
the Convention, and Coulombeau read aloud the
decree.   At the expression, "*Louis Capet* will be
taken, etc.," the King said, "*Capet* is not my name;
one of my ancestors bore it, but it is not that of my
family.   I would have wished, monsieur," he continued, addressing the Mayor, "that my son had
been left with me during the two hours I have

spent in waiting for you.   However, such treatment is on a par with that which I have experienced for the last four months.   I shall follow you, not to obey the Convention, but because my enemies have forced my hand."

The sound of the carriage was now heard in which the King of France was to be taken before the hastily convoked tribunal of his rebellious subjects.   The feelings of the royal ladies in the apartment above may be conceived, but in the presence of their gaolers they could give them no expression.   Cléry was presently taken to them by a Commissary, who, being more gentle and polite than the rest, informed him that Louis would probably not see his family again, although it was not quite settled.   Dinner was served as usual in the King's room, and the ladies then returned to their apartment.   Here only one guard was in attendance ; it was his first turn of service, and the Queen spoke to him, asking about his position, his family, etc.   Meanwhile Mme Elizabeth entered her own room, beckoning Cléry to follow, and heard from him what we have already related.   "The Queen and I," she said, "are prepared for everything, and we have no illusions regarding the fate which is being prepared for the King—he will die the victim of his goodness and of his love for his people, for whose welfare he has never ceased working since he ascended the throne.   How cruelly the People are deceived.   The King's faith and his great confidence in Providence will sustain him in this supreme trial; Monsieur Cléry," added the Princess, thinking she was addressing him for the last time, "you alone will now be near my brother; redouble, if it be possible, your care for him; do not neglect any way by which you can send us news of him, but do not expose yourself to risk for any other purpose, for then we should have no one left in whom to confide." The Princess and Cléry then discussed the means by which communications could be kept up, and Turgy was named as alone worthy of being in the secret. It was settled that Cléry should, as before, keep in his charge the Dauphin's clothes, and every other day, when sending up a change of articles, should endeavour to send information also. "If the King were to be indisposed, I wish particularly to hear of it," added Mme Elizabeth; "take this handkerchief, and keep it as long as my brother is well. Should he become ill, send it to me with my nephew's linen. Take care to fold it in this way if the indisposition is slight, and in that manner if it is more serious. Have you heard the officers speak of the Queen?" went on the Princess. "Do you know what fate they reserve for her? Alas, what can they reproach her with?" "Nothing, Madame," returned Cléry, "but with what can they reproach the King?" "Oh, nothing, nothing; but perhaps they look upon the King as a victim necessary to their projects, or even to their safety. Whereas the

Queen and her children are no obstacle to their ambition ;" and when Cléry expressed a hope that the King might only be banished, Mme Elizabeth replied sadly, " Oh, I keep no sort of hope."[1]

This was the longest interview she had dared to have with Cléry, and the fear of the arrival of the officials now brought it to a close, not a moment too soon, as Tison remarked upon its length to Cléry, who put him off with some words about the probability of the Dauphin now remaining with the Queen.

At half-past six the King was brought back to the Temple. He begged at once to be taken to his family, but was refused. He begged that at least they might be told of his return, and this was permitted ; and the Queen, on her side, vainly sought permission to descend. With extraordinary calm, and in spite of the presence of four warders, Louis quietly began to read as usual. At half-past eight, when supper was announced, he said, "Will not my family come down?" To this there was no answer. After his meal Louis again pressed for leave to see them, and was told that they awaited the decision of the Convention. The King retired to bed as usual. Upstairs the Princesses were in deep distress. The Queen had given her bed to her son, and remained standing all night in a state of such silent grief and misery that her daughter and Mme Elizabeth did not like to leave her ; but she insisted on their

[1] De Beauchesne, vol. ii. pp. 72-3.

going to their room, where the little Princess alone
was able to sleep.

In the course of the following day the King
received notice that he might appoint counsel to
defend him.   At first Louis named MM. Target and
Tronchet, or both.   Target refused, and Tronchet
was absent ; but many other great lawyers hastened
to beg the Convention to allow them to have the
privilege of defending the King.   Among these loyal
souls was M. de Malesherbes.   " I am sensible of
the offers which these persons make to me to be
my defenders," replied Louis to the deputation of
the Convention, "and I beg you to assure them
of my gratitude.   I accept M. de Malesherbes as
my Counsel.   If M. Tronchet cannot give me his
services, I will consult with M. de Malesherbes
on the choice of another advocate."

On 14th December both M. Tronchet and
M. de Malesherbes visited the Temple separately,
and were taken up to the King after being searched.
"Ah, it is you, my friend," exclaimed Louis, when
de Malesherbes entered, embracing him and taking
him aside into the turret : " You come to help me
with your advice ; you do not fear to risk your life
to save mine ; but all will be useless."   " No, Sire,
I do not expose my life to any risk, and I wish to
believe that your Majesty's own runs no danger.
Your cause is so just and the means of defence so
powerful."   " Yes, yes, they will make me perish ;
but to leave a spotless memory will be to win my
cause.   My sister," continued the King, "has given

me the name and address of a non-constitutional priest who could assist me in my last moments. I beg you to go and find him for me; to give him this note and to persuade him to give me his help. It is a strange commission for a *Philosophe*, is it not? Ah, my friend, how much I wish you could think like me. Religion instructs and consoles in a very different way from philosophy." "Sire, this commission is not at all pressing," replied Malesherbes. "Nothing is more so for me," said Louis. The note was addressed to "Monsieur Edgworth de Firmont, aux Récollects, Paris," with whom our Princess had managed to keep up communication from time to time.

In the course of the day the Convention considered the King's request to see his family, and it was accorded; but being afterwards opposed, a half-measure was adopted, which the King's unselfishness forbade him to accept. "The National Convention decrees that Louis Capet shall see his children, who are not, until a final judgment is given, to communicate with their mother and aunt." On hearing this, the King said to Cléry, "You see what a cruel alternative they place before me. I cannot make up my mind to keep my children with me; for my daughter it is impossible, and as for my son, I feel the grief it would cause the Queen; I must therefore consent to this fresh sacrifice. Let his bed be moved into his mother's room."

This generous order was obeyed. The

Dauphin had passed the three last nights on a mattress. Cléry from this time sent up his clothes every other day, according to the arrangement with Mme Elizabeth. In the afternoon a deputation from the Convention arrived to question the King, who had Tronchet beside him, and the dreary examination went on without interruption until nine o'clock in the evening, when the King asked if the officials would take supper. This Cléry prepared for them in the dining-room, "cold chicken and some fruit." Tronchet would not take anything, and remained with the King. After supper the interrogation continued till midnight was striking, and the long, miserable day came to an end. Louis then took some food. He asked Cléry if the family supper had been delayed, and on his replying that it had not, the King added, " I should have feared that such delay would have made the Queen and my sister uneasy." He then said his prayers, retired to bed, and slept quietly.

De Malesherbes and Tronchet were alarmed, if not at the gravity, at the number of accusations brought against the King; especially as the Convention had declared that it would hear Louis on 26th December for the last time. The King's advocates therefore asked his approval of their seeking aid from M. de Sèze, a young and brilliant lawyer. Louis, who only knew him by reputation, replied with a smile, " Do so. The doctors come in numbers when the danger is great. You prove to me that the sick man is at extremity :

I will show you that I am a good patient." M. de
Séze was permitted to join the King's advisers,
and the three came every day to the Temple until
26th December. Their loyalty and zeal comforted
Louis but did not alter his opinion of his impend-
ing fate. One day he took M. de Malesherbes
apart and reminded him that in their first interview
he had charged him with a commission which was
of great importance. " If I have not sooner
rendered an account of my mission to the King,"
was the reply, " I have all the same obeyed his
orders. M. Edgworth does not live at the
Récollects, he has a lodging in the Rue du Bac. . . .
I gave him a rendezvous at my sister's, Madame de
Sénozan. There, Sire, I gave him your message,
which, to anyone, would no doubt have seemed
a pressing invitation, but to one like him was, and
is, an order. He hopes, as I do, that human
perversity will never require that he should give
you so cruel a proof of devotion. He charged me
to place at your feet his heart-felt sentiments of
sorrow and respect." " Thank him for me,"
replied Louis, "and beg him not to leave Paris
just now."

That the Abbé Edgworth was well aware of
the danger he would incur by assisting the King,
we may gather from the following letter written by
him to a friend in England on 21st December :

" My unfortunate master has chosen me to prepare him for death, if the iniquity of his subjects
goes so far as to commit this parricide. I prepare

myself too for death, for I feel convinced the
popular rage will not permit me to survive the
horrible scene for an hour ; but I am resigned ; my
life is nothing. If by losing it I could save that
which God has given *for the ruin and the re-
surrection of many*, I would willingly make the
sacrifice, and I should not have died in vain." [1]

Meanwhile, Cléry had found a means, through
Turgy, of sending news to Mme Elizabeth, and
on this day learnt, in return, that the Princess had
managed to slip a note for the King into Turgy's
hand as she gave him her dinner napkin. It
contained only a few words written with a pin,
begging Louis to write her one word himself.
At bedtime Cléry gave this to the King, who
since his trial commenced had been supplied with
pens and ink, and he was able next morning to
send a few lines to his sister. He gave the note
unsealed to Cléry, saying, "There is nothing in
this which could compromise you : read it"; but
the faithful valet took the liberty of disobeying
this order, and he gave the note to Turgy. It
must have brought a ray of consolation to the
unhappy wife and sister, in their anguish, to see the
King's handwriting again.

---

[1] See *Biographie Universelle*, Paris, 1815. The Abbé Edgworth
died in England in 1807, a victim to his priestly zeal during an
epidemic. Marie Thérèse, Duchesse d'Angoulême, was present at
his funeral.

CHAPTER XI

THE KING'S LAST DAYS

NECESSITY, as we know, is the mother of invention, and presently the two faithful dependants found other methods of communication for the Royal Family. Turgy, being freer than Cléry, was able to transmit notes to the King, who would say to him kindly, " Take care ; you expose yourself to too much risk,"—but it was Cléry who invented a way of sending notes from one window to another. " The candles furnished for the King's use were delivered in packets tied up with string. Cléry preserved the string, and when he had collected sufficient he announced to his master that in future his correspondence could be more active." Mme Elizabeth's window was just above that of a little passage which ran between the King's room and Cléry's. By attaching her notes to the string, therefore, Mme Elizabeth could let them down to the window below ; and for once the terrible wooden shades or shutters were of use, as they prevented the notes from falling, or any one outside from seeing the string, to which the answer could be attached before it was again drawn up. Even paper and ink could be supplied to the Princess by the same means. She was informed of this happy contrivance and put in possession of the string, and on the morning of 20th December sent word to the King that she would make use of it at eight o'clock that evening. On that day the deputation from the Convention came again, and also the King's advocates, and at eight o'clock some of them were still with him. Cléry, however, had arranged everything discreetly, and when Louis rose and left the room for a few moments, his guests little suspected that he was holding communication with his dear ones above. " The King sent up by this aerial post sheets of white paper, which returned to him inscribed with comforting words. It was always at eight o'clock in the evening that this correspondence took place."

The King spent Christmas Day in making his will. This beautiful Christian document is well known, but we cannot refrain from quoting the paragraphs that most nearly relate to our Princess. "I beg my sister," wrote Louis, "to continue her tenderness for my children, and to be a mother to them should they have the sorrow to lose theirs. I recommend earnestly to my children, after their duty to God, which comes before all, to be always united, submissive, and obedient to their mother, and grateful for all her care and trouble for them ; and in memory of me, I beg them to look upon my sister as a second mother."

Mme Elizabeth had felt great anxiety as to how

Christmas Day would be kept in Paris.   Chaumette, indeed, forbade Midnight Mass, and officials were sent to prevent the church doors being opened, but the people were not disposed to obey.   The members of the Commune were hustled and beaten, and Mass was sung as usual.   One of the men who had suffered came on guard at the Temple on Christmas night, and recounted to Turgy how he had been treated by the " Dames de la Halle " at St. Eustache.   Mme Elizabeth remarked that " it was good for the people to know that those who pretend to make them free desire liberty neither for conscience nor for prayer."   On 26th December the King was taken again before the Convention, and on his return at five o'clock he prepared a note for his family, which could, however, only reach them three hours later.

On 1st January 1793, Cléry entered his royal master's room before daybreak, and, opening the curtains of his bed, asked in a low voice for permission to offer good wishes for an end to his misfortunes.   " I receive your wishes," said Louis, holding out his hand to his faithful attendant, who kissed it with tears.   When the King rose he begged one of the officials to go upstairs and inquire after the health of his family and give them his New Year's greetings.   The men were affected by the King's accent and his simple words.   When the messenger returned he said, " Your family thank you for your wishes and send you theirs."   " What a New Year's Day ! " exclaimed Louis.

About this time Madame Royale fell ill, and the King forgot his own troubles in anxiety for her. He received news by means of the nightly correspondence, but this did not allay his fears, and one day he spoke of them to his lawyers. They promised to ask for information from the Council ; but the next day Louis informed them that he had had better news of his daughter, and that the Queen was now easy about her. We can guess how this information had reached him.

In his intimate talks with his Advocates Louis constantly spoke of his family. " In the midst of all my trials," he said to them, " Providence has given me tender consolations. I owe the charm of my life to my children, the Queen, and to my sister. I will not speak of my children, at their age already so unhappy," he continued, with emotion, " nor of my sister, whose life has been all affection, devotedness, and courage. Spain and Piedmont both seemed to desire alliances with her. At the death of Christine of Saxony, the Canonesses of Remiremont offered to elect her as their Abbess —but nothing could separate her from me. She attached herself to my misfortunes as others were attached to my prosperity. But I desire to converse with you upon a subject which causes me cruel suffering—that is the injustice of the French people to the Queen." Louis then explained at length his wife's conduct and her natural distaste for etiquette and constraint, which had been so severely judged. " Her natural manner," he added, "so new at

court, was too much according to my own taste for
me to wish to discourage it.   At first the public
applauded the relinquishment of old customs—
afterwards it made of this a crime.   The factions
make these efforts to decry and blacken the Queen
in order to prepare the people to see her perish.
Yes, my friends, her death is resolved on.   If they
allowed her to live, it would be feared she would
revenge me.   Unfortunate princess!   Our marriage
promised her a throne.   To-day what a prospect
lies before her."

The iniquitous trial was drawing to a close.
On Tuesday, 17th January, Paris learnt that the
King's death had been voted during the night.   At
nine o'clock the three royal advocates came to the
Temple and were met by Cléry.   "All is lost,"
said M. de Malesherbes ; " the King is condemned."
They found Louis sitting at his table with his back
to the door, his face buried in his hands.   He rose
to receive them, and said, "For the last two hours
I have been thinking over the past, and have
searched my memory to see whether during my
reign I ever knowingly gave my subjects reason
for complaint.   Well, I swear to you in all sincerity,
as a man about to appear before God, I have
always desired the happiness of my people—I have
never formed a wish which was contrary to it."
The gentlemen were deeply affected by the contrast between the King's gentle words and the
terrible news they brought, and M. de Malesherbes
fell weeping at his feet, unable to speak.   Louis

lifted him up and embraced him, saying, "I was awaiting what your tears tell me; calm yourself, my dear Malesherbes. It is all for the best; yes, it is better to have no more uncertainty. If you love me, far from being sad, do not envy me the sole refuge which remains to me"; and, as M. de Malesherbes tried to persuade him that some hope remained : "No," said the King, "there is no hope, the country is misled, and I am ready to immolate myself for her." On being informed that some loyal subjects still remaining would strive to save him on the scaffold, he begged M. de Malesherbes to dissuade them from this. Such an attempt would, he said, endanger their lives without saving his. "When force might have saved my throne and my life, I refused to make use of it. Am I likely now to let French blood flow for me?"

The day passed wearily by, and the evening was still more sad. The Queen, her children, and Mme Elizabeth, who had heard the terrible sentence from the Crier outside, were plunged in grief, and the notes exchanged must have been heart-breaking in their despair.

The sentence of death was read to the King on Sunday, 20th January, and afterwards he sent a letter to the Convention. He begged to be allowed three days to prepare for death, to be permitted to see the person he should name, to see his family freely, to be relieved from the constant presence of the warders; adding other requests for the future safety of his family and the many pensioners who would lose by his death.

Being assured that his letter should be presented to the Convention, he added, "If the Convention grants my demand to see the person I wish, here is his address, M. Edgworth de Firmont, rue du Bac, 483." The reply of the Convention was couched in the grandiose and heartless terms of the period: "Louis is at liberty to call for whatever priest he wishes, and to see his family freely, and without witnesses. The Nation, always great and always just, will look after his family."

The Abbé Edgworth, who now came to the prison, shall himself tell us of his interview. "Arrived at the King's room," he says, "of which all the doors were open, I saw him standing in the midst of a group of eight or ten persons, composed of the Minister of Justice, accompanied by several members of the Commune, who had just read to him the fatal decree which irrevocably fixed his death for the next day. He stood in the midst of them, calm, peaceful, gracious even, and not one of those who surrounded him looked so much at their ease as he did. When I appeared he made them a sign to withdraw, and they obeyed. He shut the door after them, and I remained alone with him. Till then I had succeeded in controlling the agitation I felt, but now, at the sight of this Prince, formerly so great, and now so unhappy, I was no longer master of myself. In spite of my efforts my tears fell, and I threw myself at his feet without being able to use other language than my grief. This touched him far more than the decree he had been listening to. At first he replied to my tears only by his own, but soon recovering himself, he said to me, ' Monsieur, forgive this moment of weakness, if indeed it can be so termed. For a long time I have lived among my enemies and habit has in a way accustomed me to them, but the sight of a faithful subject speaks in a very different way to my heart. It is a spectacle to which my eyes are no longer accustomed, and it overcomes me in spite of myself.' "

At eight o'clock the conversation was interrupted by an official, who came to announce that the Royal Family were about to come down. Louis could not hide his emotion. " If I am not permitted to go to them, I may at least see them alone in my room ? " he said. " No," replied one of the men, " it is arranged that you shall see them in the dining-room. You will be by yourselves ; the door will be closed ; but we shall have our eyes on you through the glass lattice." The King entered the dining-room, followed by Cléry, who arranged the table and put chairs ready, and placed a glass beside a carafe of iced water which stood at hand. " If the Queen drank that water, it might hurt her," remarked Louis, " bring some plain water " ; adding, " I fear the sight of M. de Firmont might distress my family too much ; beg him, therefore, not to leave my study." While saying this, Louis walked about the room, listening eagerly for the

arrival of his dear ones. At last the door opened
and the Queen appeared, holding the Dauphin by
the hand, followed by Mme Elizabeth and Marie
Thérèse. Exclamations of sorrow mingled with the
embraces exchanged by the Royal Family. The
Queen made a motion as if to drag the King into
the next room, but he told her they must go to the
dining-room, and they entered it together, the Commissaries shutting the door on them. The Queen
sat down on the left of the King, Mme Elizabeth
on the right, the little Princess opposite, the little
Prince standing by his father's knee. For a quarter
of an hour not a word was said, nothing but
lamentations could be heard—"a piercing cry of
despair, which must have been heard in the courtyard, in the garden, in the neighbouring streets."

Presently Louis began to talk about his trial
just as if it was that of someone else : he excused
his judges and urged forgiveness for them. Marie
Antoinette implored that they might all spend the
night with him, but he refused this consolation,
saying he had need of quiet and recollection. This
heart-breaking scene lasted for nearly two hours,
and ended by a sublime lesson in Christian forgiveness. "My father," recounts the Princess Royal,
"at the moment of his separation from us for ever,
made us all promise never to think of avenging his
death. He knew well that we should look upon
the accomplishment of his last wish as sacred, but
my brother's youth made him anxious to impress
it more strongly on his memory. He took him on

his knee and said to him : '*My son, you have heard what I have just said, but as an oath is something more sacred than words, swear with your hand up that you will fulfil your father's last wish.*' My brother obeyed him in tears, and this great goodness redoubled our own."

At a quarter past ten the King rose, and the rest gathered round him. The Queen held his right arm, Mme Elizabeth the left, Marie Thérèse clung to her father, and the Dauphin held the King's and Queen's hands. The lamentations redoubled. The King promised to see them next morning, and then said Adieu. At this sad word the little Princess fell fainting at his feet. Mme Elizabeth and Cléry supported her. The King, wishing to bring this sad scene to a close, embraced them all once more and retired to his room. The doors were immediately closed, but Louis could hear the cries uttered by the royal ladies as they went up slowly to their apartments. Here the Queen's agitation was intense. Mme Elizabeth, kneeling by her, crying bitterly, implored her to calm herself, and to offer to God her anguish and implore His mercy ; but it seemed as if in her misery she could neither pray nor accept comfort. She tried to undress her son, but her weakness was so great that Mme Elizabeth had to help. When the Dauphin was asleep, the Princesses begged the Queen to go to rest ; and at last, to please them, she threw herself dressed on her bed.

The terrible night wore on slowly — "from

eleven o'clock till five in the morning her sister
and daughter could hear the Queen trembling with
cold and fear." Before daybreak Mme Elizabeth
rose and prayed while the Queen dressed, and then
they both dressed the children. They could hear
the drums beating throughout Paris. The Royal
Family stood, waiting anxiously for the last interview with the King, and when the door opened at
six o'clock the moment seemed at hand ; but it was
only a messenger. "My sister," said Mme Elizabeth, "someone has come to fetch a prayer-book
for the King's Mass." They then all knelt, uniting
their prayers to those of the royal prisoner below.
At times they looked at the clock anxiously, but
Louis had determined to save them a last anguish,
and presently the noise in the courtyard and
around the prison warned them that it was too late.
The ladies endeavoured in vain to get leave to
descend, and the poor little Prince, escaping from
their arms, rushed to the warders, exclaiming, "Let
me pass, gentlemen, let me pass ! Tell the people
not to let my father die. In God's name, let me
pass !" Such sorrow as filled the hearts of the
King's bereaved family is too sacred to dwell upon.

We must now return to the accounts of the
King's last hours, which, however well known,
should be recalled here. After the cruel leave-
taking, Louis rejoined the Abbé Edgworth in his
study, and throwing himself on a chair, he exclaimed, "Ah, monsieur, what a meeting—what

a separation! Must I then love so tenderly, and be so dearly beloved? The cruel sacrifice is made; help me now, monsieur, to forget everything so as to think only of eternity. It is there that all my affections, all my thoughts, should now be centred."

The King continued to speak in broken accents for some time. Presently Cléry came to propose supper, which, after some hesitation, he accepted. There were more officials present than usual in the anteroom, and although they talked in low voices, Louis heard this sentence: "The time is come for the People to avenge itself." "The People," said the King calmly, "the People will do justice to my memory when it knows the truth, when it is free again to show itself just; but alas, until that time comes, it will be very unhappy."

The King's supper lasted five minutes, and he then rejoined the Abbé. The latter was anxiously considering how he could procure for Louis the consolation of receiving Holy Communion before his death, and he proposed that he should try and obtain leave to say Mass in the King's room on the following morning. Louis was alarmed for the safety of the Abbé, but the latter begged him to rely on his prudence. He saw that the only way was to ask formal permission, and at last the King gave him leave to make the attempt. After some hesitation the Council gave the desired permission, on condition that the King should have concluded his devotions by seven o'clock at latest, because "at eight o'clock punctually Louis Capet must start for the place of Execution." The vestments and everything needed for the celebration of Mass were brought from the neighbouring church of St. François d'Assise.

Louis, who had waited anxiously to hear the result of Abbé Edgworth's mission, heard with joy of its success. They went together into the Turret Oratory, where the King made his last confession. By this time it was midnight, and the Abbé urged the King to take some repose, to which he consented, begging his Confessor to rest likewise in Cléry's room. Cléry helped his master to undress, and was about to dress his hair as usual, but Louis stopped him, saying, "It is not worth while." These words redoubled Cléry's tears. "More courage, Cléry," said the King; "those who love me should desire the end of my long agony"; and as Cléry drew his bed-curtains, he added, "Cléry, wake me at five o'clock." Louis at once fell asleep, but Cléry, as we may believe, could not rest. He spent the night praying for his beloved master. When he heard five o'clock strike he lit the fire, and the noise awoke the King. As he rose Louis said, "I have slept well; the events of yesterday tired me. Where is M. de Firmont?" "In my bed." "And you, where did you sleep?" inquired the King. "On a chair," replied Cléry, "could I think of myself at such a time?" The King pressed his hand affectionately. Cléry assisted him to dress and did his hair, during which Louis took a seal off his watch-chain and put it and a ring in the pocket of the white waist-coat he had worn on the previous day. He placed his watch on the chimney-piece, together with his pocket-book, glasses, and snuff-box. When he was ready he told Cléry to let Abbé Edgworth know, and they remained together in the study for half an hour. Meanwhile, Cléry prepared the temporary altar. When all was ready, he told the King, for whom an arm-chair and large kneeling cushion had been placed in front of the altar; but Louis begged him to take away the cushion, and himself fetched the small horse-hair cushion which he habitually used for his prayers. It was six o'clock, and a great silence reigned in the prison; even the officials had withdrawn to the outer room. The King heard Mass and received Holy Communion with profound devotion. After his thanksgiving, he said adieu to the faithful Cléry, holding both his hands and at his earnest desire giving him his blessing. When Abbé Edgworth rejoined the King he found him trying to warm himself by the fire. "My God," he exclaimed, "how happy I am to have my religious principles! Without them where should I be now? but with them death should appear sweet to me. Yes, there is an Incorruptible Judge above who will render me the justice refused to me by man here below."

Day was now breaking, and the beating of drums and other noises in the street could be distinctly heard in the prison, and caused terror to the priest and Cléry; but Louis was quite calm, and remarked, " It is probably the National Guard beginning to assemble." Then, faithful to his promise of the night before, he desired to see his family, but the Abbé tried strongly to dissuade him from putting the Queen to fresh suffering; and the King, after reflecting for a moment, said very sadly, " You are right, monsieur; it would give her a death-blow; it would be better to deprive myself of this sad consolation and leave her a few moments longer of hope." Taking Cléry apart, he said, " Give this seal to my son, and the ring to the Queen; tell her how greatly I feel leaving her. This little packet contains the hair of all my family; give that also. You will tell the Queen, my dear children, and my sister, that I promised to see them this morning, but that I wished to spare them the grief of so cruel a separation. How much it costs me to go without receiving their last embraces." After wiping away a few tears, he added sorrowfully, " I charge you to say good-bye to them for me."

Louis now asked for scissors that Cléry might cut off some of his hair, no doubt in order to send it to the Queen; but this was absolutely refused. He turned to the Abbé with a smile, saying, " These people see daggers and poison every-where; they think I shall kill myself. Alas, how little they know me; to do that would be a crime. I shall have the strength to die well." Two of the officials now told Cléry to get ready to accompany the King, to assist him to undress on the scaffold.

Cléry was petrified with horror, but strove to control himself and give this last sign of attachment to his royal master, who dreaded this office being performed by the executioner; but another Commissary appeared, saying, "Cléry, you will not go. The executioner is good enough for him." Every time the door opened Abbé Edgworth and Cléry feared the fatal moment had come.

At last it came. The officers, accompanied by two constitutional priests and Santerre, arrived. The King opened the door of his study, and, addressing Santerre, said, "You have come to fetch me." "Yes." "I am busy," said Louis, in a tone of authority. "I ask for a moment. Wait for me here." He shut the doors, and, throwing himself on his knees before the Abbé, said, "All is consummated, monsieur; give me your blessing and pray God to sustain me till the end." Then, rising quickly, he went out of the room and advanced to the group of officials who were awaiting him.

CHAPTER XII

DESOLATION OF THE SURVIVORS

As the King advanced into the outer room he
perceived that the officials all wore their hats, and
he asked Cléry for his, but refused his great-coat,
saying he did not require it. Addressing the group
before him, Louis inquired if any of them were
Members of the Commune. One named Jacques
Roux advanced, and the King asked if he would
take charge of his will, and give it into the hands
of the President. Roux refused, saying his duty
was only to conduct him to the scaffold. "Ah—
true," replied Louis, showing no indignation, and
he turned to another Municipal, who accepted the
commission. The King gave a paper also to one
of the warders, saying, "Give this to my wife,
please. You can read it—it contains matter which
I desire that the Commune should know." Cléry
now handed his hat to the King, who pressed his
hand in farewell and recommended him to the good
graces of the officials, saying that he hoped he
would be allowed to remain with his son, and that
the Queen ("My wife," added Louis hastily) would
be permitted to settle about this. "I commend

also my former servants at Versailles and the Tuileries to the Commune," added Louis.   No one replied, and the King, looking at Santerre, said in a firm voice, " Let us go."   At the top of the stairs, Mathey, one of the warders, met them, and the King spoke to him, saying, " I was rather hasty with you the day before yesterday, but I hope you bear me no grudge."   Mathey turned away his head and made no reply.   As Louis walked through the first courtyard, which was lined by soldiers, he was observed to look back twice as if to say adieu to those he was leaving.   In the second courtyard a carriage was waiting.   Two gensdarmes stood by it, and one entered first and sat on the front seat. Louis was surprised and pleased to find that the Abbé Edgworth was to be allowed to accompany him, and they took their seats together in the carriage.

In spite of the King's heroic wish that no one should run the risk of rescuing him, more than one loyal plot had been formed for this purpose—one notably by the Baron de Batz, who indeed made an attempt, which was quickly checked, and remained unperceived by the King—but, unfortunately, the Convention were equally well aware that there was much secret sympathy for their victim, and took every imaginable precaution to prevent a rescue. Santerre sent troops to all the entrances to Paris, while the guillotine itself was so surrounded by a strong barrier that the executioners alone could approach it.   These and other extraordinary measures show what alarm was felt on the part of the King's enemies. In the midst of so much hatred and treachery it is consoling to find instances of heroic self-sacrifice among the King's subjects and among those even who were Republicans. Many letters were sent to the Convention from persons offering to die instead of the King. We here refer to two of them : the first is from a woman who merely signs her Christian name : [1]—

"Citizen President," it runs. "I am not an aristocrat, but I am a young and sensitive woman and the misfortunes of Louis XVI. break my heart. If he is condemned—if he is to die,—I offer myself as victim in his place. Save his life, and let me ascend the scaffold. It will be in vain for you to say that the blood of a woman is not worth that of a King. We are all equal, and my soul is as pure as his. Agree to my request, I beg of you, and you shall soon know me.   JULIE."

The other writer was a certain Lieut.-Colonel Cartouzière, who offered "his life gaily to save that of Louis XVI." These letters are each endorsed thus : "*There is no occasion to consider this.*" The King probably never knew of these offers, and most certainly would not have accepted them had they been practicable, but the thought of such loyal devotion to his person would have brought a ray of consolation to him and his family.

To return to the sad procession. The carriage

[1] *Feuillet de Conches*, vol. vi. p. 422.

moved on, through streets lined with soldiers,
preceded by drummers and cannon. The houses
appeared deserted, with all windows and doors
closed, and the drums beat incessantly in order to
drown any possible loyal demonstration. The day
was dark and dreary ; Paris was wrapped in a thick
fog, and the sun "seemed to refuse its light to the
crime about to be committed." The King, shut
up in the carriage with the Abbé and the two
gensdarmes, whose presence prevented all conversation, remained silent till the Abbé offered him
his Breviary, which he gladly accepted, and asked
M. Edgworth to point out the psalms most ap-
propriate to his position, which they recited
together. The terrible drive lasted about two
hours. "The Place de la Revolution was reached
at last and the carriage stopped in the large open
space surrounding the scaffold, which had been
erected between the pedestal of the statue of
Louis xiv. and the Avenue of the Champs Elysées.
It was now twenty minutes past ten." The King,
realising that the carriage had stopped, lifted his
eyes, shut the Breviary, keeping his finger in the
place where he was reading, and turning to the
Abbé Edgworth he said, "We have arrived, if I
am not mistaken." The priest bowed his head in
silence. Louis reopened the book and read the
last two verses of his psalm. The executioners
were waiting, and one of them opened the carriage
door. The gensdarmes were about to get out first
but the King stopped them, and placing his hand

on the Abbé's knee, said authoritatively, "Gentlemen, I recommend Monsieur to you. I charge you to watch over him." Louis gave back the Breviary to the Abbé, and got out. He turned towards the Palace of the Tuileries and looked round at the armed multitude that surrounded him. "Be silent," he said in a commanding voice to the drummers ; and for a moment they obeyed, until Santerre hurried up to order them to begin again. Three executioners now surrounded the King to undress him, but he pushed them aside and himself undid his hair, took off his cravat, and opened his shirt. A terrible moment ensued, when the men wished, in spite of his protests, to bind his hands. This appeared to Louis as a worse ignominy than death itself, but here also his virtue triumphed. He consulted M. Edgworth by look, and at last the latter through his tears said, "Sire, in this new outrage I only see a last resemblance between your Majesty and the God who will be your reward." At these words Louis looked up to heaven with inexpressible sadness, saying, "Assuredly it needs His example for me to submit to such an outrage." Turning to the executioners, he added, "Do what you will, I will drink the chalice to the dregs ;" and they bound his hands with his handkerchief. From the scaffold the King spoke to the crowd as follows : "I die innocent of all the crimes which are imputed to me. I forgive the authors of my death, and I pray God that the blood you are about to shed may never fall on France; and you, unhappy people," but here Santerre's loud voice enforced silence, and the noise of the drums and the clamouring of the crowd drowned the King's words. The executioners now seized him, and while the Abbé uttered the words, "Son of St. Louis, ascend to Heaven," the King of France ceased to breathe.

In a remarkable statement of the King's death written by the chief executioner Sanson, soon after the event, he says, "To render homage to the truth I must say that he endured everything with a *sangfroid* and firmness which astonished us all. I remain convinced that he drew this courage from the principles of religion with which no one was more penetrated than he was." Sanson never recovered the King's execution. He came down from the scaffold "more dead than alive," and each time in future that he had to perform his awful functions, he suffered greatly. At last in 1795 his health gave way, and he retired into private life. Sanson lived until 1796. As soon as the churches were reopened for public worship, he had Mass said for the King on each anniversary of the fatal day, and after his death his son, Henri Sanson, who had succeeded to his father's office, also succeeded to his work of reparation and yearly assisted at Mass with all his family on 21st January.[1]

To return to the prisoners. The noise of the carriage leaving the Temple had been audible to

[1] These particulars, as well as the details of the King's last days, are taken from M. de Beauchesne's *Louis XVII.*

14

them in their rooms, and as it died away they
realised that each moment took the King nearer to
his death.   The Dauphin had taken possession, as
it were, of his mother from early morning, and
made every effort to console her : he "kissed her
hands, which he bathed with his tears, and tried to
comfort her by his caresses more than by words."
"These tears," said Marie Antoinette, "can never
cease ; the torture is for those who survive."
Presently the Queen, fearing that her children's
strength would give way, begged them to take
some food; but they refused, and began to weep
afresh.   About half-past ten the sound of guns
and shouts of joy warned them that all was over.
Mme Elizabeth, according to a contemporary
narrative, "lifted her eyes to Heaven," and exclaimed, "Now the wretches are satisfied !"   The
poor children were overcome with grief, but the
Queen remained motionless, with bent head and
haggard eyes, in a silent despair which resembled
death itself.

In the afternoon the Royal ladies asked to see
Cléry.   The sight of this faithful soul, who had been
with the King to the last moment, in a way both
consoled and increased their grief, and the recital
of Louis's last word made their tears flow.   They
begged to have the articles he had left for them, and
the Queen asked for mourning ; but both requests
had to go to the authorities.   Municipal Goret,
who was one of the warders whose secret respect
for the Royal Family renews one's wonder that

something was not effected for their escape, has left the following interesting account of his interview with the Queen on the evening of the execution :—

"The widow invited me to approach, which I did. She and Mme Elizabeth and the children were near a table, and all burst into tears. 'Madame,' I said to the Queen, 'you must preserve yourself for your family.' That is all I could say to her, and she only interrupted her sobs to say, 'We know the sorrow that has befallen us ; we heard all the preparations this morning, the sound of men and horses. Our misfortune is certain and we want to have mourning clothes.'[1] Being unable to dissimulate, I only said these few words : 'Alas, Madame—alas, Madame,' and I retired, assuring the Queen that I would at once see to her request for the mourning she desired, which was to be of the simplest, she added."

Goret also tried to comfort Cléry, and passed the night with him. "All I could hear him say," he writes, "were these words : 'Alas, my good and dear Master could have saved himself had he wished. It is only fifteen feet from the windows in this part to the ground—all was prepared to save him while he was still here, but he refused because they could not save his family with him. There,' he said, showing me it, 'is his Breviary, which he

---

[1] Articles demanded by the Queen on 21st January : "A cloak of black taffetas, a black fichu and petticoat, a pair of black silk gloves, two pairs of black kid gloves, two hoods of black taffetas, a pair of sheets (refused), a piqué coverlid (refused)."—De Vyse, *Histoire de Marie Antoinette.*

has left me, and his watch, and other little things.'
Cléry seemed to place the greatest value on
this Breviary, which he said he had the intention
of offering to the Pope." Cléry's allusions to a
possible escape are obscure, but there is a curious
letter extant from Hoste de Beaumont de Versigny
to the Maréchal de Richelieu, written in 1816, in
which he says, that on hearing that the King was
to be tried, he came to Paris and planned a rescue
at the Temple ; that he even entered it with a false
guard and with the countersign, and reached the
tower itself, but that, being too few in number,
they had to retire and the project hopelessly failed.

The long day of anguish wore on, and at two
in the morning the ladies were still awake. The
little Princess had gone to bed from obedience, but
could not sleep ; while the Queen and Mme Elizabeth sat beside the Dauphin's bed, mingling their
memories and their tears. The child slept peacefully, and as she watched him, the mother's thoughts
went back to her eldest son. " He is now the age
of his brother when he died at Meudon," she said,
"happy are those of our House who died early.
They have not seen the ruin of our family." Surprised to hear talking so late, Tison's wife had risen,
and now knocked at the door, followed closely by
her husband, who had also roused the Commissaries.
Mme Elizabeth half opened the door, and said
gently, " In mercy let us weep in peace." These
words disarmed the gaolers, and they retired again.

On the following morning the Queen said to

her son, as she embraced him, "My child, we must think of the good God." "Mama," he replied, "I also have thought much of the good God, but when I call upon Him, it is always my father I see before me." The Queen was in a state of great bodily weakness; after three sleepless nights she could hardly bear the daylight. A few days later, however, she found the strength to nurse her daughter, who became very unwell, and to follow all the directions of the doctor, M. Brunyer, who at last was permitted to enter the prison. "Happily," wrote the young Princess later, with a charming simplicity, "grief increased my illness, so that it made a diversion to my mother's despair." On 23rd January the request for mourning was granted, and some of the garments reached the Temple on the 27th. When she saw her children in black for the first time the Queen said to them, "Poor children, you will wear it for long; but for me it is for always." During this sad time Marie Antoinette could not look at the children without heart-breaking sorrow, and no doubt she felt the prevision of her separation from them, for she said to Mme Elizabeth one day, "Perhaps in the past I did not give all the necessary advice to the King for his safety, but I shall rejoin him on the scaffold. Yes, my sister, I shall ascend it also." At this time two municipal officials distinguished by their zeal and devotion to the Royal Family, Lepitre and Toulan, were able to regain admittance to the Temple. They

had discovered that the other warders were glad
to escape the Sunday duty, and managed to secure
that they should be nominated for this day and the
previous Friday or Saturday.　Before the King's
death they had had the courage to warn the Queen
of his danger, hence her words at their first interview after the fatal event.　Lepitre thus describes
it :　"We found the royal family plunged in the
profoundest grief.　On perceiving us the Queen,
her sister, and the children burst into tears.　We
dared not advance, but the Queen made us a sign
to enter the room.　'You did not mislead me,' she
said ; 'they have allowed the best of Kings to
perish.'"　They had brought various newspapers,
and for the first time the bereaved ladies had the
sad comfort of reading all the heart-breaking details
of Louis's last moments.　"Cléry, who was still
in the Temple," continues Lepitre, "gave me the
communion cloth which had been used by Louis
XVI. on the morning of January 21st.　I took it
to Joisy, to his wife, whom I had seen sometimes
at the Temple.

"I have not yet spoken of the Song composed
for the young King after the death of his august
father, and to which Mme Cléry, who was a clever
musician on the harpsichord and harp, added the
music.[1]　I took it to the Temple and offered it to
the Queen.　Eight days later, when I returned,
Her Majesty made me enter Mme Elizabeth's
room.　The young prince sang the *romance* and

[1] The words were by Lepitre himself.

Mme Royale accompanied it.   Our tears fell and we kept a mournful silence.   Who could depict the scene I had before my eyes.   The daughter of Louis at her harpsichord, her august mother seated by her, holding her son in her arms, her eyes filled with tears and directing with effort the playing and singing of her children; Mme Elizabeth standing by her sister and mingling her sighs with the sad accents of her august nephew.   No, never will this picture fade from my memory."

Without giving the poem, which is long, we may be permitted to quote the last lines, which were addressed specially to our Princess.

À Madame Elizabeth

"Et toi, dont les soins, la tendresse,
    Ont adouci tant de malheurs,
    Ta récompense est dans les cœurs
Que tu formes à la sagesse . . .

Ah ! souviens-toi des derniers vœux
    Qu'en mourant exprima ton frère
    Reste toujours près de ma mère
Et ses enfants en auront deux."[1]

One of the warders heard of this incident, and said to Marie Antoinette, " You sang yesterday, and made your children sing.   No doubt the songs were only *romances*, for you have never

[1] Souvenirs de Jean François, Lepitre.   See *Captivité et Mort de Marie Antoinette*, Lenotre.

Another Royalist song had an immense success early in 1793, and reached the ear of the King, affording him a moment of consolation. It was that beginning, " Oh, my people, what then have I done to you," and was sung to the air of " Pauvre Jacques."

had patriotic songs. I would bet that you cannot even play the air of the *Marseillaise*." The Queen, without replying, went to the piano and played the air, adding, "Are you satisfied?" and as the man said little in return, she rose, saying gently, "At least, monsieur, you should thank me for my complaisance."[1]

"It was on 7th March," continues Lepitre, "that I received from the royal family the sweetest recompense for my zeal and devotion. The Queen and Mme Elizabeth each deigned to cut off a small lock of their hair, which they added to that given me by Madame and the young prince." Toulan obtained the same favour. He placed his in a box bearing this device : *Tutto per loro* (All for Them) ; but Lepitre had a ring made for his precious gift, and inscribed on it a motto given to him by Marie Antoinette : *Poco amore ch'il morir teme* (He loves little who fears to die). "I have never ceased to wear this ring," he says, "it is the only jewel which has ever adorned my finger ; what diamond could be so precious?" Lepitre had already received a present of another kind from Mme Elizabeth. It seems that the ladies, who, as we know, felt keenly the deprivation of their work things, had implored Lepitre and Toulan to befriend them in this manner, but amidst the more important duties that occupied them the request had escaped their memory ; and on the following week when they returned to the Temple they were

[1] *Recherches Historiques sur le Temple*, E. J. J. Barillet.

astonished to find that the Queen and Princesses were knitting.   Another friendly warder had meanwhile come to their aid, and the royal ladies playfully reproached Lepitre for his forgetfulness. "Ah, messieurs," said Mme Elizabeth, "is it thus that you wish to condemn us to a painful idleness —but everyone is not like you, and the excellent M. Paffe, himself a tradesman, has been more complaisant than you." . . . "Mme Elizabeth had begun what she called a stocking," says Lepitre, "when she asked my advice about her work.   I could not help smiling when I saw the width of this supposed stocking, and I said it was probably a cap she wished to make.   'Very well—a cap, then,' she replied, 'and it shall be for you.'   She finished it during the day and gave it to me as we were leaving, telling me to give to the poor the amount which a cap would cost at that time.   I obeyed scrupulously, and it cost me the modest sum of ten francs in *assignats*."

At this time Mme de Tourzel, who from the moment she recovered her liberty had been living near Paris in the hopes of sometimes receiving news of the Royal Family, heard with joy that Mlle Piou, who had formerly been in attendance on Mme Royale, had managed to find a way of entering the prison, under the pretext of altering one of the Queen's gowns.   This piece of work took two days, and she was able to give tidings of the prisoners to the Duchess.   "I cannot tell you," she said, "all that I felt when I perceived that the

sight of my insignificant person brought a ray of
consolation to this august family—their looks said
more to me than their words could have done, and
Mgr the Dauphin, whose age excuses a piece of
fun, profited by the opportunity, under the pretence
of a game, of asking me all the questions desired
by the royal family. He ran first to me, then to
the Queen, then to the two Princesses and even to
the warder. Each time that he approached me he
asked a question regarding the persons interesting to the royal family. He charged me to embrace
you for him as well as Mlle Pauline, forgetting no
one he loved, and playing his part so well that
no one could tell he had spoken to me."

Mme Elizabeth found much consolation at this
time in feeling that the Queen was able to devote
herself to her children and was left in peace after
her bitter sorrow, though she must also have
intuitively realised that the calm was not to last
for long. The Princess aided her sister with her
usual affection and devotion, and as the King's
last wish that Cléry might attend his son had
been refused by the Commune, they did everything
for the little Prince. Mme Royale, so early
trained in the school of sorrow, was already "strong
and resigned," while her brother, in spite of his
precocious knowledge of danger, was still child
enough to cheer them all by his liveliness. The
lessons went on as before, and the King's recom-
mendations were ever kept in mind. Not only
did the mother and aunt dwell constantly on the

forgiveness of injuries, but in their daily study of the history of France they took special care to draw attention to the heroic deeds and acts of clemency they came across. Such lessons appeared to touch even the warders who assisted at them. The Queen, who, like all Maria Theresa's daughters, had learned Latin, likewise gave her son his first lessons in this language. A few words written by Marie Antoinette on a copy of de Séze's Plea for the King still exist, and are striking by their significance : *Oportet unam mori pro populo.* St. John, xviii. 14.

Since the fatal 21st of January the Queen had not been able to make up her mind to go for a walk. She dreaded to have to pass the door of the King's room as she went down, and feared she might meet Santerre in the garden ; but, anxious that her children should not suffer from want of fresh air, she begged to be allowed to take them up to the tower, from whence, as we know, they could see the sky alone. Lepitre usually accompanied them thither, and on one occasion got into disgrace for an accidental expression. "I had taken the young prince up in my arms," he says, "so that he could look down at the streets near the Temple, where people would assemble to look with interest at the tower. In the garden were some Sentinels whose appearance denoted misery and want. The cold was great, and I could not help saying to my companion, ' How can they thus expose poor *Sans Culottes* to the weather?' "

These words were overheard by another warder, and Lepitre was accused of using them in a tone of contempt, and it was even said that the Queen, on seeing his meaning, had looked at them with disdain and ill-will.   This absurd story brought Lepitre into some disfavour with the Convention.

CHAPTER XIII

PLANS FOR ESCAPE

SOME time before the incident related in the last chapter the indefatigable Toulan had thought of a plan of escape for the prisoners, destined, alas! to fail, as were all efforts on their behalf. "The imagination of Toulan was not idle," writes Lepitre. "He conceived the project of carrying off Louis's family from the Temple, and acquainted me with his ideas. We met in my house to discuss it with M. le Chevalier de Jar . . . and a clerk in Toulan's bureau called, I think, Guy, a zealous Royalist, whose aid was necessary to us and on whose fidelity we could reckon." Under the above names we may recognise the Maréchal de Jarjayes, a devoted adherent of the Royal Family, and Ricard, whose wife was a cousin of Lepitre's. After two long consultations de Jarjayes and Toulan formed their plan. The former undertook to have men's dresses made for the Queen and Mme Elizabeth, and he and Lepitre undertook to bring them to the Tower concealed under their own pelisses. In these disguises, to which the tricolor scarf was to be added, the Princesses were to pass out, by the aid of cards similar to those always used by the officials who were authorised to enter the prison. So far the project did not seem difficult of realisation, but the chief danger lay in the rescue of the children. The King in particular was so closely watched that it seemed almost impossible to hope for success. However, at last a plan suggested itself to Toulan's fertile brain. A man called Jacques came every morning to clean the lamps and returned in the evening to light them. He was generally accompanied by two children, and here was the opportunity. Toulan suggested that after the lamp-lighter had gone away, and after the guard had changed at seven o'clock, a man dressed like Jacques, and bearing his tin case, should enter the Tower and ascend to the Queen's room. " I shall be there," continued Toulan, "and will scold him in a loud voice for not coming to arrange his own lights. 'Are you not ashamed,' I shall say to him, 'of having sent your two children to do your work in your place,'—and then I shall confide the Queen's children to him, and the pretended lamp-lighter will go off with the two 'apprentices,' and all three will go to the corner of the Boulevards where M. de Jarjayes will await them."

The dresses were prepared very carefully, and three cabriolets were secured. It was arranged that the Queen and her son should be in the first, driven by M. de Jarjayes; Mme Royale in the second, whose driver should be Lepitre; and

Toulan was to drive Mme Elizabeth in the third. Lepitre, who was "President of the Commission of Passports," had no difficulty in preparing suitable ones, and a large sum of money had been provided for the expedition. The plan was to make for Normandy, from whence Jarjayes had arranged means for reaching England. A boat was to meet the party near Havre.

Everything, in short, was ready, and in the hands of those concerned in the rescue there was every reason to hope for success. "If Toulan and Jarjayes had been charged to conduct the royal family to Varennes," says M. de Beauchesne, "I have no doubt that they would have succeeded in placing them beyond the reach of danger"; but in this case also no devotedness on the part of their friends could save the prisoners. This time the failure of their hopes came from a sudden excitement in the capital on 7th March, caused by news of the defeat of the Republican troops at Aix-la-Chapelle and Maestricht, and to an alarming rise in the price of food. The next day, the 8th March, had been fixed for the escape, and we can realise that it now became an impossibility. "The violent scenes in the Convention, the violence of the Commune and the tumults in the streets, kept the Government on the *qui-vive* and redoubled its watchfulness." Unfortunately, also, as on every occasion of excitement in Paris, this watchfulness was exercised specially at the Temple. The prisoners, hearing the tumult outside, feared their plot had been discovered, and were greatly relieved to see Toulan appear and to hear that no suspicion had been aroused. " I should have been distressed to leave this place," said the Queen to him, "without taking with me some things which are precious to me and which were left to me by one who was dear to me and whose memory is sacred. I speak of the nuptial ring and the seal which the King always wore, and which he had charged Cléry to give me, together with the hair of my sister Elizabeth and of my children." Toulan made no reply to this, but he was aware that these articles had been sealed up and placed in the King's former room, and he brought them to the Queen two days later. One wonders whether he also told her that he had, with great courage and ingenuity, caused copies to be made in the interval, which he had put back in the King's room in place of the originals.

Mme Elizabeth had felt no illusions as to the difficulty of the escape, but she deeply regretted its failure, especially as the loss of a chance of safety for the Queen, whose danger constantly filled her thoughts. After the troubles of 7th March, the surveillance exercised over the little King became stricter than ever, and M. de Jarjayes and his loyal accomplices concentrated their remaining hopes on the deliverance of the Queen and our Princess, which appeared alone possible. But, as need hardly be said, nothing could persuade Marie Antoinette to leave her children. As for Mme Elizabeth, who never thought of herself, " she employed her eloquence to persuade her sister to profit by this opportunity that still offered her an escape from her enemies." "Your life," she said, "may be in danger, while those of your children and my own are exposed to none. Your children's are safe on account of their age—mine because of my unimportance. No doubt, sister, the odious reports which at times reach your ears are coloured by popular exaggeration, but they have, however, some truth when they express the animosity of the People which is excited against you. The unreasoning prejudice of the People in your regard is such that you would do wrong to wait for its effects. You have great confidence in M. de Jarjayes, and, as you see, he sends you his earnest supplications to beg you to agree to the new plan of which Toulan brings you the details. Perhaps it is the invisible hand of Providence which holds out to you this plank in the shipwreck. Do not push it aside, I implore you. I beg this of you in the name of your children, in the name of him whose memory is so sacred to you, and if you will allow it, in the name of my love for you." The Queen was touched, and agreed to attempt her escape. The day was fixed; it came.

The evening before, the royal ladies were seated as usual by the King's bed as he slept. The young Princess was in the next room with the door open, but she could not sleep, for her mother's sad and abstracted looks during the day had made her uneasy. She thus overheard the following words, as

15

she afterwards related : "God grant," said the
Queen, as she watched her son, "that this child
may be happy." "He will be, my sister," said
Mme Elizabeth, in her happy ignorance of his
future. "Youth is short, like joy," murmured the
mother. "Happiness ends, like everything else.
And you yourself, my good sister," she continued,
pacing the room, "when and how shall I see you
again? . . . it is impossible . . . it is impossible."
Marie Thérèse heard the words, but it was not till
later that she realised their import. The Queen's
last ejaculation showed that once more her mother-
love had triumphed over every other feeling, and
she resolved to remain where she was. On the
following day, when Toulan arrived, "full of
emotion at the great action he was about to
perform," she said to him, "You will be dis-
pleased with me, but I have considered it all.
Here there is only danger to be feared; better
death than remorse." Wishing in every way in
her power to show her gratitude to her would-be
preserver, Marie Antoinette found an opportunity
of whispering to him during the day the following
words, which he recalled when he too ascended
the scaffold to pay the penalty of his loyalty : "I
shall die unhappy," she said, "if I cannot prove to
you my gratitude." "And I too, Madame, if I
have not been able to show you my devotion," was
the reply. "From all that now takes place," added
the Queen, "I may expect from moment to moment
to see myself deprived of all means of communica-

tion.   Here is the ring, the seal, and the little packet
of hair, whose recovery I owe solely to you.   I
charge you to give them into the hands of M. de
Jarjayes, begging him to have them sent to
Monsieur or to the Comte d'Artois, with the
letters which my sister and I have written to our
brothers."   The Queen wished also to thank
M. de Jarjayes for his help, and to explain the
cause of her refusal ; she therefore wrote him the
following note, which she charged Toulan to give
to him : "We have made a beautiful dream, that
is all ; but we have gained much by finding in this
occasion a new proof of your devotion to me.   My
confidence in you is boundless.   You will always
find firmness and courage in me, but my son's
interest alone guides me.   However great the
happiness I should feel at being out of this
place, I cannot consent to separate myself from
him.   I could enjoy nothing without my children,
and this feeling leaves me even without a regret." [1]

Mme Elizabeth had written the following lines
to Monsieur : " I rejoice in advance at the pleasure
you will feel on receiving this token of affection and
confidence.   To be reunited to you and to see you
happy is all I desire.   You know if I love you.   I
embrace you with all my heart.   E. M. " : and to the
Comte d'Artois, " What happiness for me, my dear
friend, my brother, to be able after such a long
time to speak to you of all my sentiments.   How
I have suffered for you.   A time will come, I hope,

----

[1] De Beauchesne, vol. ii. p. 115.

when I can embrace you and tell you that you will never find a truer or more tender friend than me. You do not doubt it, I trust.   E.M."

In the following May M. de Jarjayes was able to send these Royal letters to their destinations: the seal and the packet of hair to Monsieur, and the ring and the piece of the King's hair to the Comte d'Artois.

Monsieur himself wrote a letter to M. de Jarjayes, dated from Hamm, 14th May 1793, to express his thanks, saying, "You have procured for me the greatest happiness I could have in this world; the first real consolation I have felt since our sorrows.   Their note and the other token of their affection and confidence have penetrated my heart with the sweetest sentiments. . . . Continue to serve our young and unhappy King as you served the brother I shall weep for all my life."

The little King's accession had been already recognised abroad, and he had been proclaimed in some parts of France; but, poor child, he had "as his palace a prison; in place of courtiers, ministers, or guards, only a mother assailed by every anguish but whose soul was as great as her misfortunes." The loyal rising in La Vendée, with which the South of France appeared to sympathise, helped to accentuate the anxieties of the Commune, and once more increased its zeal for the prisoners' safety.   The guard at the Temple was redoubled. The wretched Tison and his wife continued to be the trial of the Royal Family.   The little King could not bear them, and in spite of the counsels of his mother and aunt, he could not quite hide his feelings. One evening, when the Tisons had been reprimanded by one of the warders, they imagined they owed their scolding to Louis, and coming into the Queen's rooms they complained bitterly of him, calling him even *spy* and *reporter*. The Queen replied with dignity, " Know that none belonging to us would strike at anyone in the dark, nor would I tolerate it." The Tisons retired, abusing Marie Antoinette and her son. The latter was very indignant. "They are in a rage," said Mme Elizabeth gently, "forgive them." Tison heard these words and came back exclaiming, " Forgive them ! Where are we then ? Do you forget that the People alone have the right to forgive ? " The wretched man continued to act as a spy on the Royal Family, and Toulan's plans, although conducted in the most secret manner, did not altogether elude his vigilance. Although his suspicions were still somewhat vague, Tison and his wife wrote to the Council on 19th April, saying " the wife and the sister of the late tyrant have won over some of the municipal officers, who inform them of everything that takes place ; that they have been furnished with newspapers by them and that by their means they can keep up a correspondence." In proof of these allegations Mme Tison took to the Council a candle found by her in Mme Elizabeth's room, and showed the Commissaries a piece of sealing-wax which had fallen on the candlestick. We know by Turgy's Memoirs that the

Princess had, in fact, given him that morning a sealed note, begging him to send it to the Abbé Edgworth.

Next day Hébert made a surprise visit to the prisoners, not during the day, when they were always on the *qui-vive* and prepared for anything, but at half-past ten at night. Possibly he hoped to find them writing secretly at that time. He found nothing of the sort, but proceeded to overhaul everything in the room. Mme Tison was told to search the ladies, and she found in the Queen's pockets a red morocco pocket-book and a small *nécessaire*. In searching Mme Royale's possessions they found a sacred picture and a prayer : "They took from me a Sacred Heart and a Prayer for France," she says. When searching the room "of Elizabeth Marie, sister of the late Louis Capet," they found the stick of red sealing-wax already alluded to, and some powder of boxwood. The poor little King was pulled out of bed, where he was sleeping soundly. His mother held him in her arms while the men searched the mattresses and his clothes, without result. This went on for hours, as we learn by the closing words of the official reports :—

"And about two hours after midnight we closed this present *procès Verbal*, in presence of the above-mentioned ladies, who signed with us.

Ainsi signé   MARIE ANTOINETTE,
ELIZABETH MARIE,
BENOÎT, etc. etc."

Three days later, the Commissaries who were sent to the Temple to take off the seals which had been placed on the door of the late King's rooms, made a further search. Their only discovery was a man's hat, which they found in a box under Mme Elizabeth's bed. "Where does this hat come from?" they asked her. "It is a hat which belonged to my brother," she replied. "Who gave it to you?" "He himself when we inhabited the small tower." "Why is it there, and of what good is your brother's hat to you?" "I keep it in order to have something which belonged to him." The officials, however, declared that the King only possessed one hat, which he left on the steps of the guillotine, and appeared deaf to our Princess's pleading.

A slight illness of the little King's occupied his mother and aunt for some weeks at this time. The Queen's request for Dr. Brunyer was refused and the prison doctor sent, "as it would wound equality to send him another"; but fortunately this physician, M. Thierry, was excellent and well known, and he consulted with Dr. Brunyer as to the child's treatment. On 31st May the royal ladies were alarmed by a great noise and tumult outside the Temple. Mme Elizabeth questioned the warders on the cause. "Bah," replied one of them, "it is the Commission of Twelve that causes all this row." In fact, Paris was in a turmoil owing to the fall of the Girondins and the triumph of the *Montagnards*. One of the officials, Michonis, who

was on guard, informed the Princess of the events
which were agitating Paris, and tried to reassure
her as to the intentions of the *Montagnards*.
"Monsieur Michonis," said Mme Elizabeth, "the
revolutionists who have lost sight of Almighty God
no longer belong to themselves, and they themselves know not whither God is leading them."
When he told the Queen that the Emperor of
Austria would probably secure her safety, Marie
Antoinette replied coldly and sorrowfully, "What
does it matter to me?   At Vienna, I shall be what
I am here, what I was at the Tuileries; my only
desire is to rejoin my husband when Heaven
judges that I am no longer necessary to my
children."   These words made a profound impression upon Michonis.   He thought that there
remained no hope of safety for the royal prisoners
save by their escape from the Temple; and he
joined with the Baron de Batz, who had vainly
tried to save Louis XVI., in yet another effort for
rescue, which was destined to be frustrated by
Simon, who, according to his account of the
affair, received warning by an anonymous paper
which was found outside the great door of the
Temple and which bore these words: "Michonis
will betray you to-night. Watch!" This fresh
failure was followed by the worst trial which could
have befallen the Queen—the separation from her
son. In their alarm, "the Committee of Public
Safety" decreed that "the young Louis Capet
should be separated from his mother and placed

in a room apart—the best defended in the Temple, and should likewise be put under the care of a tutor to be chosen by the General Council of the Commune."

These two decrees were put into execution on 3rd July. On that night, about ten o'clock, the little King had been in bed for about an hour, and was fast asleep. As there were no curtains to his bed, the Queen had hung up a shawl to shade his eyes from the light, as she and Mme Elizabeth intended to sit up later than usual in order to mend the clothes of the family, while Marie Thérèse read aloud to them. After reading several pages of the *Dictionnaire Historique*, the Princess had opened a Holy Week book, and was beginning some liturgical prayers.[1] Her mother and aunt, while listening, often glanced towards the bed, to look at their beloved charge. Suddenly steps were heard, doors flew open, and six Commissaries appeared. One of them said, "We come to notify to you an order of the Committee of Public Safety decreeing that Capet's son shall be separated from his mother and family." At these words the Queen rose, pale and trembling, and cried, "Take away my child from me! no—no—it is not possible." Marie Thérèse stood by her mother's side, protesting by her looks against the cruel order. "Mme Elizabeth, her heart aching, looked on silent and immovable, with her hands

---

[1] This book belonged to Mme Elizabeth, and had been secretly sent to her in March, before Easter Sunday.

on the holy book." After a moment's silence Marie Antoinette spoke again : "Messieurs, the Commune surely cannot think of separating me from my son? he is so young and weak and my care is so necessary to him." But the orders admitted of no doubt. Then she cried again, "I can never resign myself to this separation ; in the name of Heaven, do not demand from me so cruel a trial." Mme Elizabeth, placing herself by the child's bed, said, "In the name of those you hold most dear, in the name of your wives, of your children, do not take from this mother what she so loves." Then tears choked her utterance : but nothing availed. "These weepings do no good," was the reply ; "your child will not be killed. Give him to us of your own free will, or we shall know how to take possession of him" ; and the men forcibly surrounded the bed. In the struggle the shawl fell down on Louis's head and awoke him. At the sight that met his eyes, the poor child threw himself out of bed into his mother's arms, crying, "Mama, mama, do not leave me." The Queen pressed him to her and comforted him. "Do not let us fight women," said one of the officials who had been a silent witness of the scene ; "Citizens, let us send for the guard." "Do not do that," said Mme Elizabeth ; "we must accept what you urge by force, but in mercy give us breathing time. This child has need of sleep, and he could not get it elsewhere. To-morrow morning he shall be given up to you. At least let him pass to-night in this room and get leave for him to be brought back each evening." A silence succeeded these words, which were uttered in touching accents, and the Queen spoke again : " Promise me," she said, "that he shall remain within the boundary of the Tower and that each day I may be allowed to see him, even if only at dinner-time." " We are not bound to give an account of ourselves to you," was the rude reply, "and it does not belong to you to question the intention of the Country. *Parbleu*, you are very unhappy just because your child is taken from you, and ours go every day to get their heads broken by the cannon-balls of the enemies you draw to our frontiers!" "My son is too young as yet to serve his country," said the Queen gently, "but I hope one day, please God, he will be proud to consecrate his life to her interests." Prayers and tears were useless. The child had to be dressed and given over to his new and rough attendants by his heart-broken mother and aunt. At last the Queen, summoning her courage, sat down on a chair, and placing Louis by her, she laid her hands on his shoulders and said to him in a grave voice, "My child, we are going to be separated. Remember your duties when we are no longer near you to remind you of them. Never forget the good God who is trying you, or your mother who loves you, or your aunt and sister who have given you so many proofs of their love. Be good, patient, honourable, and your father will bless you from heaven." She then kissed him,

and pushed him towards Mme Elizabeth, who did
the same, as well as his sister. The poor child
came back to his mother, and clung desperately
to her knees. She said to him, gently and firmly,
" My son, we must obey—it must be "; and the
officials, protesting against the delay, forcibly
dragged him off. One of them, who had kept
silence till now and seemed more humane, said to
the unhappy mother, " Do not distress yourself.
The Nation is generous ; it will see to the education
of your son."

When the door was shut upon her child, the
Queen could no longer control herself, and she
gave way entirely to her grief. Mme Elizabeth
once more tried to comfort her. Placing herself by
the King's bed, on which the unhappy mother had
thrown herself, the Princess said nothing for a time,
but contented herself with weeping with her sister
and pressing her hand ; but when the latter was
a little quieter, she said, " My sister, just now I
admired your courage and firmness, and I thanked
God for this token of His mercy ; and certainly in
God's sight, who sees us and tries us, you have no
less courage than you have shown to these men.
Do not let us ask Him wherefore He chastises us.
He knows ; that is enough. Without searching
into His design, let us accept the cross which He
sends us, and do not let us hesitate to carry it.
One does not become the heir of Jesus Christ
without having been the companion of His suffering. Let us place ourselves of our own free will

in His hands and bear everything, thinking of Him."
Marie Antoinette was now calmer, and these words
found the way to her heart. She replied by embracing her sister and then her daughter, whom
she told to go to bed; but as Mme Elizabeth
gathered together the little King's clothes and put
them away before retiring to rest, the two mothers
wept afresh at the thought of their darling.

CHAPTER XIV

THE QUEEN TAKEN TO THE CONCIERGERIE

For four days the Queen was kept in ignorance of her child's whereabouts, not even knowing whether he was still in the Temple or not. At the end of this time a rumour spread through Paris that the young Louis had been rescued from his prison and had been conducted in triumph to St. Cloud. To calm the excitement produced by this story, a deputation from the Committee of Public Safety visited the Temple in order to declare officially that he was still there. After ordering that the child should be taken down to the garden so as to be seen by the guard, two Deputies, Drouet and Chabot, ascended to the Queen's room. "We are come," said Drouet, "to see if you are in want of anything, or have too much of anything." "My son is wanting to me," replied the Queen; "it is really too cruel to take him from me for so long." "Your son wants for nothing. He has been given a Patriot as tutor, and you have no more reason to complain of the way in which he is treated, than of that in which you are treated here."

Drouet thus reported his visit to the Con-

vention : " We went up to the women's apartments, and we found Marie Antoinette, her sister
and daughter, in perfect health.   It has been said
abroad that they are ill-treated, but from their own
avowal, in presence of the Commissaries of the
Commune, nothing is wanting to their con-
venience."   He kept strict silence as to the
unhappy Queen's demand.   She continued to
implore leave to see her child ; but although filled
with fear in his regard, neither she nor Mme Elizabeth could ever have imagined the depths of cruelty
with which he was to be treated.   Tison had been
so touched by the kindness and resignation of the
Royal ladies, that from being their enemy he now
became their friend, and through him they at last
obtained news of the child, though at first he told
only the good news, carefully concealing Simon's
cruel behaviour.   Mme Tison had also ceased to
be a trial to the prisoners, for the poor woman had
gone off her head from fear and remorse.   Turgy
gives a graphic account of this incident.

After referring to Mme Tison's betrayal to the
Council of the drop of sealing-wax she had found
in Mme Elizabeth's room, he continues : " On
coming upstairs from the Council Room, the
woman Tison entered the princess's room.   She
perceived the Queen, and, becoming excited, threw
herself at the feet of this princess, crying out,
regardless of the presence of the warders :
' Madame, I ask pardon of your Majesty.   I am
a wretch.   I am the cause of your death and of

that of Mme Elizabeth.' The Princesses raised her kindly and tried to calm her. A moment later I entered with my two comrades, Chrétien and Marchand, bringing the dinner of the Royal Family, and accompanied by four Commissaries. The woman Tison threw herself on her knees before me, saying to me: 'M. Turgy, I beg pardon. I am the cause of the death of the Queen and of yours.' Mme Elizabeth lifted her up, saying, 'Forgive her, Turgy.' The princesses not only pardoned the poor creature, but gave her every care and attention in her illness. Mme Elizabeth, especially, took charge of her and comforted her by consoling words. Mme Tison spoke thus one day of her benefactors to a friend : " I pity them with all my heart. It is a generous family which the poor will not see replaced. If you could see them here as I do, you would say that there is nothing greater on earth. Those who saw them at the Tuileries saw nothing. One must have seen them at the Temple, as I have done." After the scene we have described, the poor woman fell into convulsions, and was removed some days later to the Hôtel Dieu. By the date on the register of the hospital, she entered it on 8th July.[1]

As Turgy's name has again come before us, we may here relate some of his efforts to keep up communications with the prisoners, and the ingenious methods invented by them and him to enable them

---

[1] Rélation de Turgy, *Captivité et Mort de Marie Antoinette*, Lenotre, pp. 108–9.

to receive news from outside ; these contrivances take us back as far as to the early days of the captivity. "Often it happened to me," he says, "to substitute one piece of paper placed as a cork in a bottle for another, on which had been written some news, or advice, written either in lemon juice, or with extract of gall. Sometimes I rolled a note round a little leaden ball, covered it with another piece of strong paper, and threw it into the jar of almond milk. A sign indicated what I had done. When the paper corks bore no writing, they served for the Queen and Mme Elizabeth to give me orders or to write to some-one outside. In spite of the surveillance of eight or ten persons, hardly a day passed during the fourteen months that I managed to stay at the Temple that the royal family did not get some note from me, either by the stratagems I have ex-plained, or when I handed them articles belonging to my service (as Cook), or when I received them from their hands ; or again in a reel of cotton which I would hide in a corner of the cupboard, under the marble table, etc." Turgy's office, allowing him, as it did, to go into town for provisions, enabled him to hear all that was going on, and he could meet M. Hue and receive information from him to be transmitted to the King. "Mme la Marquise de Sérent," he continues, "was the chief person in whom centred the correspondence of the Queen and Mme Elizabeth. At her house I passed as her man of business, and her servants

16

had orders to let me in at any hour of day or night. It is known what a fine character and what noble devotion this lady showed in all the dangers of the royal family and in so many circumstances full of danger for herself."

We thus owe to Turgy's zeal and devotion the few notes that remain to us written by our Princess, the survival of her large and happy correspondence of former days. About the time of Mme Tison's illness, Turgy thought of asking to be actually imprisoned in the Tower, so as to devote himself more entirely to the service of the royal ladies ; but the Queen dissuaded him from this, pointing out to him that they would then hear nothing from the outer world. "Your proposition would be agreeable to us," she wrote, "but by you we hear of everything, and if you were shut up we should know nothing. Should they send us into exile and you cannot start with us, come and rejoin us wherever you may be, with your wife, your son, and all your family." In another note the Queen asks anxiously whether Mme Tison "is well cared for."

We will here gather together the more interesting of the little notes written by Mme Elizabeth, although they belong to a somewhat later date. *Fidèle* is the designation of the faithful Toulan.

I

"Give Fidèle this note from us. Tell him,— my sister wishes you to know it,—that we see every day the little —— [Louis XVII.] through the window of the stair in the *garde-robe*, but do not let this prevent you from giving us news of him. Why have they been drumming since six this morning? Answer this if you can do so without compromising Mme de Serent and yourself. Write to her from me to say I implore her not to remain in Paris for me. The motion of the "Cordeliers" against the nobles torments me for her sake."

II

" Tell Fidèle how much his last note touches us. We do not need this assurance, to count always and entirely on him. His signals are good.[1] We will say simply, ' *To arms, citizens*,' in case they think of uniting us, but we greatly fear this kind of precaution will not be needed."

III

" If you want me to ask for Almond Milk, you will hold your napkin low when I pass. What has happened to the English fleet? [illegible] and to my brothers? Have we a fleet in any sea? What do you mean by saying everything goes well? Does it mean you hope for a speedy end— a change in public opinion? How is Mme 'S' [de Serent] and my Abbé [Edgworth]? Has he by

[1] Toulan had taken a room near the Temple, and, according to his signals, he played certain airs on his horn.

chance received news of Mme de Bombelles, who is near St. Gall in Switzerland? What has become of the ladies of St. Cyr? ... As to Fidèle, ask him if Michonis sees my sister and if he is the only one who is on guard over her." [This allusion to the Queen shows that this note was written after her removal from the Temple, as was also the following letter.]

IV

"What you tell me of the person [the Queen] gives me much pleasure. Is it the gendarme or the woman who sleeps near her? Could one send by the person Constant [M. Huë] saw, anything besides news of those she loves? If you cannot be of use to her here, place yourself in some safe place where you will not be forced to move on, but let me know where, in case we need you. I do not believe as regards myself that I shall be exiled, but if so, come and join me if you are not necessary to the Person. . . . Tell me if it is through Mme S. [Serent] that you have news of a Being [M. l'Abbé Edgworth] who, like me, knows how to appreciate faithful friends."

In October, when there was every prospect of Turgy being sent away by the Commune, the Princess wrote: "I am very distressed. Take care of yourself for better days, when we shall be happier and when we can reward you. Take with you the consolation of having served good and unfortunate Masters. Advise Fidèle not to risk too much in making me signals. . . . Adieu, honest man and faithful subject."

A few days later, on 12th October 1793, Mme Elizabeth wrote her last note to Turgy. It ends with these words: "I hope that God, to whom you have been ever faithful, will support and console you in what you have to suffer." On the following day Turgy received an order to leave the Temple immediately. This he did; "heartbroken at what he had seen, and overcome with fear for the future of his Royal mistresses." He never again saw Mme Elizabeth, but in later years he was privileged to follow the fortunes of her niece, Marie Thérèse, Duchesse d'Angoulême.

To return to the little King's position. He was, as we know, in the Temple, but all that the Queen had been able to learn was that he was "in good hands, and wanted for nothing." Tison, however, in his endeavour to atone for his former conduct, soon gave further information to the poor mother. "He brought her news nearly every day, but the respectful sympathy which had now found place in his mind taught him a delicacy which his previous conduct would not have led one to expect; he took care to hide from her the horrible treatment endured by the child, and which made Tison indignant. He spoke of Simon before the princesses, but without naming or describing him; without letting them know that the Mentor given to the Dauphin was no other than the Municipal who had always affected in their presence, and that of the King, the most insulting language."

Tison, keeping to the bright side of the picture, told them of the child's daily walks in the garden; his games at ball; his occasional walks on the top of the tower, where the air was excellent; adding that he appeared to be in good health. This mention of the excursions to the battlements suggested to the Princesses a hope of seeing the child by means of the little staircase which led from the *garde-robe* to the roof, and which is alluded to in one of Mme Elizabeth's notes to Turgy. There was a small aperture in the wall of the turret, from whence it was possible to get a glimpse of the person walking on the parapet. Of course it was very difficult to know at what moment Simon would take his charge thither, and many fruitless journeys were made by the prisoners. "All the same," writes Mme Royale, "we went up always. We did not know if the little one would come—but he might come. What hours were taken up in watching for him to pass. How often, with ears glued to wooden partitions, the poor recluses, silent, listening and attentive, felt their hearts beat at the smallest sound on the staircase. . . . Then the time for recreation was over, and we had to go down again under lock and key." This went on for days, but the Queen would not despair of success.

At last her wish was realised, but alas! only to increase her sorrow tenfold. On 30th July she

at last saw her child, but under what cruel circumstances!   He was no longer in mourning ; he wore
the Republican red cap, and was followed by the
wretched Simon, so well known to her for his
insolence.   By a singular coincidence, Simon had
at that moment heard of the entrance of the Duke
of York into Valenciennes, and he was venting his
anger on the unhappy child by oaths and blasphemies.   "The unfortunate Queen, speechless
with horror, fell into her sister's arms, who was
witness with her of this cruel sight, and both ladies
dragged away Marie Thérèse, who was approaching, and, by a mutual look deciding to spare her
young heart, they went to the other side of the
platform.   After a few moments, the Queen, unable
to hide her tears, turned her head aside ; and
retraced her steps in order to try and see her son
again, Mme Elizabeth remaining near her niece.
Presently the child passed again at Simon's side,
but this time with his head down and his gaoler
was silent.   His silence and the submissive attitude
of her son hurt the Queen almost as much as
Simon's former violence.   When Tison came near,
she lifted her head from her hands and cried,
"You have deceived me."   "No, Madame," he
replied, "I have not deceived you—all I said was
true, only out of kindness I did not wish to tell you
all.   Now I will tell you everything, as there is
nothing more to hide from you."   Mme Elizabeth
and Marie Thérèse now joined them, and the
former questioned her sister by a look.   A move-

ment of the eyelids which betrayed her anguish
was the Queen's only reply."[1]

The full horror of her brother's position was
not made known to Marie Thérèse, and Mme
Elizabeth tried hard to prevent everything from
reaching the Queen. "In mercy hide these
atrocities from my sister in future," she said to
Tison; "tell me all; and I will soften the pitiful
scenes and choose the moment for telling her of
them. Recommend this, if possible, to all who
give news of my nephew. I hope, Tison, you will
find in them the same pity which I ask from you
for this poor mother." Mme Elizabeth, as the
child's second mother in love and devotedness,
suffered almost as much as the Queen. "He was
ill, and they could not care for him; suffering, and
they could not comfort him; in danger, and they
could not succour him. His innocent soul was
perhaps weakening, and they could not uphold it."
Could there be any trial equal to this? The
same evening Marie Thérèse said to her aunt, "My
God, how sad my mother has been to-day." The
Queen and our Princess sat up late that night; they
paced the rooms in which they had watched over
their darling, "so lively, so affectionate, sometimes
so happy, working, singing, praying," and went
over in their thoughts the words and actions of
the child who had been so loving and thoughtful
for them. The royal ladies went back to the same
place on the following days, but the little King

[1] *de Beauchesne*, vol. ii. p. 145.

never reappeared, and Marie Antoinette had seen
him for the last time.   She was about to leave the
Temple for ever, carrying with her the poignant
memory of her son's misery and degradation.

On 1st August the Convention decreed as
follows : " Marie Antoinette is sent to the Extraordinary Tribunal.   She will be transferred at once
to the Conciergerie.   All the members of the Capet
family shall be exiled from the territory of the Republic, with the exception of Louis Capet's children,
and the members of the family who are under the
jurisdiction of the Law.   Elizabeth Capet cannot
be exiled until after the trial of Marie Antoinette."

On 2nd August, at two o'clock in the morning,
the officials came to arrest the Queen.   Her
daughter has left us an account of that sad night.
Her mother, she tells us, "heard the decree read
without emotion and without saying a single
word"; but she and Mme Elizabeth hastened to
implore leave to follow the Queen, which was
refused them.   The men would not leave the
Queen for a moment while she was making her
preparations—she was even obliged to dress before
them.   They asked for her pockets, which they
searched, and declared that their unimportant
contents should be sent to the Tribunal and
shown to her again there.   They only left her a
handkerchief and bottle of smelling-salts.   The
Queen went, after embracing her daughter, whom
she begged to be courageous, to take care of her
aunt, and to obey her as a second mother.   The

poor child was so overcome that she could not say a word in reply.   Mme Elizabeth whispered something to the Queen, and the latter left without looking at her daughter again, for fear of breaking down.   At the foot of the stairs she was stopped in order that the officers might make out a *procès verbal* for the delivery of her person.   In going out Marie Antoinette hit her head in the low doorway, but when asked if she had hurt herself, she replied in these pathetic words : " Oh, no, now nothing can ever hurt me again."[1]

While this sad scene was taking place at the Temple, preparations were being made to receive the royal captive at the Conciergerie.   In her interesting narrative, Rosalie Lamorlière, a servant in the prison, thus relates the events of that night :[2]—

" On the afternoon of August 1st, 1793," she says, " Mme Richard, wife of the chief gaoler, said to me in a low voice, ' Rosalie, to-night we shall not go to bed—you can sleep on a chair.   The Queen is to be brought here from the Temple ' ; and I saw that she was giving orders that M. le Général Custine should be moved from the *Council Chamber*,[3] so as to place the Princess there.   A warder was sent to the prison carpenter.   He asked from him a camp bed, two mattresses, a counterpane, a light coverlid, and a washing basin.

[1] All these details are taken from de Beauchesne's *Vie de Mme Elizabeth.*

[2] Declaration de Rosalie Lamorlière.   See Lenotre, pp. 228, 231, 238.

[3] Now the *cantine* of the prison.

This simple furniture was brought into the damp room evacuated by M. de Custine, and a common table and two prison chairs were added. Such was the furniture of the room destined for the Queen of France. Towards three in the morning, when I was dozing in the chair, Mme Richard pulled me by the arm and woke me, saying these words : ' Rosalie, come ! come ! wake up !—take this light, they are arriving.' I went down trembling, and accompanied Mme Richard to M. de Custine's cell, which was at the end of a long black passage. The Queen was already there. . . . The day was beginning to dawn. . . . Mme Richard and I remained alone with the Queen. She seemed to look with amazement at the horrible bareness of the room, and then she looked rather attentively at the Concierge and me. Then, standing on a stool I had brought from my room, she hung a watch on a nail in the wall. She began to undress ; I approached respectfully, and offered my services to the Queen. '*I thank you, my girl,*' she replied without pride or ill-humour, '*since I have had no attendant, I do everything myself.*'

"The daylight was growing brighter ; we took away our candles, and the Queen went to rest in a bed no doubt very unworthy of her, but which we had furnished, at least, with very fine linen and a pillow." Rosalie noticed that the Queen had brought no clothes with her. "The unhappy princess begged for fresh linen, and Mme Richard, fearing to compromise herself, neither dared to lend or procure any." At last Michonis went to the Temple, and on the tenth day a parcel arrived from there "which the Queen opened promptly; it contained beautiful chemises of *batiste*, pocket-handkerchiefs, *fichus*, etc. Madame was moved as she looked through the packet, and turning to Mme Richard and me she said: 'In the careful way these are sent, I recognise the hand and the attentions of my poor sister Elizabeth.'"

Among the things the Queen had asked for were her knitting-needles and some stockings she had begun for her son; but the officials pretended that she might use the needles to attempt her life, and they were not allowed to be sent. However, as M. de Beauchesne says, the day was a happy one to the Queen and the Princesses, as it had brought about communication between the two prisons. M. Huë was happy at this time in being able to procure some communication between the royal ladies by means of his acquaintance with Mme Richard. This good woman obtained leave from the police that the bottles of *Ville d'Avray* water usually drunk by the Queen should now be sent to her new prison. At the Temple Tison continued to keep Mme Elizabeth informed about her poor little nephew; but our Princess could hardly believe the details given to her, and thought they were exaggerated, until one day her hopes were destroyed by hearing Simon talking so loud that his oaths and wicked language were quite audible, mixed sometimes with the plaintive cries of a child.   Concealment as regards Marie Thérèse was now impossible ; she recognised her brother's voice, and could also distinguish it amidst the voices of the Simon *ménage* when they sang revolutionary songs.   "We heard him daily," she writes in the account of his captivity, "singing the Carmagnole and other horrors with Simon. The Queen happily did not hear them.   She had gone.   Heaven spared her this torture."

The poor girl's heart was full of sad thoughts of her mother and brother, and her aunt strove in vain to comfort her.   She, who was truly a valiant woman, endeavoured to strengthen her young charge by her words, but her very presence was an example in Christian heroism.   Prayer and victory over herself from her early years was the solid basis of her piety, and, ready for every sacrifice herself, she, as we know, did everything in her power to sweeten or console the suffering of others.

Presently another great trial befell the Princesses. All news of the Queen ceased.   A more rigorous surveillance prevented any of the former modes of communication, and our Princess herself was deprived of the means of writing, having destroyed her pencils and some scraps of paper which she possessed on the night of the Queen's departure, for fear of compromising the latter.   However, the Queen herself managed, by requests for articles left behind at the Temple, to open a way, and the sisters exchanged a few words once more.   Mme Elizabeth gave news of the little King, but, as we may suppose, with much left unsaid. She did all in her power to get people to intervene and to procure a change of conduct in Simon, but with absolutely no success. One good man, a mason by profession, now a Municipal officer, followed her wishes and spoke to Simon, but the wretch's only reply was as follows : " I know what I do, and what I have to do; in my place perhaps you would *go quicker.*"

Meanwhile the chains of captivity were being drawn tighter. On 21st September, Hébert, *Vice-Procureur* of the Commune, accompanied by other officers, visited the prisoners and declared to them that they were no longer to have an attendant. " In all prisons," he said, " the prisoners have no one to serve them ; the exception made for you wounds justice and public morality, as equality ought to reign in prisons as elsewhere."

The result of this fresh order was that Tison was withdrawn and shut up, a prisoner himself. The royal ladies in future made their own beds and swept the floors. On the following day a fresh decree interfered with their meals. From motives of economy, the Council forbade chickens and pastry to be served to the prisoners. They were to have only one dish for *déjeuner*; at dinner a *potage*, boiled beef, and one other dish, also half a bottle of *vin ordinaire* each a day ; at supper two dishes were to be allowed. No silver or porcelain was to be used for their meals, wax candles were no longer to be permitted, and even the linen sheets were exchanged for "stable" sheets of yellow cotton. Our Princess took all these changes with great calmness and even joy for herself, fearing such trials only for her niece.   All the time of her captivity she had always kept the laws of the Church as far as possible, and only ate bread on fish days, if other *maigre* food was not granted to the prisoners.

On the first day of their new régime she said to Marie Thérèse, "This is the bread of the poor; we are poor also, how many unfortunate people have still less."   Mme Elizabeth, although of a good constitution, often suffered from some little ailments which sorrow and anxiety had augmented. She now had a sore place on her arm, but could not obtain the necessary ointment, until at last one warder, more humane than the rest, sent her some. All these little trials, however, must have appeared as nothing in Mme Elizabeth's eyes when contrasted with the one which was now about to wound her heart.

CHAPTER XV

MADAME ELIZABETH AND MADAME ROYALE

It is not our purpose to enter into the details of the tragic scene in the Temple, when the poor little King, under the baleful influences which had been brought to bear on him, was forced unknowingly to utter odious slanders against those who were most dear to him. When Mme Elizabeth and her niece returned to their room after this bitter moment, they could not speak. "Oh, my child," exclaimed Mme Elizabeth, opening her arms, and they wept together, and then, "falling on their knees, offered their humiliation and grief to the God of the humble and the afflicted."[1]

On 11th October, as we know, the last friend of the royal captives was taken from them. Turgy was turned out of the Temple, and on the 13th the faithful M. Hüe was arrested. This was a fatal

---

[1] Although the child hated wine, Simon forced him to drink it when he wished to make him drunk, which is what happened on the day that he made him say the horrors which are related in the Queen's process. At the end of this odious scene the poor little Prince began to come back to himself, and approaching his sister tried to kiss her hand ; but Simon prevented it and carried him off. See *Memoirs de la Duchesse de Tourzel*, vol. ii. p. 318.

blow, as from that time no communication from the outer world reached them, and the fate of the Queen remained absolutely unknown to them. This was, however, really a blessing; for although the silence caused anxiety, they were spared the news of Marie Antoinette's trial and even of her death, which took place on 16th October; and it is to be noted that on this occasion all the officials, and even Simon himself, united in charitably keeping the sorrowful intelligence from the captives.

Still we cannot but regret that Mme Elizabeth had not the consolation of knowing what history has now proved—that her sister was strengthened and consoled for her combat by receiving the Sacraments before her death and by having Mass said in her poor cell.[1] A cruel thought had haunted the unhappy Queen during her last days—that of her son's apparent ingratitude to the best of aunts; and we find these touching words in the admirable letter addressed by her to Mme Elizabeth on the eve of her death, but which was never to reach its destination: "I must speak to you of something very painful to my heart," she says, "I know how much this child must have hurt you. Forgive him, my dear sister. Think of his age and of how easy it is to make a child say what one wants and what he does not even understand." Mme Elizabeth had no need to forgive. She, like the mother, knew and understood.

[1] See the interesting declaration of the Abbé Mangin and others in Lenotre's *Captivité et Mort de Marie Antoinette*.

17

One evening about this time Mme Elizabeth heard quarrelling in Simon's room, and feared he was venting his anger on his hapless victim. This idea haunted her that night and the next day, and she once more ascended the little staircase we have before mentioned, to try and see the child. On the second day she was rewarded by seeing him pass with his gaoler, but could not be certain whether she was also seen by them, though they both looked in her direction. Alas! the change in his appearance, and still more the sad deterioration in his ideas and language, of which she now had knowledge, were calculated to cause deep suffering to his second mother. No trial, perhaps, had been so acute, but Mme Elizabeth practised in her own life the resignation she had urged upon the Queen, and thanked God for the consolation she felt in being allowed to remain still with her niece. She knew how precarious was her position even here ; Chaumette had already alluded to the Temple as "a special, exceptional, and aristocratic refuge, contrary to the spirit of equality proclaimed by the Republic," and in November he again discussed the matter from the point of view of economy, "representing to the General Council of the Commune the absurdity of keeping three persons in the Temple Tower, who caused extra service and excessive expense." The Committee of Public Safety, however, resolved to maintain the prison in its present state.

During these last days of her imprisonment

Mme Elizabeth seems to have had the consolation of receiving a book which must have had a deep interest for her. This was the Life of her much-loved Carmelite aunt, Mme Louise.

The author, Abbé Proyart, who had known our Princess in her happier days, and who seems to have foreseen the mission of mercy which was reserved to her, wrote her the following letter at the same time. History, however, does not tell us whether it too reached her :—

"À Madame Elizabeth, Sister of Louis XVI.

"MADAME,—Providence, whose just rigours you so well know how to adore, does not permit me to have the advantage of myself presenting you with the Life of Mme Louise. But everything assures me, Madame, of the kind reception which awaits this work, whatever official hand undertakes to introduce it into your solitude,—the story of a Christian Princess of France, of a courageous soul who surprised her generation by the generosity of her sacrifice, and who, already known to the world by the repute of her virtues, became still more celebrated in the obscure dwelling to which the Spirit of God had conducted her. There, Madame, lie resemblances which, while escaping the eyes of piety and modesty, are appreciated with the most touching interest by all French hearts. Live, then, Angel of France, worthy follower of the Angel of Carmel, live. Live for yourself, for your country ;

live for those precious ones whom the good Louis in dying recommended to you. Fulfil the glorious duty which Heaven imposes on you of *perpetuating heroic Virtues in the House of St. Louis.*" [1]

From the time Turgy was removed Mme Elizabeth's life "entered into a phase of abandonment and solitude, impossible to describe; misery, monotonous and gloomy, and deprived of all the dignity which generally surrounds royal sufferers;" but she thought only of her little companion. She spoke to her with that gentle piety with which she was penetrated: "The sufferings of this world," she would say, "have no proportion with the future glory which they merit for us. Has not Jesus Christ gone before us bearing His cross? Remember, my child, the words your father spoke to you [on the day of her First Communion]. 'Religion,' he said, 'is the source of happiness and our support in sorrow. Do not think you will be sheltered from it. You do not know, my daughter, for what Providence destines you.'" Prophetic words, which must have now found their echo in the young girl's heart.

One day Mme Elizabeth opened a little packet which she always wore, containing the hair of the King and Queen, and with, perhaps, a presentiment of the future, she cut off a lock of her own hair and added it to the others. She then gave the little packet to Marie Thérèse, saying, "My

[1] See Preface to *Vie de Mme Elizabeth*, de Beauchesne, p. vi.

MARIE THÉRÈSE, CHARLOTTE DE FRANCE, DUCHESSE D'ANGOULÊME.
Née le 19 Dec., 1778.

daughter, keep these sad souvenirs.   It is the only heritage which your father and mother, who so loved you, can leave you, and I too, who love you also most tenderly.   They have taken from me pens, paper, pencils, and I cannot leave you any written legacy ; at least, dear child, remember the consolations I have told you of, they will supply for books, which are wanting to you.   Lift up your heart to God.   He tries us because He loves us. He shows us the nothingness of greatness.   Ah, my child," she said, weeping and taking her in her arms, "God alone is true.   God alone is great."[1]

As we have said, no echo of the horrors being enacted reached the prisoners.   They were not aware of the deaths of Danton and Hébert, and all the cruelties which accompanied this worst period of the Reign of Terror.   "Eleven thousand four hundred 'aristocrats' are crowded together in the palaces and convents of Paris, which are now prisons. Crime and fear are everywhere in the streets, where people try not to see each other, or if they greet someone exchange two words in a low voice.   They walk on quickly unless a Crier is heard proclaiming the arrest of the condemned, when they stop to hear the name of a relation, a friend, perhaps their own !"

For our Princess the hour of supreme sacrifice was approaching.   She had desired to partake in all the sorrows and dangers of her family, and had

[1] *Les derniers Régicides*, etc., par M. le Chevalier de M. (London, 1796), quoted by M. de Beauchesne, vol. ii. p. 176.

nobly kept her resolve.   At Versailles, in Paris, at Varennes, and in the closing scenes at the Tuileries, Mme Elizabeth had been at hand to cheer and support those dear to her.   She was to be permitted now to follow them to the end and to offer her life for her misguided country.

Hébert seemed to have been determined on this crime, although he eventually fell before his victim ; and it is said that Robespierre would have avoided the useless cruelty of taking Mme Elizabeth's life, but the moment was so critical for the revolutionary chiefs that he " hid his thought of reprieve under words of insult.   He dared not claim that innocent woman from the ferocious impatience of Hébert," says M. Louis Blanc, " without insulting the victim he desired to save. He called her the 'despicable sister of Capet'; such a word," adds M. Blanc, "applied to such a woman in the situation made for her was an injustice, and, to be plain, a cowardly act."[1]

On 9th May, towards seven in the evening, " Monet went to the Temple, accompanied by Citizens Fontaine, Adjutant-General of artillery in the Paris army, and Saraillée, aide-de-camp to General Hanriot.   He presented to the following Members of Council, Mouret Eudes, Magendie, and Godefroi, a letter from Fouquier, Public Accuser to the Revolutionary Tribunal, requesting them to give over the sister of Louis Capet to the above-named."

[1] See *Prisoners of the Temple*, by O'Connor Morris, p. 141.

The usual preliminaries took some time, and while the officials were discussing them in the Council Room, Mme Elizabeth and her niece were preparing for bed. Suddenly they heard the bolts withdrawn, and hurriedly dressed again to receive the unwelcome visitors. "Citizeness," said one of the Commissaries, opening the door of Mme Elizabeth's room, "come down at once, you are wanted." "Is my niece to remain here?" "That is no affair of yours. She will be seen to afterwards." Mme Elizabeth embraced Marie Thérèse, saying, "Don't distress yourself. I will return." "No," exclaimed Commissary Eudes, "you will not return; take your cap and come down." She obeyed, first raising her niece, who was clinging to her, and saying, "Come, show courage and firmness; hope always in God; make use of the good religious principles given to you by your family and be faithful to your father's and mother's last counsels." The aunt and niece clung to each other for a moment, and then Mme Elizabeth walked rapidly to the door, saying, "Think of God, my child." Such was the last parting between aunt and niece, and we have now to follow our Princess into the wet, cold night, on her way to the dreary prison and to the scaffold that awaited her.

What a contrast between what we have known of her happy, brilliant youth at Versailles and Montreuil and the last hours of her life; but if

her charm and goodness were bright then, they
have now a deeper and holier radiance; and
although her work for her own dear ones is
finished, we shall find her helping and consoling
others to the very end.

In the Council Room the Princess was searched,
and the *procès-verbal* drawn up by which she was
made over to Fouquier-Tinville's envoys. She
was then conducted through pouring rain across
the garden and the first court to a carriage and
taken to the Conciergerie. On her road to the
fate which she well knew awaited her, the gentle
Princess raised her heart to God, we are told,
and, to use her own expression, "clasped hands in
heaven with resignation." She repeated her daily
prayer of union with God's Holy Will, her thoughts
turning likewise to the beautiful prayer to the
Sacred Heart of Our Lord which she had given
long before to Mme de Raigecourt.[1] It was now
eight o'clock, and at ten she was taken before the
Council of the Revolutionary Tribunal. Here,
before the judge Gabriel Deliége, assisted by
Ducray and in presence of Fouquier, she under-
went her first interrogation, which we will give in
full, for, wearying as it is, it strikingly illustrates the
spirit in which these terrible and quite futile proceedings were conducted. Asked her name, age,
profession, country, and dwelling, Mme Elizabeth
replied that she was called "Elizabeth Marie

[1] See Introduction to *Correspondance de Mme Elizabeth*, by
Feuillet de Conches.

Capet, sister of Louis Capet,[1] aged thirty, native of Versailles, department of Seine et Oise."

" Did you conspire with the late Tyrant against the safety and liberty of the French people?"

"I do not know to whom you give the title, but I have never desired anything but the good of the French."

"Have you entertained correspondence with the enemies, internal and external, of the Republic, in particular with the brothers of Capet and your own, and have you not furnished them with help and arms?"

"I have only known the friends of France. I never sent help to my brothers, and since the month of August 1792 I have had no news of them nor have I given them news of me."

"Did you not send them Diamonds?"

" No."

"I must observe to you that your reply is not exact upon this question of the diamonds, as it is notorious that you had your diamonds sold in Holland and other countries abroad, and that you sent the proceeds by your agents to your Brothers to assist them to keep up their rebellion against the French people."

"I deny the fact because it is false."

"I would have you observe that in the *Procès* which took place in November 1792 relating to the

[1] Mme Elizabeth only signed this declaration in her usual way, "Elizabeth Marie," and it is doubtful if she used the word *Capet* herself.

pretended theft of the diamonds in the *ci-devant garde robe*, it was established and proved that a portion of the diamonds with which you used to adorn yourself had been abstracted; it was also proved that the price of those had been transmitted to your brothers by your orders. I summon you therefore to explain yourself categorically as to those facts."

"I am ignorant of the thefts which you speak of. I was at that time in the Temple, and I persist besides in my preceding denial."

"Were not you aware that the journey to St. Cloud determined on by your brother Capet and Marie Antoinette on April 18th, 1791, had been imagined only in order to seize a favourable opportunity for leaving France?"

"I knew of this journey only as regards my brother's intention to go into the country for his health, which was not good."

"I ask you if, on the contrary, it is not true that this journey was fixed only by the advice of the persons who used then habitually to frequent the *ci-devant* Chateau of the Tuileries, and especially Bonal the ex-Bishop of Clermont, and other Prelates and Bishops? and you yourself, did not you urge your Brother's departure?"

"I did not urge my Brother's departure, which was only decided upon according to the Doctor's advice."

"Was it not equally at your solicitations and those of Marie Antoinette, your sister-in-law, that

Capet, your brother, fled from Paris in the night of June 20–21 1791?"

"I learnt on the day of June 20th that we were all to start the following night, and I obeyed my brother's orders in this respect."

"Was not the motive of this journey to leave France and to reunite yourselves to the Emigrés and the Enemies of the French people."

"My brother and I never had the intention of leaving our country."

"I would observe that this reply does not seem exact, as it is notorious that Bouillé had given orders to different parties of troops to find themselves at the point agreed upon to protect this flight so as to be able to help you as well as your brother and others to leave French Territory, and also that all was prepared for your reception at the Abbey of Orval, situated in the territory of the Austrian Despot. I observe besides that the names you and your brother took leave no doubt of your intentions."

"My Brother was to go to Montmedi and I know of no other intention of his."

"Are you aware that secret councils were held in the room of Marie Antoinette *ci-devant* Queen, which were called 'Austrian Committees.'"

"I have absolute knowledge that none ever took place."

"I observe that it is, however, notorious that these Consultations took place on two days—one from midnight till three in the morning, and even

that those who were admitted to them passed through
what was then called the Picture Gallery."

" I have no knowledge of it."

"Were you not at the Tuileries on February
28th, 1791, June 20th and August 10th, 1792?"

"I was at the Château these three days, and
notably on August 10th, 1792, till the moment
when I went with my Brother to the National
Assembly."

"On the above-named 28th of February were
you aware that the assembly of the *ci-devant*
Marquises, Chevaliers, and others, armed with
sabres and pistols, was also to favour a fresh flight
of your Brother and all the family, and that the
Vincennes affair which took place that same day
was only imagined in order to make a diversion?"

"I have no knowledge of this."

"What did you do on the night of August
9–10?"

"I remained in my Brother's room, and we stayed
up all night."

"I observe that as you all had your own apartments it seems strange that you should have
assembled in your Brother's, and no doubt this
meeting had a motive which I summon you to
explain."

"I had no motive except always to be with my
Brother when there was trouble in Paris."

"Were not you and Marie Antoinette that same
night in a Hall where the Swiss were occupied
in making cartridges? and, in particular, were not

you there from half-past nine till ten o'clock in the evening?"

"I was not there and know nothing of this at all."

"I would observe that this answer is not exact, as it is proved in several *Procès* which took place at the Tribunal on August 17th, 1792, that Marie Antoinette and you, several times in the night, visited the Swiss guards, and gave them drinks, and that you joined them in making cartridges, of which Marie Antoinette 'bit' several."

"This did not happen, and I have no knowledge of it."

"I must represent to you that the facts are too notorious for me not to remind you of the different circumstances belonging to them which you deny, and for us not to know the motive which actuated the assembly of troops of all kinds who found themselves at the Tuileries that night. I therefore summon you afresh to declare whether you persist in your previous denials and deny the motives of the assemblage."

"I persist in my former denials and I add that I knew of no motive for an assemblage. I know only, as I have already said, that the body of troops formed for the safety of Paris had come to warn my Brother that there was a movement on the Faubourgs, and that on these occasions the National Guard assembled for his safety as the Constitution prescribed."

"At the time of the flight of June 20th, was

it not you who took the children?" [from the Palace].

"No, I went alone."

"Have you a defender, or will you name one?"

"I know of none."

[We therefore named Citizen Chauveau to her as Counsel.]

> "ELIZABETH MARIE,
> DELIÉGE,
> H. G. FOUQUIER,
> DUCRAY."

After signing each page of the Procès, Mme Elizabeth was taken back to her prison. She had no delusions as to her coming fate, and thought only of preparing for death. She knew she could expect no spiritual help, as none but a constitutional priest would have been allowed to approach her had she asked for one. The favour accorded to Louis XVI. would now have been considered a crime in the eyes of the nation. Our Princess resigned herself, therefore, to this last trial. She offered to God the sacrifice of her life, and found in her great faith the strength of which she had need, for herself and those she was also to help to die nobly.

It is difficult for us to realise the horrors of the prisons of the Revolution. In the year 1793, Citizen Grandpré, in his report of the Conciergerie, where our Princess now was, says, "The horrible impression which I received at the sight of the poor people crowded together in this frightful dwelling is inexpressible." Three hundred and eighty prisoners were then in this prison, and M. de Grandpré saw with horror that in one room "twenty-six men were lodged with twenty-one mattresses between them, breathing shocking air and covered with wretched rags : in another were forty-five men on ten miserable couches : in a third thirty-eight dying persons, etc." The state of things at the moment we write of was different, if no less terrible. "The agony of waiting was spared to those under suspicion, and long terror to the condemned. The prisons were filled each day, but each day also they were emptied by the executioner."

On entering the Conciergerie the waiting room lay to the left. This room was divided in two by bars. One part was reserved for documents, in the other were placed the condemned. It is here that they sometimes waited for thirty-six hours for the fatal moment, and it was here that Mme Elizabeth spent the first two hours after her arrival and before her Interrogation.

It is a relief to know that she was allowed to spend the last night alone, and was thus saved some of the horrors depicted by M. Grandpré. The Concierge, Richard, has left some pathetic details of this night. Mme Elizabeth's first thought on entering the prison had been for the Queen, and she had anxiously inquired for her, and asked Richard if it was long since he had seen her. Afraid of telling her the truth, he replied, " She is

very well, and wants for nothing." All through
the night the Princess seemed uneasy, and often
asked Richard the time. He slept in a dark little
room next the "Alcove" in which she was. She
was about early in the morning, and when she
again asked the time, Richard brought his watch
to show her the hour and made it repeat. "My
sister," said Mme Elizabeth, "had one very like it,
only it did not repeat." She took a little chocolate
for her breakfast, and towards eleven o'clock
went to the prison entrance. Many great ladies,
who were to go to the scaffold with her, were
already there. Among others were Mme de
Sénozan, sister of Minister Malesherbes, the King's
defender, the best and most charitable of women.
Mme Elizabeth charged Richard to present her com-
pliments to her sister ; but one of the ladies present
said to her, "Madame, your sister has suffered the
same fate that we ourselves are about to undergo."[1]
Such news, as far as the Queen herself was concerned, must have been almost a relief to the faithful sister, although it added a new pang to her
grief for the children left behind.

[1] See Lenotre, *Captivité et Mort de Marie Antoinette*, pp.
380–81.

CHAPTER XVI

THE END

THE passage quoted in the preceding chapter makes no allusion to the hours of agony that had passed between Mme Elizabeth's rising and the moment that she joined the other victims, and which were spent in face of her judges. As we have seen, she had refused the offer of Counsel, but by some coincidence, some one who said he was authorised by the Princess had gone to warn M. Chauveau-Lagarde that he was named to defend her. The latter, therefore, hastened to the Conciergerie in order to confer with his client, but was not allowed to speak to her. He appealed to Fouquier-Tinville, who replied, " You cannot see her to-day. There is no hurry; she will not be judged so soon." The trial, however, followed immediately, and when M. Chauveau-Lagarde, impelled by some vague presentiment and fear, made his way to the court on the following morning, he saw to his surprise Mme Elizabeth, dressed in white and surrounded by a large number of accused persons, seated at the top of the seats, where she had been placed to be visible to all. He

18   273

could no longer hope to speak to her, and saw
that she was no doubt quite ignorant that there
was a man present who would rise in her defence.
Among those near her were a few persons she
had known in other days, such as Mme de Crussol
d'Amboise ; M. de Loménie, former Minister of
War ; and Mme de Montmorin, widow of the
Minister of Foreign Affairs who had been massacred at the *Abbaye* on 2nd September 1792.   To
most of the prisoners the King's sister was unknown,
but that morning, some one having been heard to
pronounce her name, the news had run through
the prison, and now all looked at her with earnest
attention.   Mme Elizabeth was not troubled ;
always mistress of herself, she remained so serene
and calm that she communicated this peace of mind
to the most agitated.   " She thought only of giving
consolation—peace of soul and the grace of God to
these unfortunate ones who were without hope ; for
whom all doors were closed, except that which was
open towards heaven."

Renée François Dumas, President of the Tribunal, presided, supported by the Judges Gabriel,
Deliège, and Antoine Marie Maire.   Dumas,
addressing the Princess, said, " What is your
name ? "

" Elizabeth Marie."   Although it is not stated
in the *Moniteur*, a great many of those present
affirmed that, in making this reply, Mme Elizabeth
added the following words : " I am called Elizabeth
Marie de France, sister of Louis xvi., aunt of

Louis xvii., your King." "I knew a person myself," adds M. de Beauchesne, in relating this incident, "who was most trustworthy; he assured me he had heard those words, and I have an intimate conviction that they were pronounced."

"Your age?"

"Thirty."

"Where were you born?"

"At Versailles."

"Where do you reside?"

"In Paris."

The Act of Accusation was then read. As has been already seen, the accusers did not even pretend to find the Princess guilty of any personal crime. She was the sister of Louis xvi. and of Marie Antoinette, that was enough; and her case was prejudged from the first. Twenty-four persons besides the Princess are included in the accusation, but her name, of course, it is that is insulted by the fury of her enemies in the long and dreary indictment. "It is to the family of Capets that the French people owe all the miseries under the weight of which it has groaned for so many centuries. . . . Elizabeth has partaken in all its crimes; she has co-operated in all the plots of her infamous brother. . . . Elizabeth, together with Capet and Antoinette, planned the massacre of the citizens of Paris on the immortal 10th of August . . . and finally, she has been seen, since the well-merited execution of the most guilty of tyrants who ever dishonoured human nature, trying to secure the re-establishment of tyranny by paying, together with Antoinette, the homage due to royalty and the pretended honours of the throne to the son of Capet."

When the Act of Accusation had been read in a "high and intelligible voice" by the Gréfier, the President said to the prisoners, "This is what you are accused of. You will now hear the charges which are brought against you." The charges brought against Mme Elizabeth were much like those of the night before : her sympathy with her brother, the fate of the diamonds, etc. ; and the President repeated his efforts to make her acknowledge that she was not telling the truth. We select from this wearying list of questions and answers the two last on the list as being the most interesting.

"Did you not," asked the President, "take care of and dress the wounds of the assassins who were sent to the Champs Elysées against the brave Marseillais by your brother?"

"I am not aware that my brother sent assassins against any persons, whoever they may be. I gave succour to several of the wounded. Humanity alone prompted me to dress their wounds. In order to comfort them I had no need to enquire into the origin of their misfortunes. I claim no merit for this, and I cannot imagine that this can be imputed to me as a crime."

After a long diatribe, Dumas concluded his next remarks by these words : "Will the accused Elizabeth, whose plan of defence it is to deny everything with which she is charged, have the good faith to acknowledge that she has encouraged the little Capet in the hope of succeeding to his father's throne, and that she has in this way tried to bring back royalty?"

"I talked familiarly with the poor child, who was dear to me on more than one account; I therefore gave him the consolation which appeared to me capable of comforting him for the loss of those to whom he owed his being."

"That is to say, in other words," retorted the President, "that you nourished the little Capet with the projects of vengeance which you and yours have not ceased to form against Liberty, and that you flattered yourself with the hope of raising again a broken throne by inundating it with the blood of patriots."

The other prisoners were now asked some insignificant questions to give a semblance of justice to the trial to which Mme Elizabeth's fate gave its only importance in the eyes of the judges.

According to the report given above, and by the silence of the *Moniteur* and historians of the period, one might believe that the Princess was not defended by counsel. It is, however, well known that after the Interrogation Chauveau-Lagarde rose and pleaded her cause in a short speech of which he has himself given us the substance :—

"I observed," he says, "that the *Procès* consisted of a list of *banal* accusations, without documents, without questions, without witnesses, and that, in consequence, where there existed no legal element of conviction there could be no legal conviction. I added that therefore they could only offer in opposition to the august accused, her replies to the questions they had made to her, as it was in these replies alone that the whole matter consisted; but that these answers themselves, far from condemning her, would, on the contrary, bring her honour in everyone's eyes, as they proved nothing but the goodness of her heart and the heroism of her friendship. Then, after developing these first ideas, I concluded by saying that instead of a Defence of Mme Elizabeth I had only to present her Apology, but that, in the impossibility of discovering one worthy of her, it only remained for me to make one remark, which was, that the Princess who in the Court of France had been the most perfect model of all virtues, could not be the enemy of the French.

"It is impossible to describe the fury with which Dumas apostrophised me," continues M. Chauveau-Lagarde, "reproaching me with having had *the audacity to speak* of what he called *the pretended virtues of the Accused and to have thus corrupted public morality.* It was easy to see that Mme Elizabeth, who till then had appeared calm, and as it were insensible to her own danger, was moved by that to which I had now exposed myself."

After the Public Accuser and the Defender

had been heard, the President declared the case closed. He made the résumé of the *Procès*, or rather of the different proceedings, as there was one for each accused person ; then he handed to the President of the Jury the following paper, which served as a preamble to the fatal question which was the same for all the accused :—

"Plots and conspiracies have existed formed by Capet, his wife, his family, his agents, his accomplices, in consequence of which there have been provocations to war from the allied Tyrants abroad, and civil war at home. Succours in men and arms have been furnished to the enemy ; troops have been assembled ; dispositions taken ; chiefs named to assassinate the people, annihilate liberty and re-establish despotism. *Anne Elizabeth Capet* —is she an accomplice in these plots?"[1]

The Jury, after a few minutes' deliberation, returned to the hall, and declared Mme Elizabeth and all the accused guilty. The Tribunal, "according to the fourth Article of the second part of the Penal Code," condemned the Princess and her companions to the pain of death.[2]

These terrible words, to which were added, *execution within twenty-four hours*, caused a slight movement among the prisoners, but Mme Eliza-

[1] Why Mme Elizabeth should be called *Anne* on this occasion is unexplained.

[2] The names of ten women appear on the list of the condemned, but one who was shortly to become a mother, but who had refused to plead for herself, was reprieved at the request of our Princess, who warned the judges of her condition.

beth remained perfectly calm. Her thoughts were fixed on God and on her fellow-sufferers, with whom she was now taken back for a few moments to the prison. As she left the court Fouquier-Tinville remarked to the President, "One must allow that she has not uttered a complaint." "Of what should Elizabeth of France complain?" retorted Dumas ironically; "have we not to-day given her a court of aristocrats worthy of her? There will be nothing to prevent her fancying herself still in the salons of Versailles when she sees herself, surrounded by this faithful nobility, at the foot of the holy guillotine."

Meanwhile the twenty-four prisoners left the hall in slow procession between two lines of curious spectators who had rushed to see them pass. They were conducted to the "Hall of the Condemned" to wait for the executioner. This room, "long, narrow, dark," was furnished only by wooden benches which ran along the walls. The sad company seemed to turn instinctively to Mme Elizabeth for comfort. "She spoke to them with inexpressible gentleness and calm, dominating their mental suffering by the serenity of her look, the tranquillity of her appearance, and the influence of her words."

Such as she had ever been—at Versailles, at Montreuil, in the Temple—she was now, thinking only of others, her brow already radiant with the light of heaven. "She encouraged them to hope in Him who rewards trials borne with courage, sacri-

Louise Marie de Cousans
Mariée le 28 Fev. 1784
au Marquis de Raigecourt

fices accomplished." Under her inspiring words, Mme de Sénozan, the oldest of the victims, felt her courage return, and offered her short remaining span of life to Almighty God as cheerfully as MM. de Montmorin and Bullin, two quite young men of twenty, resigned their hopes for this world. M. de Loménie felt great indignation, not at his condemnation, but at the way in which Fouquier had imputed to him as a crime the affection and gratitude evinced for him by his former constituents in Brienne. Our Princess approached and said gently, "If it is grand to merit the esteem of one's fellow-citizens, it is much finer, believe me, to merit God's mercy. You showed your countrymen how to do good. Now show them how one dies when one's conscience is at peace."

Madame de Montmorin, who had lost nearly all her family on the scaffold, could not reconcile herself to her son's death, although he strove tenderly to reassure her. "I am ready to die," she said, sobbing, "but I cannot see him die." "You love your son," said Mme Elizabeth, "and you do not wish him to accompany you? You are going to enjoy the joys of heaven, and you wish him to remain on this earth, where there is now only torments and sorrow!" These words brought a ray of comfort to the poor mother. Throwing her arms round her son, she exclaimed, "Come, come, we will ascend together." [1]

[1] A maid in the service of the Marquis de Tinoul, and who had been imprisoned for refusing to give witness against her master, was

Mme de Crussol d'Amboise was most timorous by nature : she made two of her maids sleep in her room ; a spider alarmed her, and even an imaginary danger filled her with terror ; but Mme Elizabeth's example helped her to meet her death heroically.   To all these sorrowing souls the Princess brought strength and healing.   "We are not asked to sacrifice our faith like the early martyrs," she said, "but only our miserable lives ; let us offer this little sacrifice to God with resignation"; and, thanks to her, they all followed her with faith and courage, a grace which must have brought her ineffable consolation.   The fatal moment was approaching, and the melancholy preparations — the "funeral toilette" — was completed.   The gates of the Conciergerie opened for the entrance of the tumbrils, or "living biers," as they were termed.   The Princess found herself in the same cart as Mme de Sénozan and Mme de Crussol, and conversed with them on the way. When complaints escaped some of the prisoners, she gently exhorted them to resignation.   As the carts approached the Pont Neuf, the white kerchief which covered Mme Elizabeth's head was blown off and fell at the feet of the executioner, who

present at this scene, and related these particulars to M. de Beauchesne. Can the Pauline de Montmorin who shared Chateaubriand's literary labours and who died young be one of this family? Her epitaph in the Church of S. Luigi dei Francesi in Rome records that she faded away after having seen all her family perish on the scaffold —her father, mother, two brothers, and a sister. See the *Month*, p. 678, June 1908.

kept it, says an eye-witness.   As the Princess
was now the only person with bare head, she
attracted special attention from the passers-by,
who all bore witness to her calm and serene
aspect.

When the Place de la Révolution (Place Louis
xv.) was reached she got out first, without accepting
the help of the executioner.   At the foot of the
scaffold was a bench for the condemned ; it had
been placed there in prudence, it is presumed, as
so many were to be executed that it was feared
some would lose courage and faint, but no one
faltered.   Encouraged by the presence and the
look of the King's sister, each went bravely to
death.   The first name called was that of Mme de
Crussol.   She rose at once, and, bowing before the
Princess, asked whether she might embrace her.
"Very willingly and with all my heart," was the
reply, and she gave her the "kiss of adieu, of death,
and of glory."   All the women who followed were
given the same mark of affection ; the men, as they
mounted the steps, bowed reverently to their
Princess.   One of the spectators, anxious to know
who was being so honoured by the victims,
approached near enough to recognise Mme
Elizabeth, and exclaimed aloud, "They may make
her salaams if they like, but she will share the fate
of the Austrian."[1]   The Princess overheard, and
rejoiced to think that her sister had ceased to suffer
and that she would find her in heaven.   While her

[1] This account differs a little from Richard's report, Chap. XV.

companions were going to death she was repeating the psalm "De Profundis" as she waited for her turn.   As the twenty-third victim bowed before her, she said, "courage, and faith in the mercy of God!" and then rose to be ready for her summons. She went up the scaffold steps with a firm step, and, looking up to heaven, allowed the executioner to seize her and bind her.   As he did so her *fichu* fell off, showing a little silver medal of the Immaculate Conception and a small key which she wore round her neck on a silk cord.   As the executioner's assistant tried to take this from her, she said, "In your mother's name, monsieur, cover me."   These were her last words, and immediately afterwards the pure soul of Elizabeth de France passed to its reward.   No other execution, it is said, caused so much emotion amidst the bystanders : no one cried " Vive la République " ; every one went sorrowfully away.[1]

All the accounts and all the *mémoires* of the time agree in saying that at the moment when

[1] It is known that Robespierre dreaded the effect of Mme Elizabeth's death.   On the evening of the execution he and Barère went to the library of Maret in the Palais-Royal, a shop often visited by Robespierre.   Here, while examining some brochures, he asked Maret what people were saying.   "They murmur ; they cry out against you," was the reply ; "they ask what Mme Elizabeth did to offend you ; what were her crimes ; why you sent this innocent and virtuous person to the scaffold."   "Well," retorted Robespierre, addressing Barère, "you hear, it is always me.   I assure you, my dear Maret, that, far from being the cause of the death of Mme Elizabeth, I wished to save her.   It was that wretch Collot d'Herbois who snatched her from me."   See Preface to *Vie de Mme Elizabeth*, by de Beauchesne, p. xvi.

Mme Elizabeth received the fatal blow an odour
of roses was diffused over the Place Louis xv. ; and
her gentle life has likewise left a fragrant memory
in the hearts of her countrymen and throughout the
world.

CHAPTER XVII

AFTERWARDS

Mme Elizabeth and her companions in death were buried in the piece of ground destined for the victims of the guillotine, ground recently opened near the Parc de Monceau. Here Danton, Chaumette, Mme Camille Desmoulins, and the excellent M. de Malesherbes had, with many others, been already interred. It is sad to think that the Princess's remains could not be recovered in 1817, when those of the other royal martyrs received the honours due to them. In life Mme Elizabeth effaced herself as far as possible, and in death also her last resting-place is known only to God; but, to use the words applied two centuries earlier to another royal martyr, "Her effigy and that of her virtues are better engraven on our hearts than they could be in marble."[1]

As the sombre procession of carts moved along the streets, the few shouts of "Vive la République" which had been started by the police soon died away, and Mme Elizabeth was taken to her grave in silence. A few persons could be observed

---

[1] Funeral Oration for Mary Queen of Scots by R. P., 1587.

looking from the half-closed windows, "silent motionless, and perhaps on their knees," as the remains of the once much-loved Princess, the *Ste. Géneviève of the Tuileries*, passed by. The Revolution had gained another innocent victim, and France a fresh intercessor in heaven.

The news of the murder of Mme Elizabeth was received throughout Europe with sorrow and consternation, and by her family with the deepest grief. The sorrow of the Princess of Piedmont, Mme Clothilde of France, has been specially chronicled. This Princess and her husband had cherished the hope that their sister's life, so justly dear to France and of comparatively no political importance, was safe from the fury of the Revolutionaries, so that the evil news came as the greater blow. The Prince heard it first and was obliged to break it to his wife. He went to her " with bent head, eyes wet with tears, and a crucifix in his hand," and said simply, " We must make a great sacrifice." Mme Clothilde understood ; overcoming her feelings, she raised her eyes to heaven and replied, " The sacrifice is made "; but she had hardly uttered the words when she fell fainting. A public Procession of Penance had already been arranged for that day in Turin, and the Princess insisted on taking part in it. She had the courage to do this, and when the Church of the Père Philippins was reached, she herself announced to the Fathers the death of her sister and begged prayers for her. After this the Princess, exhausted by her grief, could no longer keep up, and retired to her apartments.

" From this moment she spoke of Mme Elizabeth only to bring to memory the fine qualities which had adorned her and to praise her virtues. She kept entire silence as regards her executioners, seeing in this tragic event one of those blows which divine Providence sometimes inflicts for the purification of souls. . . . She desired to possess a copy of the prayer she had composed—which she had recited each day of her long captivity and had also repeated at the foot of the terrible scaffold." [1]

At the Château of Wartegg, in St. Gall, Switzerland, where the Bombelles family were now residing, the news caused intense sorrow. The newspaper containing it arrived one morning, and the sorrowful event was quickly known by all except Mme de Bombelles herself, who was still in bed. " A servant entered her room, and his tears and the name of Mme Elizabeth told Mme de Bombelles all. She gave a cry and fell insensible on her pillows." M. de Bombelles rushed to give her every attention, but the shock had been too severe, and she recovered consciousnes only to alarm her husband by an attack of hysterical laughter. He had the happy thought to send for the children, whose tears and caresses brought consolation to their mother. The whole family went into mourning for their dear Princess, whose memory became their constant topic of conversation

[1] Lodovico Bottiglia. See M. de Beauchesne, vol. ii. pp. 236-38.

and the thought of whose charity inspired Mme de Bombelles to emulate her works of mercy among the poor, in spite of the extreme poverty to which she was reduced. She died in 1800, at the early age of thirty-eight, at Brünn, "where her memory has remained in veneration."[1]

Mme de Raigecourt and Mme de Moutiers suffered equally at the loss of their faithful friend and benefactress. The former wrote in 1796 to condole with Mme Royale, then released from prison, and received a touching reply, in which Marie Thérèse says, "I know well the love you had for my virtuous aunt Elizabeth. She loved you much also, and often spoke of you and her sorrow at being separated from you. . . . I share in all the troubles you have suffered, and assuredly I shall always take the greatest interest in all that happens to you, as the friend of my dear aunt Elizabeth. You say that you possess a portrait of her which is very like. I wish that you would send it to me. I promise to return it."[2]

Mme de Tourzel, as we need hardly say, had a special share in this general mourning for the death of our Princess.

"We had also the sorrow to weep for Mme Elizabeth, that Angel of courage and virtue," she writes in the concluding portion of her *Mémoires*. She goes on to relate an interesting visit paid by her and Mlle Pauline de Tourzel to the young

[1] *Gazette de Brünn*, 1st October 1800.
[2] M. de Beauchesne, vol. ii. p. 242.

Princess Royale when they obtained leave to re-
enter the Temple in 1795. The Duchess took the
precaution of first seeing Mme de Chantereine—
the lady who had now been sent to keep the
Princess company — and of ascertaining that the
latter "was aware of all her misfortunes." Marie
Thérèse, whom they found had grown "handsome,
tall, and strong," and who resembled her parents
and also Mme Elizabeth, was delighted to see her
old friends and embraced them tenderly. She spoke
very simply and touchingly of her losses, and when
Mme de Tourzel remarked that she longed to see
her free and able to leave France, she replied, "I
feel a consolation in being in the country in which
rest the remains of those most dear to me in the
world"; adding, as she burst into tears, "I should
have been happier in sharing the fate of my beloved
parents than in being condemned to weep for them."
Her words touching her aunt, and Mme de Tourzel's
reflections on them, have a special interest for us,
and we shall be pardoned if we give them in full.
When the Duchess asked the young girl how she
had been able to bear such sorrows, this was her
reply : "Without religion it would have been impossible. It was my only resource, and procured
for me the only consolations which my heart was
capable of receiving. I had kept my Aunt
Elizabeth's pious books. I read them—I thought
over her counsels, and I tried not to omit anything
but to follow them exactly. As she embraced me
for the last time she exhorted me to have courage

and resignation, and advised me seriously to ask to
have a woman about me. Although I infinitely
preferred to be alone to having such a person as
would have then been given me, my respect for my
Aunt's wishes did not permit me to hesitate; but
they refused my request, and I confess I was very
glad. My Aunt, who foresaw only too well the
misfortunes to which I was destined, had accustomed
me to wait on myself and to require no one. She
had arranged my day so as to have each hour
employed. The care of my room, my prayers,
reading, work, all was planned. She had taught
me to make my bed alone, to do my hair, and dress
myself, and she had also neglected nothing which
could preserve my health. She made me throw
water about my room to freshen the air, and
required also that I should walk about very quickly
for an hour, watch in hand, to prevent stagnation
of blood."

"These details," adds Mme de Tourzel, "so
interesting to hear from Madame's own lips, made
us weep. We admired the courage of that holy
Princess, and the farsightedness which extended to
everything that could be useful to Madame. She
was the consolation of her august family, especially
of the Queen, who, less pious than she on her
entrance to the Temple, had the happiness to
emulate this Angel of virtue, who, not content with
assisting those dear to her, employed her last
moments in preparing those condemned with her
to appear before Almighty God, and exercised the

most heroic charity till the moment in which she went to receive the rewards promised to a virtue so striking and so tried as was that of this virtuous and holy princess."

Before concluding this little history of Mme Elizabeth, it may be interesting to trace, in the light of present historical research, the fate of the long and admirable letter addressed to her by Marie Antoinette on the morning of her execution. This letter, which fills two quarto pages and still bears traces of the Queen's tears, may be regarded as the writer's last will and testament. It runs as follows :—

"This 16th of October, at half-past four in the morning. It is to you, my dear sister, that I write for the last time. I have just been condemned, not to a shameful death—that is only for criminals —but to rejoin your brother. Innocent as he was, I hope to show the same firmness as he did in his last moments. I am calm as those are whose consciences are free from reproach. I regret profoundly that I must leave my children—you know that I live but for them—and you, my good and kind sister, you who in your affection have sacrificed all to be with us, in what a position do I leave you ! I have learned by the pleadings in my trial that my daughter has been separated from you.[1] Alas, my poor child, I dare not write to her : she would not get my letter. I do not even know if this will reach you. Receive here my blessing for both of

---

[1] This was a mistake, happily.

them. I hope that some day when they are older they may rejoin you and freely enjoy your tender care. Let them both think of what I have never ceased to teach them, that principle and the exact performance of duties are the basis of life ; that their affection and mutual confidence will be their happiness. Let my daughter feel that at her age she should always assist her brother by the advice which her greater experience and her affection will enable her to give. Let my son in his turn render to his sister the devotion and services that his affection will prompt. Let them both feel, in short, that in whatever position they may find themselves they will only be truly happy in being united. Let them take example by us. In our troubles what consolation we received from our friendship, and in happiness there is double enjoyment if it is shared by a friend ; and where is a tenderer or dearer friend to be found than in one's own family ? Let my son never forget the last words of his father which I expressly repeat to him : That he must *never* seek to revenge our death. I have to speak to you of what is very painful to my heart ; I know how much grief this child must have caused you. Forgive him, my dear sister ; think of his age and how easy it is to make a child repeat what is required of him, and what he does not comprehend. A day will come, I hope, when he will feel all the more the great value of your goodness and your tenderness. I have still to confide to you my last thoughts. I wished to write them at the beginning

of my trial, but besides the fact that I was not allowed
to write, the procedure was so rapid that I should not
really have had time.   I die in the Catholic, Apos-
tolic and Roman Faith, in that of my fathers, in that
wherein I have been brought up and which I have
always professed.   Not having any spiritual consolation to expect, not knowing if there are still
any priests of that religion, and the place where I
am endangering them too much if they once entered
here, I sincerely ask forgiveness of God for all the
faults which I may have committed since I was born.
I hope that in His goodness He will receive my last
prayer as well as those which for a long time I have
offered that in His mercy and goodness He would
receive my soul.   I ask pardon from all whom I
have known, and in particular from you, my sister,
for all the sorrow which, without willing it, I may
have caused you.   I forgive all my enemies the
evil they have done, and I here bid farewell to my
aunts and to all my brothers and sisters.   I have
had friends ; the thought of being separated from
them for ever and of their sufferings is one of my
greatest regrets in dying.   Let them at least know
that to my last moment I thought of them.   Farewell, my good and kind sister—may this letter reach
you.   Remember me always.   I kiss you with all
my heart as well as those poor and dear children.
O my God, how hard it is to leave them for ever.
Farewell—farewell.   I will henceforth occupy myself
only with my spiritual duties.   As my acts are not
free, a [constitutional] priest may be brought to me,

but I here protest that I will not speak one word
to him, and that I shall treat him as an absolute
stranger." At the end the Queen added these
words as a last charge to her son : " Let my son
never forget the last words of his father, which I
emphatically repeat to him. Let him never think
of revenging our death. I forgive all my enemies
the evil they have done me."

We see that the Queen does not allude to the
fact that she had heard Mass and received the
Sacraments. As the Abbé Mangin says, this was
due, no doubt, to the fear of imperilling the zealous
priests who had visited her, and she could with
truth say that "she did not expect spiritual helps,
as she had already received them."[1] In further
proof of the Queen's meaning, we may quote her
words to the constitutional priest, M. Girard, who,
on the part of the constitutional bishop of Paris,
Gobel, went to see her at half-past six on the
morning of her execution to offer her his services.
She thanked him, but refused them, and when he
said to her, " But, Madame, what will be said
when it is known that you have refused spiritual
succour in this supreme moment?" the Queen
replied, " You will tell those who speak of it to you
that the mercy of God has provided for my needs."[2]

M. Lenotre gives the following curious account

[1] Déclaration de l'Abbé Mangin, Lenotre, p. 332.

[2] M. Girard, who repented of his errors and re-entered the Church,
repeated the Queen's answer to M. de Lagny and others. See
Lenotre, *Captivité et Mort*, p. 333.

of the fate of the Queen's letter. From her anxious
questions regarding her sister, it is evident that it
never reached Mme Elizabeth. The Concierge
Bault, to whom the Queen had confided it, gave
it over to Fouquier-Tinville, who inscribed it with
his signature and kept it for some time.[1] After
the fall of Robespierre, the commission appointed
to examine his papers named Edme-Bonaventure
Courtois, bootmaker at Arcis and Deputy of the
Aube, to report on them. His report filled two
volumes, but what he seems *not* to have reported
was that having gone one day to the house Robespierre had occupied, he examined his room minutely,
and in a secret place, cleverly contrived beneath the
bed of the " Incorruptible," he found papers and other
things which had belonged to the Royal Family,
and among them, apparently, the precious letter of
the Queen to Mme Elizabeth, which Robespierre
had begged from Fouquier-Tinville, who could
refuse him nothing. We shall never know what
Robespierre purposed doing with it ; but Courtois,
who at once recognised its value, " folded the paper,
which still bore traces of the tears of the Condemned,
and, without saying a word, carried off to his house
the only legacy which the poor woman had left to
her children." Years later, Courtois tried to turn

[1] " My husband," writes Mme Bault, "was present when the
Queen returned to her cell. She asked him for writing materials,
and was obeyed at once. He said to me the same day of her death,
'Your poor Queen has written. She gave me her letter but I could
not take it to its destination. I had to take it to Fouquier.'"—*Journal
de Cléry*, p. 328.   Cf. footnote to vol. vi. Feuillet de Conches.

the letter to his own profit by offering to restore it to the Royal Family, but his manœuvres failed, and the precious document was removed from his house on the occasion of a search made by orders of the Prefect of the Meuse.[1]

Twenty-five years had passed since the paper, now yellowed by age, had left the hand of the dying Queen, when it reached—not the sister for whom it had been written—but the daughter who had survived both mother and aunt. Marie Thérèse fainted, it is said, when she received this precious "voice from the dead"; and Louis XVIII. desired that it should be read in all the churches in France on the 16th of October of each year. The letter itself was placed among the State Archives of France, where it still remains, the memorial of a great soul and of the affection which united the two royal ladies whose trials we have recorded.

Our task is now ended, and we lay these pages at the feet of Mme Elizabeth, in reverence for her virtues and her sufferings.

[1] For further details see Lenotre, *Captivité et Mort de Marie Antoinette*, pp. 381–93. According to Courtois' son, his father and Danton had planned the escape of the Queen and Mme Elizabeth. See Feuillet de Conches, vol. vi. p. 519.

INDEX

ADELAIDE, Madame, 4, 22, 39, 51, 22, 101–2; leaves France, 78–80.

Aix-la-Chapelle, French defeat at, 223.

Alais, Bishop of, 50.

Angoulême, Duchesse de, *see* Marie-Thérèse, Madame Royale.

Aosta, Duc d', proposes for Mme Elizabeth, 19.

Artois, Comte de (Charles X.), 3 *note*, 38, 104 *note*; in exile, 79, 106, 137 *note*, 228; letter to, of Mme Elizabeth, 227.

Artois, Comtesse de, 32.

Asselin, M., music by, 48.

Aumale, Mme de, 32.

BARNAVE, 99, and Mme Elizabeth, 92–95, 103.

Basire, Mme de, escape of, 156.

Bastille taken, 61; toy from stones of, 85, 143.

Batz, Baron de, plans rescue of King, 205, and of Queen, 232.

Bault, Mme, on the Queen's last letter, 296 *and note*.

Beauchesne, M. de, 20, 125.
On appearance of Mme Elizabeth, 24, on her trial, 275.

Beauvais, Bishop of, prayer by, used by Mme Elizabeth, 151–52.

Beauvan, Maréchal de, as Minister, 62.

Berry, Duc de (Louis XVI.), 3 *note*, 6.

Bombelles, Madame, friend of Mme Elizabeth, 9, 20; Mme Elizabeth's rich gift to, 30–31; farewell to the former, 61–63.
Life in Switzerland, 4, 288, early death, 289.
Letters to her husband—
On birth of Dauphin, 29.
Referring to Mme Elizabeth, 20, 21, 25, 26, 43, on her proposed

Bombelles, Madame—*continued*.
marriage, 27–28; on life at Montreuil, 34; on the fall of the French Royal Family, 49.
Letters to, of Mme Elizabeth, *see* Elizabeth Marie, letters of.

Bombelles, M. de, ambassador at Ratisbon, 25, 61.

Bordeaux, Archbishop of, as Minister, 62.

Bosson, Jacques, and wife, 60, fate, 68 *note*.

Bouillé, M. de, 101.

Boutin, M., garden of, 86.

Brienne, M. Loménie de, 58.

Brisson, faithful servant, 54–55.

Brunyer, Dr., 213, 231.

Buccleuch, Duke of, owner of painting by Mme Elizabeth, 104 *note*.

Burgundy, Duke of, 3, 7.

CALONNE, M. de, and the centenarian, 37.

Campan, Mme, on intimacy of the Royal Family, 22.

Cartouzière, Lieut.-Colonel, offers his life for the King's, 206.

Causans, Mme de, 42, 43, death of, letters of Mme Elizabeth on, 46, 47.

Causans, Mlle de, *see* Raigecourt, Mme de.

Cazotte, M., friendliness of, 91.

Cecilia, read by royal prisoners, 148.

Chabot, Deputy, 124, 238.

Chambon, Mayor of Paris, 179.

Chamilly, M. de, 139, 146.

Chamisot, M. de, 81, praised by Mme Elizabeth, 82.

Chantereine, Mme de, companion of Mme Royale in the Temple, 290.

Chartres, Duc de, 45.

Chaumette, 179, 190, 258.

Printed by MORRISON & GIBB LIMITED, *Edinburgh*

Telegrams :
'Scholarly, London.'

41 and 43 Maddox Street,
Bond Street, London, W.,
September, 1908.

Mr. Edward Arnold's List of New Books.

THE REMINISCENCES OF LADY RANDOLPH CHURCHILL.

By Mrs. GEORGE CORNWALLIS WEST.

Demy 8vo.   With Portraits.   **15s. net.**

The title of this delightful book gains point from its contents. Mrs. George Cornwallis West is unable to bring her recollections down to the immediate present, and so she brings them to a close when she ceased to be Lady Randolph Churchill. But that was only a few years ago, and it is doubtful whether any volume of reminiscences of Society has ever described the life of the interesting and distinguished people so close to our own day.

Lady Randolph Churchill's earliest experiences were in Paris during the last gay days of the Empire and the horrors of the Franco-German War. Then came her marriage and introduction to all that was best and highest in English Society. In 1876 Lord and Lady Randolph accompanied the Duke of Marlborough to Dublin, and her account of life at the Viceregal Court is full of entertainment. Then come recollections of political society in London, of the formation of the Primrose League, and anecdotes of well-known politicians, such as Mr. Balfour, Sir William Harcourt, Mr. Chamberlain, and others.

Lady Randolph visited the Royal Family both at Windsor and at Sandringham : she has also many interesting glimpses to give of Continental Society, including an audience of the Czar in Russia, Court functions at Berlin, a dinner-party with Bismarck, a friendship with General Boulanger. Such are some of the varied items that catch the eye as one turns over the pages. They are samples from a mine of well-chosen topics, handled with tact, courage and grace.

LONDON : EDWARD ARNOLD, 41 & 43 MADDOX STREET, W.

EIGHTEEN YEARS IN UGANDA AND EAST AFRICA.

By the Right Rev. ALFRED R. TUCKER, D.D., LL.D.,
BISHOP OF UGANDA.

With over 50 Full-page Illustrations from the Author's Sketches, several of them in Colour. In Two Volumes. Demy 8vo. **30s. net.**

This is a book of absorbing interest from various points of view, religious, political and adventurous.   It will appeal to the Churchman and the philanthropist as a wonderful record of that missionary work, of which Mr. Winston Churchill has recently said:

'There is no spot under the British Flag, perhaps in the whole world, where missionary enterprise can be pointed to with more conviction and satisfaction as to its marvellous and beneficent results than in the kingdom of Uganda.'

It will interest the politician as a chapter of Empire-building, in which the author himself has played no small part.   Lastly, it will delight all those who travel or who love reading about travel.   The Bishop describes his wanderings, mostly afoot, through nearly 2,000 miles of tropical Africa.   He tells of the strange tribes among whom he dwells, of the glories of the great lakes and the Mountains of the Moon.   He tells of them not only with the pen, but also with pencil and brush, which he uses with masterly skill.

ON SAFARI.

Big=Game Ibunting in British East Africa, with Studies in Bird Life.

By ABEL CHAPMAN, F.Z.S.,
AUTHOR OF 'WILD NORWAY,' 'BIRD LIFE ON THE BORDERS,' 'WILD SPAIN,' ETC.

With about 200 Illustrations by the AUTHOR and E. CALDWELL.
Demy 8vo. **16s. net.**

The author of this fascinating book is a well-known ornithologist, as well as a mighty hunter and traveller.   He takes us 'on safari' (*i.e.*, on trek) through a new African region—a creation of yesterday, Imperially speaking, since British East Africa only sprang into existence during the current decade, on the opening of the Uganda Railway.   'The new Colony,' he says, 'six times greater in area than the Mother Island, is an Imperial asset of as yet unmeasured possibilities, consisting, to-day, largely of virgin hunting grounds, unsurpassed on earth for the variety of their wild fauna, yet all but unknown save to a handful of pioneers and big-game hunters.'   Much knowledge, however, can be acquired through the pages and pictures of this book, describing, as it does, the vast tropical forests, with their savage inhabitants and teeming animal life.   The numerous illustrations of African big game, owing to the expert knowledge of both author and artist, are probably the most accurate that have ever appeared.

OLD AND ODD MEMORIES.

By the Hon. LIONEL TOLLEMACHE,

AUTHOR OF 'TALKS WITH MR. GLADSTONE,' 'BENJAMIN JOWETT,' ETC.

Demy 8vo. With Portraits. **12s. 6d. net.**

One of the most brilliant men of his day, only prevented, probably, by the physical infirmity of near-sightedness, from being also one of the most prominent, gives us in this volume a collection of remarkably interesting reminiscences, which extend over half a century. They include, mostly in anecdotal form, life-like portraits of the author's father, the first Baron Tollemache (another Coke of Norfolk, but with more eccentricities), and of Dr. Vaughan of Harrow. The author's years at Harrow, of which he records his memories, were from 1850 to 1856, and those at Oxford from 1856 to 1860. The book contains, besides, a number of characteristic stories, now for the first time given to the public, of the Duke of Wellington, Lord Houghton, Lord and Lady Mount Temple, Fitz-James Stephen, to take but a few names at random from these fascinating pages.

IN SEARCH OF A POLAR CONTINENT.

By ALFRED H. HARRISON, F.R.G.S.

Illustrated from Photographs taken by the Author in the Arctic Regions, and a Map. Demy 8vo. **12s. 6d. net.**

The white North continues to exert its magnetism upon British explorers. Mr. Harrison's object was to explore the unknown region off the North American Coast of the Arctic Ocean, but he first travelled 1,800 miles by waterway through Northern Canada, till he arrived at the delta of the Mackenzie River. There he was frozen in and delayed for three months. He then continued his journey to the Arctic Ocean with dogs, but was obliged to abandon his supplies. He hoped to obtain provisions at Herschel Island, but being disappointed in this, he went into the mountains and spent two months with the Eskimo, whose manners and customs he describes. He next returned to Herschel Island and made a voyage to Banks Land in a steam whaler. There, too, the failure of an expected tender to arrive from San Francisco again defeated his hopes of procuring supplies. Consequently he once more threw in his lot with the Eskimo, between the Mackenzie Delta and Liverpool Bay, and spent a year among them.

Such are the adventures described in this interesting book, the last chapter of which, explaining the author's plans for resuming his enterprise, once more illustrates the fact that an Englishman never knows when he is beaten.

CHRONICLES OF THE HOUGHTON FISHING CLUB, 1822–1908.

Edited by the Rt. Hon. Sir HERBERT MAXWELL, Bart.,

AUTHOR OF 'MEMORIES OF THE MONTHS,' 'THE CREEVEY PAPERS,'
'THE STORY OF THE TWEED,' 'BRITISH FRESH-WATER FISHES,' ETC.

With numerous Illustrations, many in Photogravure or on Japanese Vellum, including facsimile Reproductions from Sketches by Landseer, Chantrey, Turner, etc. Demy 4to. £2 2s. net. Limited to 350 copies.

This sumptuous volume, which gives the history of one of the oldest and most famous fishing clubs, on that finest of all English streams, the Test, forms an unique addition to angling literature. The effect of angling on literature has always been genial and discursive, and these delightful Chronicles are no exception to the rule. They throw much light on the changes which have affected social habits in general, and the craft of fly-fishing in particular, during the best part of a century. They contain not only records of sport, but various contributions—literary and pictorial—to the club album, made by celebrated members and visitors. These included Penn's well-known fishing maxims, some portraits by Chantrey, several sketches by Landseer and Sir Francis Grant, and one precious drawing from the hand of Turner. In the leisurely old days of mail-coaches, the members of the club and their guests had more time for such diversions, when the weather was unfavourable to sport, than is the case in the present age of telegrams and express trains.

IN OLD CEYLON.

By REGINALD FARRER,

AUTHOR OF 'THE GARDEN OF ASIA.'

With numerous Illustrations. Demy 8vo. 12s. 6d. net.

The shrines of Oriental romance have once more charmed the pen of Mr. Reginald Farrer. His book has little concern with modern Ceylon, its industries and exports. He tells rather of the bygone glories and sanctities of ancient Lanka, when the island was the seat of a powerful monarchy and a dominant church. He gladly deserts the beaten track for the fastnesses of the jungle and the great dead cities whose bones lie lost in a shoreless ocean of green. Under his guidance, all those who love contemplation of 'old unhappy things and battles long ago' can follow the tale of the Buddhist hierarchy and the Cingalese monarchy, realizing their ancient glories amid the ruins where they lie buried, and their final tragedy in the vast jungle that now for many centuries has engulfed their worldly majesty.

Nor is the interest of the book wholly antiquarian and historic, for Ceylon—that Eastern Island of Saints—is a vast flowering garden, of whose blossoms and paradises all votaries of horticulture will delight to read in Mr. Farrer's pages.

THE BOOK OF WINTER SPORTS.

With an Introduction by the Rt. Hon. the EARL OF LYTTON,
and contributions from experts in various branches of sport.

Edited by EDGAR SYERS.

Fully illustrated. Demy 8vo. **15s. net.**

Every winter more and more visitors are attracted to Switzerland,
the Tyrol, and Scandinavia, to take part in the various winter sports
of which this book is the first and only comprehensive account in
English. Each sport is dealt with separately by an expert. Thus,
Mr. and Mrs. Syers write on Skating, Mr. C. Knapp on Tobogganing,
Mr. E. Wroughton on Ski-running, Mr. Bertram Smith on Curling,
Mr. E. Mavrogordato on Bandy, and Mr. Ernest Law on Valsing on
Ice. The various chapters give instructions in practice, rules, records,
and exploits, as well as useful information as to hotels, hours of
sunshine, the size and number of rinks, and competitions open to
visitors at the different centres. The book contains a large number
of original illustrations. It should be indispensable, not only to
experts in the various sports, but to the far larger class of holiday-
makers who engage in them as a pastime.

FIVE MONTHS IN THE HIMALAYAS.

A Record of Mountain Travel in Garhwal and Kashmir.

By A. L. MUMM,

LATE HONORARY SECRETARY OF THE ALPINE CLUB.

*Magnificently illustrated with Photogravure Plates and Panoramas, and
a Map. Royal 8vo.* **21s. net.**

The first and principal portion of this volume contains an account
of a journey through the mountains of Garhwal made by the author
in May, June, and July, 1907, with Major the Hon. C. G. Bruce and
Dr. T. G. Longstaff, whose names are already well known in con-
nexion with Himalayan mountaineering. The tour has considerable
geographical interest, which is enhanced by a magnificent series of
original photographs of scenes never before submitted to the camera,
and it was rendered memorable by the fact that in the course of it
Dr. Longstaff reached the summit of Trisul, 23,415 feet above the
level of the sea, the loftiest peak on the earth's surface whose actual
summit has, beyond all doubt or question, been trodden by man.

Later on, Major Bruce and Mr. Mumm proceeded to Kashmir,
where they climbed Mount Haramukh, whose snowy crest is familiar
to all visitors to 'the happy valley'; and made a 'high-level route'
down the range of mountains which separates Kashmir from Kagan.
Their photographic spoils were of an interest hardly inferior to those
of the Garhwal journey.

PAINTING IN THE FAR EAST.

An Introduction to the History of Pictorial Art in Asia, especially China and Japan.

By LAURENCE BINYON.

With 30 Full-page Illustrations in Collotype from Original Chinese and Japanese Pictures. One Volume. Crown 4to. **21s. net.**

This important book is a pioneer work in the artistic interpretation of the East to the West, and in the breaking down of the spiritual barriers between them. For a basis of study of Eastern art, writes Mr. Binyon, 'the public at present has nothing but a few general misconceptions.' He therefore puts forward his volume with the modest hope that it 'may not be thought too presumptuous an attempt to survey the achievement and to interpret the aims of Oriental painting, and to appreciate it from the standpoint of a European in relation to the rest of the world's art. It is the general student and lover of painting,' he continues, 'whom I have wished to interest. My chief concern has been, not to discuss questions of authorship or of archæology, but to enquire what æsthetic value and significance these Eastern paintings have for us in the West.' Besides its stimulating artistic criticism, the book is full of interesting glimpses of Eastern history and thought in so far as they have affected art, as well as of biographical sketches of Eastern painters.

MADAME ELIZABETH DE FRANCE, 1764–1793.

A Memoir.

By the Hon. Mrs. MAXWELL SCOTT,

AUTHOR OF 'JOAN OF ARC,' 'ABBOTSFORD AND ITS TREASURES,' ETC.

With a fine series of Photogravure Portraits. Demy 8vo. **12s. 6d. net.**

Among the victims of the French Revolution, perhaps the figure which excites most sympathy is that of the modest and heroic Princess whose life is told in this deeply interesting memoir. Madame Elizabeth was the sister of Louis XVI. Her life was at first one of calm and quiet. Her studies, her charities, and her intimate friendships filled her time until the storm broke over France, and she left her peaceful Montruil to take her part in the dangers and sufferings of her family, and to be their consoler in the time of trial. It was not till the King and Queen had both been executed that Madame Elizabeth was brought from prison, tried for corresponding with her brother, and condemned to the guillotine.

The fresh documents lately discovered by M. Lenotre have enabled the author, who, by the way, is a great-granddaughter of Sir Walter Scott, to throw much new light on the life of 'The Angelic Princess.'

SCOTTISH GARDENS.

By the Rt. Hon. Sir HERBERT MAXWELL, Bart.

Illustrated in Colour by MARY M. G. WILSON,

MEMBER OF THE SOCIETY OF SCOTTISH ARTISTS.

With 32 Full-page Coloured Plates. Crown 4to. **21s. net.**

Also an Edition de Luxe, limited to 250 copies, at £2 2s. **net.**

This work is the outcome of a desire to produce a volume worthy in every respect of the beautiful gardens of Scotland. Sir Herbert Maxwell, whose knowledge of the subject is probably unique, is personally acquainted with the places described, and has throughout been in consultation with the artist, Miss Wilson. Visitors to her studio in Edinburgh, or the exhibitions of her work in London, will need no further testimony to the charm of her pictures, which are here reproduced with the utmost care and on the largest feasible scale.

One of the objects of the work is to dispel certain popular fallacies as to the rigours of the Scottish climate. Its chief aim, however, is to present a typical selection of Scottish garden scenes representing all styles and all scales, modest as well as majestic, and formal as well as free, so that the possessor of the humblest plot of ground may be stimulated to beautify it, with as fair hope of success, in proportion, as the lord of many thousand acres.

ALPINES AND BOG-PLANTS.

By REGINALD FARRER,

AUTHOR OF 'MY ROCK GARDEN,' ETC.

With Illustrations. Large Crown 8vo. **7s. 6d. net.**

Like most hobbies, rock-gardening provides an endless topic of interest for its devotees, and the lore of the subject is inexhaustible. At any rate, Mr. Reginald Farrer, who is a recognized authority on the art, by no means exhausted his stock of information and anecdote in his previous work, ' My Rock Garden.' That garden, as most of his fellow-enthusiasts know, is on the slopes of Ingleborough in Yorkshire, and it is a place of pilgrimage for the faithful of this cult. As a writer, Mr. Farrer combines a light and genial style with sound practical information, so that his books are at once readable and instructive. Some idea of the scope of the present volume may be gained from the list of chapters, which is as follows: 1. Of Shrubs and their Placing. 2. Of Shrubs, Mostly Evergreen. 3. Ranunculaceæ, Papaveraceæ, Cruciferæ. 4. A Collecting Day above Arolla. 5. Between Dianthus and Epilobium. 6. From Epilobium on through Umbelliferæ and Compositæ. 7. Of Odd Treasures. 8. The Big Bog and its Lilies. 9. The Greater Bog Plants. 10. Iris. 11. The Mountain Bog. 12. More of the Smaller Bog Plants. 13. The Water Garden.

THE HISTORY OF THE 'GEORGE' WORN ON THE SCAFFOLD BY KING CHARLES I.

By SIR RALPH PAYNE-GALLWEY, Bart.,

AUTHOR OF 'THE MYSTERY OF MARIA STELLA,' ETC.

Finely illustrated in Collotype.   Royal 8vo.   **7s. 6d. net.**

A 'George,' in the sense in which it is here used, is the jewelled pendant of St. George and the Dragon which is worn by Knights of the Garter.   There are two of these 'Georges' used in the Insignia of the Order.   One is attached to the collar, and is worn only on solemn feasts: the other is called 'the lesser George,' and is worn on general occasions, attached to a chain or lace of silk.

The sovereign is, of course, head of the Order, and Charles the First was wearing his 'George' when he ascended the scaffold to be executed.   The question afterwards arose as to what had become of it, and it has since been given up as lost.   Sir Ralph Payne-Gallwey, however, who has already, in his book on Maria Stella, proved himself a skilful literary unraveller of historical mysteries, makes out a very good case, in his new volume, for identifying the missing 'George' with one that is now in King Edward's possession at Windsor.

A PARSON IN THE AUSTRALIAN BUSH.

By the Rev. CHARLES H. S. MATTHEWS

(BROTHER CHARLES).

Illustrated from Sketches by the AUTHOR, *etc.   Crown 8vo.*   **6s. net.**

The Rev. C. H. S. Matthews, better known in the bush of New South Wales as 'Brother Charles,' is one of the founders and chiefs of an Anglican Society called the Brotherhood of the Good Shepherd, formed to minister to the religious needs of those remote regions. During five years spent almost entirely in itinerating in the 'back-blocks' of the colony, he has had exceptional opportunities for studying bush-life.   Finding, on his return to England, a wide-spread interest in Australian affairs, coupled often with an astonishing ignorance of the real Australia, it occurred to him to set down his own experiences and views on various Australian problems.   Knocking about among the bushmen, camping with sleeper-cutters and drovers, visiting the stations and selections 'out-back,' Mr. Matthews has caught the spirit and atmosphere of the bush, with its mingled pathos, humour and humanity.   The book should appeal, not only to those interested in missionary enterprise, but to all who like to learn how the other parts of the Empire live.

THE ROSE-WINGED HOURS.
A Collection of English Lyrics.

Arranged by St. JOHN LUCAS,
EDITOR OF 'THE OXFORD BOOK OF FRENCH VERSE,' ETC.

Small 8vo., elegantly bound.   **5s. net.**

The special claim of this anthology, arranged, as it is, by one of our most promising younger poets, will be due to the prominence given in it to the love-lyrics of those Elizabethan and Jacobean poets whose verse, though really entitled to rank with the finest flowers of their better-known contemporaries, is unduly neglected by the ordinary reader. The love-lyric is, indeed, the only form in which a great many of the lesser poets write anything at all memorable.

Sidney and Campion, both writers of extraordinary power and sweetness, devote themselves almost entirely to this form, and the strange and passionate voice of Doune finds in it an accent of deep and haunting eloquence. And since every love-lyric from Meleager to Meredith has a certain deathless interest that is shared by every poem of its kind, no matter how many the centuries between them in this volume the great line of the Elizabethans will lead to the nineteenth century poets, to the singers of an epoch with a lyrical harvest as great, indeed, as all the gold of Elizabeth.

THE MISTRESS ART.
By REGINALD BLOMFIELD, A.R.A.,
PROFESSOR OF ARCHITECTURE TO THE ROYAL ACADEMY.
AUTHOR OF 'A HISTORY OF RENAISSANCE ARCHITECTURE IN ENGLAND.'

Crown 8vo.   **5s. net.**

The author of this interesting book, who speaks, as it were, *ex cathedrâ*, has here collected a series of eight lectures on architecture delivered in the Royal Academy. In them he has endeavoured to establish a standpoint from which architecture should be studied and practised. His general position is that architecture is an art with a definite technique of its own, which cannot be translated into terms either of ethics or of any of the other arts, and the development of this thesis involves a somewhat searching criticism of the views on architecture advanced by Ruskin and Morris.

The first four lectures deal with the study of architecture—its relation to personal temperament, its appeal to the emotions, and its limitations. In the last four, devoted to 'The Grand Manner,' the writer has illustrated his conception of the aims and ideas of architecture by reference to great examples of the art in the past.

WOODSMEN OF THE WEST.

By M. ALLERDALE GRAINGER.

With Illustrations. Demy 8vo. **7s. 6d. net.**

This is an extremely interesting personal narrative of 'logging' in British Columbia. 'Logging,' as everyone knows, means felling and preparing for the saw-mill the giant timber in the forests that fringe the Pacific coast of Canada, and it is probably true that no more strenuous work is done on the face of the earth. Mr. Grainger, who is a Cambridge Wrangler, has preferred this manual work to the usual mental occupations of the mathematician, and gives us a vivid and graphic account of an adventurous life.

ARVAT.

By LEOPOLD H. MYERS.

A Drama.

Crown 8vo. **4s. 6d. net.**

The author of this play is a son of the late Frederick Myers, the well-known authority on 'Psychical Research.' It is a poetical drama in four acts, describing the rise and fall of the hero, Arvat. The time and place are universal, as are also the characters. But the latter, though universal, and therefore in a sense symbolic, are psychologically human, and the significance of the action, heightened as it may be by interpretation through the imagination, is nevertheless independent of it. Thus Arvat's career, while providing subject-matter for a drama among individuals in the flesh, may also be taken as the symbol of a drama among ideas in the spirit.

PEEP-IN-THE-WORLD.

A Story for Children.

By Mrs. F. E. CRICHTON.

Illustrated. Crown 8vo. **3s. 6d.**

The author of this charming tale ought to take rank with such writers as Mrs. Molesworth in the category of childhood's literature. The story tells of a little girl who visits her uncle in Germany and spends a year in an old castle on the borders of a forest. There she finds everything new and delightful. She makes friends with a dwarf cobbler, who lives alone in a hut in the forest, and knows the speech of animals and birds. Knut, the cobbler, is something of a hermit and a misanthrope, but he is conquered by Peep-in-the-World, whom he eventually admits to the League of Forest Friends. She wants him to teach her how to talk to the wild things of the woods, and though she has to leave Germany without learning the secret, she gains a growing sense of the magic power of sympathy and kindness.

LONDON SIDE-LIGHTS.

By CLARENCE ROOK.

With Frontispiece.   Crown 8vo.   6s.

The author of these entertaining sketches has taken his place as an ordinary Londoner who is a journalist as well.   He has walked and ridden about London with pennies in his pocket, eyes in his head, and a brain behind the eyes.   He has found secrets of London hotels, he has pierced the problem of London traffic, he has been to queer boxing contests, and he has been present at the birth of the popular song.   He has sat in the gallery of the House of Commons, and in the newspaper office that cuts and carves its speeches.   And he knows the story of the famous block in Piccadilly.   He has found, too, the problem of the London woman who is alone.   The problem also of those London children whom the Salvation Army rescues. And at the end comes the 'Bath of Silence,' which gives the City peace.

THE DOWAGER OF JERUSALEM.

A Romance in Four Acts.

By REGINALD FARRER,

AUTHOR OF 'IN OLD CEYLON,' 'MY ROCK GARDEN,' ETC.

Crown 8vo.   3s. 6d. net.

CHRONICLES OF SERVICE LIFE IN MALTA.

By Mrs. ARTHUR STUART.

Illustrated.   Crown 8vo.   6s.

Fiction is always the more interesting the more closely it is drawn from life, and these sketches of naval and military society in Malta, depicted in the form of stories, come from the pen of a lady who is intimately acquainted with the life of which she writes.   The names of some of the stories, such as 'The Temptation of the Engineer,' 'The Red Parasol,' 'The Prince, the Lady, and the Naval Captain,' will perhaps be as good an indication as can be given of the character of the book.   It will doubtless appeal especially to those familiar with society at naval and military stations, while the fact of its having a specific *milieu* should in no way detract from its general interest.   'Plain Tales from the Hills' did not appeal only to the Anglo-Indian.

KNOWN TO THE POLICE.

Memories of a Police Court Missionary.

By THOMAS HOLMES,

AUTHOR OF 'PICTURES AND PROBLEMS OF LONDON POLICE COURTS.'

Demy 8vo.   **10s. 6d. net.**

There is probably no man living who is so well qualified as Mr. Holmes to write the naked truth about the 'submerged tenth' of our population. His are not the casual, superficial observations of the amateur, but the first-hand experiences of one whose whole life is spent among the scenes he describes. His work has lain among the hungry and thirsty; he has visited the criminal in prison, and been face to face with the Hooligan and the Burglar in their own haunts; but through all the gloom and shadow of crime he has contrived to preserve a fellow-feeling with humanity in its most depressing garb. Every chapter is full of interest, of strange and quaint narratives in chequered pages of despair and hope.

VEGETARIAN COOKERY.

By FLORENCE A. GEORGE,

AUTHOR OF 'KING EDWARD'S COOKERY BOOK.'

Crown 8vo.   **3s. 6d.**

Some are vegetarians for conscience' sake, and others for the sake of their health. Miss George caters for both these classes in her new book; but she does not strictly exclude all animal food, since eggs, butter, milk, cream and cheese form a large part of her dishes. As far as possible, dietetic foods have been avoided in the recipes, as they are often difficult to procure. Every recipe given has been tested to ensure accuracy, and the simplest language is used in explaining what has to be done. A special feature of the book is the large number of vegetable soufflés and creams. The various chapters deal with Stock and Soups; Sauces; Pastes, Borders and Garnishes; Casseroles, Patties, Pies, Puddings and Timbales; Curries, Stews and Scallops; Galantines; Croquettes; Vegetables; Aspics, Creams and Salads; Soufflés, Omelettes and Egg Dishes; Aigrettes and Fritters; Savouries; Macaroni and Rice; Sweets; and Menus.

THE SEEKERS.

By FRANK SAVILE,

AUTHOR OF 'THE DESERT VENTURE,' ETC.

Crown 8vo. 6s.

This is a stirring novel of adventure in Eastern Europe. A learned Professor astonishes the British Association by announcing that he has located the famous lost treasure of Diocletian, as buried somewhere in the principality of 'Montenera.' This little State with its brave Prince is hard pressed for funds to defend itself against more powerful neighbours who aim at absorbing it, and the treasure would be invaluable. Whether it was discovered or not, the reader learns in the course of a spirited and exciting story. In reviewing the author's last novel, 'The Desert Venture,' the *Times* said: 'When you have agreed to treat it as crude adventure, it is really as good as you can wish.' The *World* said: 'If Mr. Savile's style is to some extent modelled on that of Merriman, this is no fault, but a virtue. And the reading world will find that it may safely welcome such work as this on its own account—as it assuredly will.'

THE WITCH'S SWORD.

By DAVID KERR FULTON.

Illustrated. Crown 8vo. 6s.

This work, by a new author, is of a highly imaginative and romantic tendency, and deals with a most interesting period in Scottish history. The hero, who tells his own story, is an All Hallows child, born in the one weird hour which makes him kith and kin to the spirits of the air. The mystery of Flodden and the strange events grouped round the ancient tradition as to the fate of the gallant James are stirringly told, and lead up to the dénouement, which comes with vivid unexpectedness at the close of the book.

The lonely orphan of a wronged father is unwittingly schooled to vengeance by the fiery Welsh swordsman Jevan, who, at the instigation of the dying old nurse, forges the wizard steel that gives the story its name.

A tender love idyll is woven into the tale and relieves the scenes of violence through which the wearer of the Witch's Sword must fight his way to honour and acceptance.

AMABEL CHANNICE.

By ANNE DOUGLAS SEDGWICK,

AUTHOR OF 'VALERIE UPTON,' ETC.

Crown 8vo. 6s.

Readers of ' Valerie Upton ' will turn eagerly to Miss Sedgwick's
new novel. The scene is laid in England, and the principal characters are four — Amabel Channice, her son, her husband, and
another woman, Lady Elliston. The relations between mother
and son form the basis of the story, and the dramatic situation
begins when the son, a youth of nineteen, broaches to his mother
the question why she and his father do not live together. Curiosity
is thus awakened, and the emotional atmosphere charged with uneasy
expectation. Thereafter events move quickly, reaching a dramatic
climax within the space of a week. Further than this it would not
be fair to the author to reveal her plot.

A ROOM WITH A VIEW.

By E. M. FORSTER,

AUTHOR OF 'THE LONGEST JOURNEY,' 'WHERE ANGELS FEAR TO TREAD,' ETC.

Crown 8vo. 6s.

A novelist's third book, when its predecessors have shown great
promise, is generally held to make or mar his reputation. There
can be no question that Mr. Forster's new story will effectually
establish his position. It is a comedy, having more affinity in style
with his first book, ' Where Angels Fear to Tread,' than with ' The
Longest Journey.' The author's whimsical humour, and unexpected
turns of satire, have attained a still more piquant quality. He excels
especially in satirizing the banalities of ordinary conversation, and
his dialogue is always deliciously amusing.

MIRIAM.

By EDITH C. M. DART.

Crown 8vo. 6s.

This is a promising first novel by a new writer, whose style is
remarkable for delicate workmanship. The story moves round the
dying fortunes of an old country family and its ancestral home. The
hero belongs to another branch of this family, and there is a mystery
about his birth. The heroine is an orphan, the daughter of a yeoman
father and a French mother. Another important character is a
scheming lawyer, and with these threads of love and intrigue the
author has woven an interesting plot which is cleverly worked out.

THE DRESSING OF MINERALS.

By HENRY LOUIS, M.A.,

PROFESSOR OF MINING AND LECTURER ON SURVEYING, ARMSTRONG COLLEGE,
NEWCASTLE-ON-TYNE.

With about 400 Illustrations. Royal 8vo. **30s. net.**

The object of this book is to fill a gap in technological literature which exists between works on Mining and works on Metallurgy. On the intermediate processes, by which the minerals unearthed by the miner are prepared for the smelter and for their use in arts and manufactures, no English text-book has yet appeared. The present work should, therefore, be very welcome to students, as well as to miners and metallurgists.

THE GEOLOGY OF ORE DEPOSITS.

By H. H. THOMAS and D. A. MacALISTER,

OF THE GEOLOGICAL SURVEY.

Illustrated. Crown 8vo. **7s. 6d. net.**

This book belongs to a new series of works under the general editorship of Dr. J. E. Marr, F.R.S., for students of economic geology, a subject which is receiving more and more attention in our great educational centres. It is also hoped that the series will be useful to students of general geology, as well as to surveyors and others concerned with the practical uses of geology. The chapters in the present volume treat severally on the Genesis of Ore Deposits, Segregation, Pneumatolysis, Metasomasis, Deposition from Solution, Sedimentary Deposits, and Secondary Changes in Lodes.

STEEL ROOF AND BRIDGE DESIGN.

By W. HUME KERR, M.A., B.Sc.,

LECTURER ON ENGINEERING, DRAWING AND DESIGN, UNIVERSITY OF EDINBURGH.

With detailed Drawings. Demy 8vo. **10s. 6d. net.**

In accordance with a need long felt by engineering students, this work presents the complete designs of four typical structures—two roof trusses and two bridges—worked out with full arithmetical calculation of stresses. There is a minimum of theory, and the author's object has been to make the methods of design so clear as to enable students and engineers to proceed to design independently.

THE BODY AT WORK.

By Dr. ALEXANDER HILL,

RECENTLY MASTER OF DOWNING COLLEGE, CAMBRIDGE.
AUTHOR OF 'AN INTRODUCTION TO SCIENCE,' 'THE PHYSIOLOGIST'S NOTE-BOOK,' ETC.

With Illustrations, about 500 pages, Demy 8vo. **16s. net.**

This is a book for the non-professional reader, not a regular text-book for the medical student. It does not assume any technical knowledge of the sciences, such as chemistry, physics and biology, which lead up to a formal study of physiology. Dr. Hill describes the phenomena of life, their interdependence and causes, in language intelligible to people of general education, and his book may be compared in this respect with Dr. Hutchison's well-known work on ' Food.' There is perhaps a prejudice against the ordinary popularizer of scientific knowledge, but when a master of his subject takes up his pen to write for the public, we cannot but be grateful that he has cast aside the trammels of the text-book, and handled subjects of vital interest to humanity in so broad and philosophic a manner.

A TEXT-BOOK OF EXPERIMENTAL PSYCHOLOGY.

By Dr. C. S. MYERS,

PROFESSOR OF PSYCHOLOGY AT KING'S COLLEGE, LONDON UNIVERSITY.

Crown 8vo. **8s. 6d. net.**

The lack of a text-book on Experimental Psychology has been long felt, the literature of the subject having been hitherto so scattered and profuse that the student has to collect a small library of books and periodicals. The present work gives an account of the more important results obtained, and describes methods of experiment, with practical directions for the student.

APPLIED PHYSIOLOGY.

A Handbook for Students of Medicine.

By ROBERT HUTCHISON, M.D., F.R.C.P.,

PHYSICIAN TO THE LONDON HOSPITAL, AND ASSISTANT PHYSICIAN TO THE HOSPITAL
FOR SICK CHILDREN.
AUTHOR OF ' FOOD AND THE PRINCIPLES OF DIETETICS,' ETC.

Crown 8vo. **7s. 6d. net.**

The author of a standard work on diet is not likely to err by being too theoretical. The principle of Dr. Hutchison's new book is to bring physiology from the laboratory to the bedside. ' Physiology,' he writes, ' is studied in the laboratory, and clinical medicine in the wards, and too often one finds that the student is incapable of applying his scientific knowledge to his clinical work.'

LONDON: EDWARD ARNOLD, 41 & 43 MADDOX STREET, W.

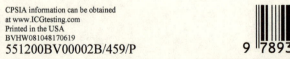

9 789353 706135